Restructuring in the Classroom

Restructuring in the Classroom

Teaching, Learning, and School Organization

Richard F. Elmore

Penelope L. Peterson

Sarah J. McCarthey

Jossey-Bass Publishers • San Francisco

Substantial discounts on bulk quantities of Jossey-Bass books are available to corporations, professional associations, and other organizations. For details and discount information, contact the special sales department at Jossey-Bass Inc., Publishers (415) 433–1740; Fax (800) 605–2665.

For sales outside the United States, please contact your local Simon & Schuster International Office.

TCF Manufactured in the United States of America on Lyons Falls Pathfinder Tradebook. This paper is acid-free and 100 percent totally chlorine-free.

Library of Congress Cataloging-in-Publication Data
Elmore, Richard F.
    Restructuring in the classroom : teaching, learning, and school organization / Richard F. Elmore, Penelope L. Peterson, Sarah J. McCarthey. — 1st ed.
        p.   cm.
    Includes bibliographical references (p.   ) and index.
    ISBN 0-7879-0239-X
    1. School management and organization—United States—Case studies.   2. Educational change—United States—Case studies.
3. Teachers—United States—Case studies.   4. Teaching—United States—Case studies.   5. Learning—Case studies.   I. Peterson, Penelope L.   II. McCarthey, Sarah J., date.   III. Title.
LB2805.E456 1996
371.2'00973—dc20   95-46898
                                                     CIP

FIRST EDITION
HB Printing 10 9 8 7 6 5 4 3 2 1

Contents

Preface ix

The Authors xix

1 Introduction: The Puzzle of Organization 1
and Practice

Part One: Lakeview School

√2 A Principal Leads the Way 17

3 Teams and Themes 35

4 Self-Esteem and Self-Expression 51

5 Structure and Practice 68

Part Two: Webster Elementary School

6 The Development of a District's Flagship 77

7 Active Learning in Mathematics 92

8 Developing Teams 112

√9 A Model of School Restructuring? 132

Part Three: Northeastern Elementary School

10 An Alternative School Is Born 141

11 Reading and Writing 158

12 Learning Science 184

13 Fitting Structure to Practice 207

14 Conclusion: Restructuring Teaching 213

Notes 245

References 247

Index 251

To the teachers, administrators, students, and parents at Lakeview, Webster, and Northeastern, who are dedicated to the continued improvement of education

Preface

Origins

Restructuring in the Classroom was conceived in the late 1980s, during the heyday of school restructuring, a time of great optimism about the capacity of schools to change their fundamental patterns of organization so as to accommodate new and adventurous kinds of teaching. The conventional wisdom at the time was that the country had been pursuing an educational reform strategy since the early 1980s that was essentially top-down in character, mandating changes in graduation standards for high school students, changing entry requirements for teachers, instituting merit pay for teachers, and the like. For a number of reformers, this top-down view of reform had a fundamental defect: it overlooked the everyday conditions of teaching and learning in schools, and it failed to address day-to-day issues that really mattered for teachers and students. The school restructuring movement, if it can be called that, was in part a response to the perceived excesses of top-down reforms. The essential theory of school restructuring, which we explore in depth in the introduction, was that for teachers to teach in new ways reforms had to change the basic structure of schools.

In 1985, the Center for Policy Research in Education (hereafter the Consortium for Policy Research in Education [CPRE]) was embarking on its second five-year grant from the Office of Educational Research and Improvement (OERI) of the U.S. Department of Education. Senior researchers in CPRE decided that we should attempt to shed some light on the basic premises of school restructuring. Out of that initial motivation, the present study was conceived, although actually as two related studies. One, by Prof. Penelope Peterson at Michigan State University, explored how teachers in "restructured" schools thought about their teaching practice and how they responded to the initiative their schools were taking. The other study, by Prof. Richard Elmore, then at Michigan State University and later at Harvard University, explored how schools went about the process of restructuring. As the design developed, we decided to collaborate more closely. In the process we were joined by Sarah McCarthey, then a graduate student at Michigan State and later a professor at the University of Texas, Austin.

In traditional academic terms, it was a highly improbable collaboration. Peterson and McCarthey come from a tradition of studying teaching and learning of subject matter at close hand by observing individual teachers working with students. Elmore comes from a completely different intellectual tradition of studying how organizations respond to policy. The collaboration was always fruitful, but never easy. We spent long hours, sandwiched between our other commitments, sitting face-to-face around a conference table working out difficult issues of design, data collection, analysis, and interpretation of findings. We also spent many hours in conference calls, reviewing drafts of our results, often laboriously, line-by-line. This collaboration had an enormous intellectual influence on all of us. In effect, we had to create out of our very different intellectual backgrounds a common language for talking to each other, and for talking to our readers, about what we thought we were finding. It was energizing, complicated, and rewarding, but never simple.

Research Context

When we began this book, there was little empirical research on the actual processes and effects of school restructuring, and virtually no research on the detailed relationship between structural change in schools and what went on inside the classroom. Since then, two major federally funded research centers have done large-scale research projects on questions of organization and teaching practice: the Center for the Study of the Context of Teaching, at Stanford University (see for example Cohen, McLaughlin, and Talbert, 1993) and the Center on Restructuring Schools, at the University of Wisconsin, Madison (see for example Newmann and others, 1995). Both centers have produced a number of studies of organization and teaching practice, and their findings run parallel to ours. Our book is at once much more modest than these bodies of research and more ambitious. It is more modest in that it focuses only on three elementary schools in a detailed way. It is more ambitious in that it attempts to subject the main tenets of school restructuring to careful scrutiny by looking at how specific teachers respond to changes in structure in specific schools. Our work, then, should complement that of the others by providing a window into the world of specific schools.

Readers should expect to find in this book a detailed view of the broader issues treated in other, parallel research. We hope our focus on the microcosm also provides some grounding for broader discussions of school organization and teaching.

We also hope that our study, in tandem with the growing body of parallel research, incites others to take up the questions we have raised about the slippery, indeterminate relationship between organizational change in schools and teaching practice. We argue in our concluding chapter that school reformers persist in making structural reforms because they believe that the way schools are organized exerts a potent influence—or a potent constraint—on how teachers teach. We find little evidence in our schools of such a connection, but we do think it is possible that structural change operating in tandem with other kinds of change might have the effect that reformers hope for. We feel we have only scratched the surface of this question, and we hope that our research and the work of others stimulates a broader conversation among researchers, teachers, administrators, and policy makers about the aims and effects of school reform.

Research Design

At the core of this book are three extensive case studies of schools at various stages of restructuring, with detailed studies of how four teachers in each school responded to the organizational changes going on around them.[1] We visited each of our three schools on at least four occasions over a three-year period, in the 1988–89, 1989–90, and 1990–91 school years. In these visits, we interviewed principals, teachers, parents, support staff, and district personnel about their general perceptions of the changes occurring in the school. We also attended at least one staff meeting, spent time informally in the teachers' lounge, and attended assemblies and other school activities held during our visits. Out of these interviews and observations, we compiled case studies of what the school had done to change its structure and how those changes had occurred. In addition, from an initial sample of teachers we had interviewed, we selected four at each school for closer observation and discussion about their teaching practice. They were recommended by their principals as exemplifying some aspect of what the school was trying to accomplish; each participated in the study voluntarily. We tried to get a cross section of teachers, by age, experience, race, and ethnicity.

We conducted full-day classroom observations of each teacher three times over the course of the study. During these sessions the teacher wore a wireless microphone, to provide a complete record of her or his interactions with students. In addition, we used "dish" microphones to capture student-to-student interactions. Students knew they were being taped. All audiotapes were transcribed verbatim. Our observations focused on the tasks that teachers set for students, on discourse between teachers and students, on the choices that students were offered in their work, and on student-to-student interaction around classroom work. We also collected samples of student work for later analysis.

We conducted interviews with each of the teachers we observed, before and after the observations. In the pre-observation interviews, we asked teachers about their goals for students, the concepts or ideas they were teaching, the materials they were using, and their rationale for these decisions. In the post-observation interviews, we asked each teacher follow-up questions about the classroom activities we observed. After each of the three observations, we also asked each teacher a set of detailed questions in three separate domains. The first interview asked teachers to describe their personal histories, their roles in the school, and the influence they had over decisions at the school in such areas as resources, curriculum, and evaluation. In the second interview, we focused on teachers' interactions with their colleagues. Third, we asked teachers to reflect on their own learning and on students' learning.

Thus for each school we constructed a record both of what the school was doing to change its structure and what a small number of teachers judged as being exemplary within that school were doing in the classroom. Both the schools and the teachers we studied were considered by various scholars and practitioners with whom we consulted to be exemplars of some feature of school organization or classroom practice. Hence we have deliberately chosen the "best" cases we could, to maximize the likelihood that we would find both significant structural changes in schools and significant changes in teaching practice in classrooms. We cannot speak with complete authority on how teachers' practices changed as a consequence of changes in school structure, since we did not observe teachers before school restructuring started. We did, however, ask teachers to explain to us how they thought their teaching practices had changed. We asked teachers and others in the school how they thought teaching practice should be different as a consequence of the restructuring activities they were engaged in, and, during the course of our study, we used these characterizations to form some conclusions about what the schools and teachers aspired to.

Our claims for the social science merits of this study are modest. We deliberately chose to focus on a small number of very special schools where serious structural change was happening and where teachers were committed to trying new kinds of practice. We also chose to focus on a small number of teachers within those schools, because we were doubtful that a broader-scale study would produce the level of detail necessary to understand how schools and teachers grapple with the relationship between organizational changes and changes in teaching practice. So this study should be seen as one part of the broader picture of how changes in school structure might relate to changes in teaching practice—a picture that we hope will be filled in by other studies designed to capture other levels of detail and generality. We have tried to present a revealing and compelling picture of what it is like to live and work in a school that is trying to change structure and hence teaching practice, and to draw from that picture some ideas about how to think about this relationship between school structure and teaching practice.

We hope this book gives a picture of what the process of school restructuring looks like, from the perspectives of the school and of individual teachers and students within the school. In doing so, we subject the basic premises of school restructuring to careful, systematic scrutiny. And from this analysis we have tried to deduce some guidance about how educators might think about the relationship between the way schools are organized and the way teachers teach.

We think these are important issues because schools seem to be reforming or restructuring themselves, even in the absence of an actual "restructuring" movement. Any time a teacher gets together with another teacher to devise a common strategy for working with students, some kind of restructuring is going on. Any time a group of teachers decides to organize the school day differently, for example creating a thematic curriculum that cuts across several periods of the day, that is a kind of restructuring. Any time a school decides to change the way it groups students for purposes of instruction, some restructuring occurs. Often the assumption is that these changes will make it possible for teachers to teach in new ways. This connection between changes in school structure and changes in teaching practice is the central focus of this book.

Audience

Teaching, Learning, and School Organization should be useful to anyone interested in school reform, or in the relationship between school reform and teaching and learning. We have deliberately sought to minimize academic jargon, both because we believe in clear writing and because we would like to appeal to a broad audience of people interested in school reform. Specifically, we hope our detailed focus on how teachers teach in restructured schools appeals to teachers and academics who do research on teaching, and we hope to bring them more centrally into the conversation about how the work of teaching relates to the broader context of school reform. By putting detailed studies of teaching in the context of organizational reforms, we hope to appeal to principals and other school administrators interested in the role that school reform might play in the improvement of teaching and learning for teachers and students. Framing this as a study of school restructuring should engage the interests of policy researchers and policy makers; we hope they will see the possibilities of viewing their ideas for reform through the microcosm of the school. In other words, this is a book that should appeal to anyone who is curious about how the general and often ephemeral ideas of policy get enacted in the concrete world of specific schools.

Organization of the Book

The structure of the book is relatively simple. In the Introduction, we lay out the basic issue of the relationship between structural change in schools and changes in teaching practice, reviewing the literature on school restructuring and setting the context for how we view these issues in schools.

The body of the book is divided into three sections of four chapters each, providing detailed case studies of restructuring in three schools. Within each section, the first chapter describes the school's restructuring agenda and the context in which the school operates; the next two chapters then provide case studies of two teachers each in each school; and a final chapter gives an overview and analysis of the school and the teachers. The book's concluding chapter then draws conclusions about the main issue in the book: the relationship between changes in organizational structure and changes in teaching practice.

How to Use This Book

One way this book might be read is from front to back as an argument about school restructuring. When we wrote this book, we envisioned its use as a conventional research study, in which the reader proceeds more or less from beginning to end and uses the evidence presented in the main body of the book to evaluate the authors' thesis as it is presented and developed at the beginning and end.

Alternatively, by focusing on the case studies, it can be read as offering a series of provocative portraits of schools restructuring and teachers practicing. This could stimulate researchers and practitioners to form their own explanations of what they observe, and compare them to ours. This approach focuses more on the book's value as a device for teaching professional teachers and school administrators how to think about problems of structure and practice. In this use, one might ask practitioners to read the chapters that relate to specific schools first, to form their own ideas about what is going on in those schools, and then to read the analytical chapters (that is, the final chapter in each part) later. In other words, the book can be a collection of teaching cases on the subject of school structure and teaching practice. It might be used to engage students in their own thinking about what they observe going on in specific schools and how they think about the key relationships *before* they are "taught" what we, as authors, think about those relationships.

We hope the book proves useful in both ways, and possibly in others we have not anticipated.

We have maintained a largely unsentimental and skeptical posture toward what we observed happening in the schools, despite our own personal and professional sympathy with what the schools and the teachers in them were trying to do. We have deliberately tried to keep some distance between ourselves and the participants of the study because we wanted to be inquisitive and analytical about relationships that others regarded as self-evident.

Acknowledgments

We have dedicated this book to the teachers, principals, students, and parents in the schools we studied, because we believe that they are engaged in important work that is central to the improvement of American schools. We would also like to acknowledge their help in doing our research. They were cooperative and supportive, even though it was not always clear to them what we were doing.

Among the people who supported this research, two deserve particular thanks: Susan Fuhrman, director of the Consortium for Policy Research in Education (formerly the Center for Policy Research in Education [CPRE]), and Jim Fox, who has been CPRE's project officer since 1985 at the Office of Educational Research and Improvement (OERI) in the U.S. Department of Education. With the typical foolhardy optimism of researchers, we thought we could do the research and produce a book in a relatively short period of time. We soon discovered that we needed to think and talk about what we were finding and to work systematically through an argument about it; these tasks proved to be time consuming, coupled with our other commitments. Throughout what must have seemed like a millennium, Susan Fuhrman and

Jim Fox were staunch supporters and loyal colleagues. We could not have asked for more.

CPRE is a unique collegial environment. Its researchers are spread across several institutions, doing many projects related to school reform in the United States. At the core of the organization, though, is a group of colleagues from whom we have gained immeasurable intellectual support over the course of this study. Martin Carnoy, William Clune, David Cohen, Susan Fuhrman, Michael Kirst, Allan Odden, Andrew Porter, Arthur Powell, and Brian Rowan were among those with whom we discussed various versions of our findings and arguments over the course of the research. In general, CPRE has provided an incomparable set of colleagues.

Lesley Iura and Christie Hakim, of Jossey-Bass, have been loyal, valuable contributors to this and other projects. Lesley, in particular, brought her talents as an editor, reader, and parent to making this a better book. We also thank Michelle Parker, who assisted with data collection in one of the schools, and Lisa Roy, who provided technical assistance throughout the project.

Fred Newmann, of the Center on Restructuring Schools of the University of Wisconsin, Madison, was always generous, and never competitive, in providing us with comments on various versions of the cases and the argument. Fred opened the work of his own center to discussion, and we benefited from his generosity. Larry Cuban and David Tyack of Stanford University provided their incomparable collegueship, both by responding to pieces of the book and by sharing the manuscript of their own book on school reform, *Tinkering Toward Utopia*. Finally, Emily Browder, Susan Kenyon, and Mark Melchior provided invaluable help in the preparation of the manuscript, bringing their considerable talents with the English language as well as their good humor to the project.

January 1996

RICHARD F. ELMORE
Austin, Texas

PENELOPE L. PETERSON
East Lansing, Michigan

SARAH J. MCCARTHEY
Austin, Texas

The Authors

Richard F. Elmore is professor of education and chairman of programs in administration, planning, and social policy at the Graduate School of Education, Harvard University. He is also a Senior Research Fellow of the Consortium for Policy Research in Education, a group of universities engaged in rescarch on state and local education policy, funded by the U.S. Department of Education, Office of Educational Research and Improvement. He earned his A.B. degree (1966) in political science at Whitman College, his M.A. degree (1969) in government at Claremont Graduate School, and his doctorate in educational policy (1976) from the Graduate School of Education, Harvard University.

Elmore's research focuses on state-local relations in education policy, school organization, and educational choice. He was previously on the faculty of the Graduate School of Public Affairs, University of Washington (1975–1985), where he received the University's Distinguished Teaching Award (1985). He was also on the faculty of the College of Education, Michigan State University (1986–1990). He previously held positions in the Office of the Secretary, Department of Health, Education, and Welfare; and in the Office of the Commissioner, U.S. Office of Education (1969–1971). He teaches regularly in programs for public-sector executives. His government advisory positions have included the City of Seattle, the State of Washington, the U.S. Department of Education, the National Research Council of the National Academy of Sciences, and the Organization for Economic Cooperation and Development. Elmore is the coauthor, with Milbrey McLaughlin, of *Reform and Retrenchment: The Politics of School Finance Reform in California* (1981) and of *Steady Work: Policy, Practice, and the Reform of American Education* (1988).

Penelope L. Peterson is University Distinguished Professor of Education at Michigan State University. She received her B.S. degree (1971) in psychology and philosophy from Iowa State University and her M.A. and Ph.D. degrees (1976) from Stanford University in education. Prior to her current position, Peterson was Sears-Bascom Professor of Education at the University of Wisconsin, Madison.

Peterson's research focuses on learning and teaching in schools and classrooms, particularly in mathematics and literacy; teacher learning in reform contexts; and relations among educational research, policy, and practice. In 1986, Peterson received the Raymond B. Cattell Early Career Award from the American Educational Research Association (AERA) for her outstanding programmatic research on effective teaching. In 1992, Peterson was given the Distinguished Research Award by the Association of Teacher Educators. For six years, she served as editor of the *Review of Educational Research,* a major journal of the American Educational Research Association. Peterson is currently president-elect of AERA.

Sarah J. McCarthey is an assistant professor in the Department of Curriculum and Instruction at the University of Texas, Austin. She teaches reading and language arts courses to undergraduates and sociolinguistics and research in reading to graduate students. She received her Ph.D. in teacher education from Michigan State University in 1991, where she developed her interests in literacy and culture with an emphasis upon classroom discourse. Previous research, published in *Reading Research Quarterly* and *Language Arts,* examined the ways students from diverse backgrounds internalized the dialogue from writing conferences. She has also published with James Hoffman in the *Journal of Reading Behavior* and *Reading Research and Instruction* from a project funded by the National Reading Research Center, investigating changes in teachers' practices and student learning connected to the adoption of the new basal readers in Texas. She is currently conducting a study, funded by the National Academy of Education and the Spencer Foundation, in a multi-age, team-taught setting to understand the ways in which teachers and students make connections between home and school literacy practices.

Restructuring in the Classroom

Chapter One

Introduction
The Puzzle of Organization and Practice

Changing Teaching by Changing Schools
What is School Restructuring?

This book is about a simple, seemingly plausible idea: that we can change how teachers teach and how students learn by changing how schools are organized. This idea has heavily influenced educational reform over the past decade, and it lies at the center of what has been called the "school restructuring" movement. As with most complex reforms, it is difficult to decipher exactly what advocates of school restructuring want by way of school reform. Some reformers want more parental influence over schools through increased parental choice. Some want better working conditions for teachers through more collegial interaction and more collaboration with administrators. And some want more decentralized, less bureaucratic structures for administering schools through increased school-site management and accountability (Elmore and Associates, 1990). At some basic level, though, all advocates of restructuring believe that changing the way schools are organized will cause teachers to teach differently; hence students will learn differently, and the overall performance of schools will increase. This belief is the central concern of this book.

While *restructuring* means many things in debates about educational reform, we use the term in this book to mean something quite specific. We mean quite literally changes in the structure of schools—for example, changes in the way students are grouped for purposes of learning, the way teachers relate to groups of students and to each other, and the way the content or subject matter of education is allocated time during the school day.

To cite examples, many educators believe that grouping children across traditional age groups makes it possible for teachers to respond better to the developmental differences of children and to teach in ways that respond more appropriately to these differences. Many educators believe that dividing the school day into discrete periods of time in which specific subjects are covered makes it difficult for teachers to engage students in sustained problem solving and inquiry, and that using longer periods of time, and having a cross-subject focus, makes it possible for teachers to teach in ways that keep students engaged in serious learning. These structures are the basic building blocks of school organization. When we talk about restructuring at the school level, it seems implausible that we could change school organization without changing these building blocks. Indeed, all of the schools in our study made significant changes in these building blocks, each in its own way and to a differing degree. We decided to focus on these basic structural building blocks of schools because we thought they were likely to be the ones most directly related to teaching practice. If we were to find a relationship between structural change in schools and changes in teaching practice, we surmised, we would find it in schools that were changing those structural features of schooling closest to teaching.

When we speak of teaching practice in this book, we mean the way teachers define the purpose of their work with students, the ways they engage students in learning, the ways students relate to content or subject matter while the teacher is teaching, and the ways students relate to each other in the teacher's presence. These are the basic problems that any teacher must solve in deciding what to teach and how. If changes in school structure are really related to teaching and learning, then we should be able to observe teachers doing things with students that reflect different solutions to these problems as a consequence of their working in different structures. All of the teachers in our study thought that their teaching practice had changed as a consequence of working in a school that had changed its organizational structure. Whether their practice actually did change, and what the relationship was between changes in school organization and changes in teaching practice, is the central problem of this book.

Changing Traditional School Structure

Reformers need enemies, and for advocates of school restructuring the enemy is the traditional school structure. In particular, there are three main elements of traditional school structure that reformers find most troubling.

The first element is the "egg-crate" structure of classrooms within schools, in which students and teachers work in isolated groups for most of the school day, without significant contact around academic content with other groups in other classrooms. The egg-crate structure creates inflexibility in responding to student differences, and it isolates teachers from one another.

A second element of school organization that critics find problematical is the grouping of students by prior ability. Most schools sort students into groups, either within classrooms or in separate classrooms, whether based on teachers' judgments about students aptitudes or on some kind of measurement of ability. Critics of this practice argue that inflexible grouping practices rob low-achieving students of access to high-achieving students, who can act as role models, and that low-achieving students are stigmatized and given less challenging work that deprives them of opportunities to achieve at higher levels.

A third element of school organization that critics find problematical is the organization of academic content into discrete chunks confined to short periods of time, each isolated from the others. The typical school schedule is divided into specified periods of time, often an hour or less, for each subject. Students' work in one subject is isolated from their work in other subjects; the amount of time available for work in a given subject is often not related to the amount of time it takes a student to master knowledge in that subject.

All the schools in our study were deliberately engaged in changing these three elements of traditional school structure. They saw themselves as inventing alternatives to structures they thought worked badly for students. The schools developed three alternatives to the traditional structure, and they were at different stages in the transition from the traditional structure to some alternative. So each of our schools presents a unique picture of what it means to restructure a school.

At the heart of the current school reform debate, then, is a strong belief that if teachers are to teach and students are to learn in different ways, then these traditional school structures and others like them will have to change. Hence, school restructuring, where it occurs, tends to focus on changing (1) how students are grouped, (2) how teachers relate to groups of students and to each other, and (3) how content is allocated time over the school day. These changes aim to increase opportunities for teachers to work collegially during the school day; to introduce more-flexible student grouping practices, in which teachers often take responsibility for more than one group of students or in which groups of teachers jointly take responsibility for larger groups of students; and to make more flexible use of instructional time during the school day, for example by creating larger blocks of time or by teaching combinations of subjects together.

Stripped to its essentials, school restructuring rests on a fundamental belief in the power of organizational structure over human behavior. In this belief, traditional school structures are the enemy of good teaching practice, and fundamental structural changes are the stimulus for new practices. Changing structure changes practice.

Teaching for Understanding

Another target of school reformers is the traditional way in which knowledge and learning are defined in schools. Critics assert that most teaching focuses on the assimilation and repetition of isolated facts, devoid of connection to any broad scheme or context for knowledge, or of any application to problems that engage students' interests. The result of this view of knowledge, critics argue, is that students acquire factual knowledge but do not understand what this knowledge means in a broader context. Nor do they understand how to use it in solving problems in the world.

Reformers argue that curriculum and teaching should change fundamentally to reflect a greater emphasis on students' deep understanding of content, rather than on rote learning and memorization of facts. The proponents of this view of teaching and learning generally argue that "understanding" is manifested when students engage in intentional learning, or the active management of different types of knowledge and processes of cognition around concrete problems. Understanding, or intentional learning, occurs when students themselves exercise considerable control over their own learning, when they are able to make judgments about what types of knowledge are required to solve problems, and when they are able to construct explanations of their own and test those explanations against facts or against the explanations of other students. In this view of learning, the teacher's role is to enable students to engage in a high degree of self-directed learning and to promote the active engagement of students in their own learning, rather than simply to present the subject matter. Students are expected not simply to demonstrate the ability to recall facts but also to draw inferences from facts, approach unfamiliar problems in a deliberate and thoughtful way, and construct explanations for why they approach problems as they do. Students learn to do these things not by operating in isolation from one another, or from the teacher, but by actively engaging in discussions with the teacher and other students. The teacher's responsibility is to create a social environment in the classroom that promotes active engagement and risk taking on the part of students, as well as a high level of interaction among students around problems (Resnick, 1987; Bereiter and Scardamalia, 1987).

Classrooms that represent this view of learning are characterized, for instance, by students interacting around difficult and interesting problems that engage their interests, rather than by passive assimilation of knowledge purveyed by a teacher standing in the front of the room. Students initiate much of the learning, perhaps by constructing stories, running experiments, and using diverse sources of information to answer a question, rather than relying on the teacher to tell them what to do. Teachers operate flexibly, dealing with students in a variety of ways and in a variety of settings—eliciting students' understanding of subject matter in full class discussion, facilitating individual students as they pursue independent work, assisting small groups with coursework and innovative tasks, and the like—rather than standing before the entire class as the focal point of all learning.

For many reformers, such practices—called teaching for under-standing—or "constructivist" views of teaching (so called because of emphasis on the child's construction of knowledge) are deeply intertwined with school restructuring. That is, for these reformers the purpose of school restructuring is to enable teachers to teach in ways that approximate teaching for understanding. School orga-nization, while by no means the only influence on how teachers teach, is seen by many advocates of teaching for understanding as a key variable in determining teachers' capacities to engage in new, more ambitious practices (Talbert and McLaughlin, 1993).

All of the teachers in our study, and the principals of the schools in which they worked, subscribed to some version of this broader, more ambitious view of curriculum and teaching. They believed that they were changing the way they taught, moving from the traditional mode to some more ambitious mode characterized by such beliefs as

- Teachers taking a more active role in constructing the cur-riculum
- Students playing a more active role in constructing knowledge in the classroom, breaking down traditional boundaries among subjects
- Providing students with opportunities to cultivate a deeper understanding and appreciation for their own learning

The degree to which these beliefs were actually realized in practice is a subject to which we return in greater detail later.

This book, then, is an analysis of the relationship between structural change in schools and the development of new teaching practices aimed at enhancing student understanding. We examine how three elementary schools went about the process of restruc-turing themselves and how a selection of teachers within those schools responded to changes in school structure and grappled with the problems of learning to teach in ways designed to enhance students' understanding of academic content.

We take our point of departure from the question of whether there is *necessarily* a relationship between changes in school struc-ture and the practices that teachers pursue in classrooms. If there were such a necessary relationship between school structure and teaching practice, then teachers in schools that were engaging in significant restructuring would begin to teach in ways that more closely approximated teaching for understanding. In its simplest form, this is the central empirical question for our study: how does school restructuring affect teaching and learning?

Is There a Necessary Relationship Between Structure and Practice?

The idea that schools need to be restructured to accommodate and encourage new teaching practice has a certain practical appeal to it. It seems unlikely, for example, that teachers who are isolated from each other during most of the school day will develop ambitious new teaching strategies spontaneously and on their own—at least not on a broad scale. Likewise, it seems equally implausible that students will engage in greater interaction with each other, or more sustained interaction with teachers around challenging new content, if the structure of the school day remains compartmentalized and if each subject is taught as if it bore no relationship to the others. On face value, structural changes should have some relationship to new teaching practice.

However, those who study school restructuring have expressed doubts about the *necessary* relationship between structural change and teaching practice. Fred Newmann argues, for example, that "new organizational structures *alone* are unlikely to improve education," in the absence of what he calls new types of commitment and competence to guide teachers' practice. Teachers have to be committed to some alternative view of what education should be about, Newmann argues, and they have to have the competencies required to turn that vision into practice. He adds that structural change may be a necessary condition for changes in teaching, but it is probably not a sufficient condition (Newmann, 1993, pp. 5–6).

Similarly, critics have argued that structural change may not lead to changes in teaching practice because the changes often are not intended to affect practice. Structural change is often undertaken for political or symbolic reasons, many of which are unrelated to the improvement of teaching and learning (Elmore and Associates, 1990). Structural changes may be designed to appease certain key political constituencies, such as the reforms that have decentralized some administrative functions after parents complained about a lack of influence in school affairs (Elmore, 1993). Changes may also be undertaken to demonstrate a central administration's commitment to enlightened management practices in the face of criticisms from the community, as seems to be the case with many school-based management schemes (Malen, Ogawa, and Krantz, 1990). "Efforts at reorganization—despite prevailing rhetoric—often have more to do with politics than with greater efficiency and enhanced quality," argues Joseph Murphy. "Structural changes in and of themselves never have and never will predict organizational success" (Murphy, 1991, p. 76). In other words, one should not expect change in the structure of schools to result in changes in teaching practice unless there is some direct relationship between the purpose of the change and the problems of teaching and learning in schools.

Even if structural change is clearly aimed at changing teaching practice, there may be reasons to doubt whether changes in structure connect directly with what teachers do in the classroom. Michael Fullan suggests that "it is possible to change 'on the surface' by endorsing certain goals, using specific materials, and even imitating the behavior *without specifically understanding* the principles and rationale for the change. Moreover, . . . it is possible to value and even be articulate about the goals of the change without understanding their implications for practice" (Fullan, 1991, p. 40, emphasis in original).

Organizational changes, according to Fullan, operate in at least three dimensions: beliefs, behavior, and materials or technology. These dimensions typically operate independently of one another. Educators often subscribe to certain beliefs without those beliefs' tangibly influencing their behavior. They may use materials and technology with no real understanding of the changes in beliefs or behavior required to make them work as intended. In other words, individuals can feel as though they are engaged in substantial changes either because they are using different technologies or materials or because their beliefs about what they are doing have changed. But the educators may have changed their actual *behavior* very little, if at all.

In educational research and practice, there are abundant examples of slippage between structural change and teaching practice in schools. A few examples suffice to illustrate the elusiveness of this connection. An interesting one is from the literature on grouping and tracking practices in schools. As noted above, critics of ability grouping and tracking argue that putting students in homogeneous groups, based on some measure of prior aptitude or achievement, robs "slower" students of the stimulation and example provided by "faster" students and, similarly, robs "faster" students of the opportunity to work with students from diverse backgrounds with diverse aptitudes and interests. These critics argue that the structure of ability grouping and tracking, whatever its espoused purposes, serves to limit certain students' access to challenging academic content and therefore deprives them of opportunities to acquire the skill and knowledge necessary for further education and economic self-sufficiency (Oakes, 1985; Murphy and Hallinger, 1989).

✔ The actual empirical evidence on the effects of ability grouping and tracking are considerably more mixed than one would expect, given the arguments of critics. The evidence supports the conclusion that students in different groups are on the whole exposed to different kinds of classroom experience; for example, they study different content and they are treated differently by teachers in comparison to nontracked students (Oakes, 1985, 1990; Gamoran, 1987; Sorenson and Hallinan, 1986). But the evidence is mixed on what effect this treatment has on student learning. While secondary school tracking seems to restrict access to challenging academic content and teaching for low-track students, there is little evidence that (controlling for students' prior achievement) tracking in itself affects aggregate student performance. There seems to be little difference in measured achievement between schools that track and those that do not (Slavin, 1990).

In elementary schools, there is evidence that certain types of homogeneous grouping under certain conditions actually do have positive effects on student achievement. For example, within-class grouping in mathematics seems to have a modest positive effect on student achievement, as does grouping by reading level across classrooms for reading instruction. But the assignment of students to self-contained classrooms on the basis of ability appears to have no discernible effects, positive or negative (Slavin, 1987).

Most reformers regard these results, when they choose to acknowledge them at all, as puzzling. Clearly, the structures we use to limit students' access to certain kinds of subject matter *must* have some relationship to what students are taught, how they are taught, and therefore what they learn. Regardless of where they stand on the tracking and ability-grouping issue, most teachers and principals would say that grouping and tracking practices *must* matter. How could a structure that apparently has so direct a relationship to teaching and learning have such a seemingly ambiguous and weak effect on what students actually learn?

One possibility is that the research simply does not measure student learning, or differences in learning opportunities across tracks and groups, with enough discrimination to pick up the effects that ability grouping and tracking have on student learning. A second possibility is that grouping and tracking practices are actually a good deal more flexible in implementation than they appear to be in principle, and students are actually exposed to a more diverse curriculum than the critics of grouping practices suggest (Garet and Delany, 1988; Delany, 1991). Still another, equally plausible possibility is that teaching practices may not vary much across different grouping and tracking structures, so that the structures themselves actually have very weak effects on what teachers teach and how they teach. Researchers on ability grouping and tracking have observed that the research does not adequately address the question of how teaching practice may or may not vary independently of track or group assignment of students. Robert Slavin observes, "Unfortunately, the research comparing alternative ability grouping arrangements in elementary schools has, with few exceptions, failed to specify in detail the changes in instructional practice brought about by the various grouping methods. Clearly, the effects of grouping on achievement are mediated by teacher behaviors" (Slavin, 1987, p. 297). Adam Gamoran and Mark Berends observe with regard to tracking in secondary schools: "Another explanation for weak and inconsistent effects [of tracking] is that although instruction varies between tracks and ability levels, the instructional differences may actually be small when compared to the overall similarity of instruction at all levels" (Gamoran and Berends 1987, p. 425). In other words, teachers may pursue certain standardized teaching practices regardless of what grouping structure they are working in, and the effect of these practices on student learning may be stronger than the effect of the structures.

Another example of the slippery relationship between school structure and teaching practice comes from the research literature on the effects of class size on student learning. In general, the research finds that class size affects student achievement only at the extremes—say, fewer than twenty and more than forty students per teacher. Where they exist, class size effects tend to be modest in the primary grades—kindergarten through third—and weaker or nonexistent in later grades (Glass and Smith 1979; Finn and Achilles 1990). Again, the relationship between a major structural variable of schooling and student achievement seems to be weak or nonexistent.

Still, we believe most teachers, most parents, and many educational reformers would argue that there *must be* some relationship between what a teacher is able to teach in a class of, say, twenty versus a class of thirty students, and that these differences *must* have an effect on what teachers teach and what students learn. But as in the case of grouping, teaching practices might be more similar than different across classrooms of different sizes. If this were true, then regardless of how much teachers might think their teaching would be different in a class of twenty rather than thirty, their teaching would actually be indistinguishable in both cases, at least in terms of student learning. This seems to be so. The few studies done on the relationship between class size and teaching practice have indicated that teaching practices vary little between large and small classes. "Many teachers whose classes have been reduced, even by substantial numbers," says Glen Robinson, summarizing this body of research, "do not change their teaching techniques to take advantage of the smaller classes," by, for example, giving students more individual attention, changing the layout of their classrooms, or engaging in more personalized forms of student evaluation (Robinson, 1990, p. 87). So while it is plausible to believe, as most teachers, parents, and school reformers do, that changing class size *could* result in changing teaching practice, and hence in changing student learning, the evidence suggests that it often does not.

These examples underscore an important problem at the center of this study. While there may be compelling reasons to believe that teaching practice can only change if school structures are changed, there are also compelling reasons to believe that changes in structure do not lead inevitably to changes in practice. By the same token, to say that changes in structure have no discernible effect on teaching and learning is not to say that there *cannot* be any such effect. Under ordinary conditions, changes in structure might not produce discernible changes in teaching and learning. But it may be that certain kinds of innovative teaching practices can only occur if there are changes in structures, such as grouping practices, class size, schedules, and interaction patterns among teachers. If teaching practice is relatively resistant to change under any structural conditions, then one cannot state a simple relationship between changes in structure and changes in teaching and learning. If changing school structure does not immediately result in teachers and students behaving differently in classrooms, this does not necessarily mean that different structures are not necessary for teachers and students to begin acting differently.

We began this study expecting, as do most advocates of school restructuring, that we would find relatively direct connections between the changes we observed in structure and the teaching practices we observed in classrooms. We quickly discovered that the relationships between structure and practice are more complex and indeterminate than we could ever imagine. It may be true, as Newmann, Murphy, and others have argued, that there is no predictable relationship between changes in structure and changes in teaching practice and that structural change may be a necessary, but not sufficient, condition for change in teaching practice. However, knowing these things is only the first step to understanding how structure and practice might be linked. We have tried in this study to present this relationship in greater detail than it has been treated in other studies; in doing so, we hope to shed light on how school reformers might think about it in the future.

The Design of This Study

At stake here is the causal logic of the relationship between structure and practice in schools. Social scientists typically look, at least initially, for rather simple causal relationships of the form "X causes Y" or, in our case, that changes in structure cause changes in practice. This relationship is simple both in the sense that it involves only two factors, a cause (X, structure) and an effect (Y, practice), and in the sense that causality runs in only one direction, from X to Y. Life, however, is seldom this simple, and life in schools is at least as complex as life in general.

Complexity has many forms. People in schools may think there is a relationship between structure and practice; but upon examination we may find that this relationship does not exist, or that it does not exist with the consistency that people think it does. Also, while structure itself may have a weak relationship to how teachers teach, structure can operate in concert with other factors to exert an effect on teaching practice. Finally, structure and teaching practice may not have a simple, linear relationship to each other. The relationship may run in both directions simultaneously. Because this relationship is so complex, it is a kind of problem particularly amenable to a relatively fine-grained qualitative study, in which we try to describe in some detail how schools actually grapple with the relationship between structure and practice, rather than reducing the relationship to simple measurable variables and trying to find it in the aggregate.

Our study therefore attempts to examine the relationship between school structure and teaching practice more closely than is possible in aggregate studies, and to explore in greater detail how this relationship works in real schools that are trying to change both the way they are organized and how teaching occurs in classrooms. We chose the three schools in our study deliberately because they are schools with a reputation for being exemplars of "school restructuring." They were chosen from a list of schools recommended to us by a sample of knowledgeable scholars and practitioners. The schools are nationally renowned for being engaged in serious structural change and pursuing ambitious goals for student learning. They are also schools with quite heterogeneous student populations; they all enroll substantial numbers of low-income, minority children and diverse teaching staffs. They are all in relatively urbanized areas, one each in the western, central, and eastern United States. Because we deliberately chose schools where we were likely to find serious changes in structure and teaching practice, we make no pretense of suggesting that these schools are "typical" in any sense. Each is probably quite different from the typical elementary school, each special in its own right.

We do think, however, that the problems these schools confronted in changing their structures, and the problems teachers confronted in attempting to teach differently, are part of a class of problems that all schools confront if they try to change teaching and learning by changing structure. In other words, although these three schools may not be representative in a statistical sense their experience is germane to the experience of other schools and other teachers.

Part One

Lakeview School

"If you could do anything you wanted with this school next year, what would you do?"

–Laurel Daniels, principal, Lakeview School

Chapter Two

A Principal Leads the Way

The School and Its Community

Lakeview School nestles against a green hillside in a middle-class neighborhood of small, well-maintained homes in Clearhaven. The brick building has space for about 250 students—small for an urban elementary school. Farther up the hill, the houses become larger and more expensive. About one mile away, on the top of a steep hill, sits another, larger elementary school. Lakeview was originally built in 1914 in response to neighborhood pressure to spare the children of its neighborhood from the walk up the hill. Until the present structure was erected in 1924, the school consisted of two small, portable buildings. From its origins in neighborhood activism, Lakeview has had a history of close relations to its community. In 1986, when the school district proposed closing Lakeview, the school's parents and supporters—now drawn from across the city—mobilized to reverse the decision.

Presently, about 70 percent of its children come from outside the immediate neighborhood.[1] Under the district desegregation plan that existed from the early 1970s until 1990, Lakeview was classified as an "option" school. While other elementary schools in the city were grouped into pairs and triads for purposes of busing to promote desegregation, Lakeview and a small number of other schools were allowed to draw their students from any attendance area. A small school in a middle-class neighborhood with declining numbers of school-aged children whose parents now had the choice to send their children elsewhere, being an option school allowed Lakeview to survive. Though the majority of students reside outside the neighborhood, parents both in and beyond the neighborhood play an active role in the life the school.

Lakeview has a reputation for caring about racial diversity and children with learning and behavior problems. Its racial composition is over 40 percent African American and about 50 percent white, with a small number of students from other ethnic backgrounds. The 40 percent African American population represents a decline from the early 1980s, when about one-half of the student body was African American. About 30 percent of Lakeview's students come from families with incomes low enough to qualify for free and reduced-cost lunches. More than 50 percent come from single-parent families. The school has accepted a number of students who were referred by the district from other schools because of learning and discipline problems.

Laurel Daniels Comes to Lakeview

From 1983 to 1989, Lakeview's principal was Laurel Daniels. During this period, Lakeview developed a reputation within Clearhaven for being a highly innovative school.

Daniels began her career in education in a rural western school district at age twenty-six. She taught and went to college at the same time, while raising three children. Later, she spent time teaching in a Montessori school, an experience she credits with shaping her views about children's learning. When she moved to Clearhaven in the early 1970s, the local economy was flat and teaching jobs were scarce. Soon after she arrived, she became involved in the citizens' advisory council of her neighborhood school, joined a group of parents who were interested in starting an alternative school, and soon found herself running a small alternative program. She worked her way through a number of jobs in alternative schools in the middle-to-late 1970s, acquiring a master's degree from a local university, a principal's credential, and raising five children.

Daniels's experience in alternative schools reinforced her concern about the way schools treated children, especially urban minority children: "Kids were being asked to fit into a system that guaranteed their failure. I was interested in designing systems around kids. There was a lot of trial and error going on in alternative schools. Some of the kids didn't fit into the alternative programs any better than the traditional programs. I was increasingly frustrated and started looking for an opportunity to show what a school could really do."

Daniels applied for a principalship in 1981, a period when the district was hiring 13 new principals. She was given her first principal's assignment in an inner-city K–3 school with, in her words, "very needy kids," "a very tired staff," and a former principal who had "retired before he went there." Daniels saw that "[t]wo-thirds of our kids were in the bottom three stanines" (roughly the bottom third of the distribution) of the district's reading test. She organized a buildingwide reading program and within one year "turned the reading scores upside down."

Her reward was a transfer to the principalship of Lakeview. "I was ticked," she said. "I needed to be where I was, not at another school." Lakeview parents had expressed some dissatisfaction with the previous principal, who had been reassigned to district administrative duties. The school had a reputation, in Daniels's words, for having "great discipline" and "pushy parents."

Daniels spent her first year at Lakeview "getting to know the place. . . . It was a very discipline-oriented school," she said. "It was mainly about people learning to control themselves. The adults weren't any more independent than the children. Everyone was waiting for me to tell them what to do." As the year progressed, Daniels said, teachers and parents began to sense that she had a different attitude. "I would go out and play with the kids during recess. I would take them home with me sometimes to talk about problems in school. Things like that.

"The biggest problem I sensed," she said, "was that teachers generally didn't believe that kids could learn. We had a few arguments about that issue when I would ask about certain kinds of learning and they would say, 'Kids aren't able to do that.'"

At the end of the first year, Daniels held a series of staff meetings to plan for the following year. As she recalls,

I asked them, "If you could do anything you wanted with this school next year, what would you do?" We covered the walls with paper and made long lists. Class size came to the top. Class size wasn't something that particularly excited me, but getting students engaged in learning did. So we made a bargain. Everyone in the school would teach reading for one hour each day. We would divide the kids up into reading groups outside their regular class-rooms. By focusing all teachers on reading, including our compen-satory and special education teachers, we could lower class size. This was something I had done at the school I had come from, and I was confident that we could show results. We gave the kids a reading test at the beginning of the year. At the end of the year scores went up. Most teachers loved it. Parents loved it. We had no trouble getting the kids back and forth to class. There were very few problems.

Changing the Structure of Lakeview

Gradually, Daniels's influence at Lakeview was becoming apparent. First she began to assert control over the composition of the staff. At the end of her second year at Lakeview, a few teachers who were uncomfortable with her approach left. "I helped them go. I really worked with them, gave them choices, and we found them places in other schools. Then I went to the open staffing day at the dis-trict during the summer and actively recruited new teachers who were interested in what we were doing. We began to draw inter-esting people."

Another area where Daniels began to exert influence was cur-riculum. Lakeview had been part of a districtwide program to use Distar, a highly structured, teacher-centered reading program that Daniels thought was inconsistent with what she wanted to do at Lakeview. "I worked with the zone administrator [a regional offi-cial of the school system] to get it moved to another school."

A third area was scheduling and staffing. "We decided that if we could reduce class size and change the way we taught reading, why not do it for everything else?" Daniels said.

At the end of the second year we had a meeting similar to the one we had at the beginning of the year, and we were talking about "maybe next year we'll do both reading and language arts as well as math in blocks." So when they went away at the end of the summer, I sat down and said that there was no reason why we couldn't do that. The resources are there. Not that schools don't need more resources, but there are more resources available to us than we think there are. It is just that we are so locked into the old ways of using them that we don't think about how to do it differently. So that is when I put together a sort of comprehensive plan. When they came back [in the fall], I called them back two days early, I scrounged some money to do a two-day workshop, and said, "Here is what we have been saying for the last two years, and if we're really serious about this we could do it.

The result was a significant change in scheduling and staffing, which led to Lakeview's reputation as an innovative school and to Daniels's reputation as a mover and shaker.

The essence of the plan was to divide the schedule into morning and afternoon blocks, with reading, language arts, and math taught in the morning and all other subjects, including social studies, science, and physical education, in the afternoon. In the morning, children were placed in two multi-age groups—kindergarten through second grade and grades 3–5—and further grouped according to broad ability bands.[2] The K–2 and 3–5 teachers worked in teams, dividing students according to flexible grouping strategies, generally putting lower-ability students in smaller groups than higher-ability students. In the afternoon, students were grouped by the traditional age-grade structure. In the morning, all existing staff plus the three special-needs teachers, the librarian, and the PE teacher worked with groups of students teaching reading, language arts, and math. In the afternoon, the special-needs teachers also taught regular classes. This staffing arrangement lowered average class size from about thirty to about twenty-two students.

A fourth area where Daniels asserted her influence was staff development. "The teachers felt that changing class size was the most important thing we were doing, but I felt the most important thing was that we were beginning to gel as a school and to focus on what was best for kids. We had a dramatic change in staff development; we spent a lot of time together working on issues related to curriculum and teaching. By the end of the second year and the beginning of the third we had some respect for each other; we had begun to teach each other." The use of teams and flexible staffing arrangements created opportunities for teachers to consult with each other, and the schedule was arranged so that team members had common planning time during the school day for team meetings. The effect of these arrangements, teachers agreed, was increased consultation among teachers about curriculum and student learning problems.

Daniels's belief in staff development as the major source of innovation was also apparent in the amount of outside training and assistance the school received. Over a period of two years, Lakeview teachers received formal training in a number of areas, including Real Math (a mathematics curriculum based on the use of concrete objects to learn abstract concepts), alcohol and drug abuse, loss and grieving, Teacher Effectiveness and Student Achievement (TESA), whole-language approaches to teaching reading and writing, student learning styles, classroom management, self-esteem, and cooperative learning. Lakeview's proximity to a major state university, Daniels's leadership in the district principals' association, and her participation in a regional educational consortium to promote school restructuring brought a steady flow of new ideas into the school.

The Core Values of Lakeview's Restructuring

As these changes accumulated, Daniels and the Lakeview teachers began to agree on and to articulate a set of core values that gave meaning to the changes. One value was, in Daniels's words, "Don't label kids." Putting children in special classes according to their eligibility for remedial or special education, Daniels argued, was counterproductive. Student diversity could be accommodated much better by using the school's resources to create more flexible structures, based in part on students' progress in academic subjects and in part on their age group.

Another core value was collaboration among teachers. As the changes progressed, teachers began to take an increasingly active role in decisions about curriculum and school structure, although they depended heavily on Daniels for leadership. New ideas were being discussed in staff meetings and retreats, and changes were agreed to collectively. In Daniels's words,

> When I go to the teachers with a decision, they have just as much right to turn that down as I would if they came to me with a decision. If they come to me and want me to do something I think is wrong, basically we keep talking about it until either I get con-

vinced or I convince them. That is the same for me. If I go to them with an idea, I have to sell it in the same kind of a way and convince them that this is really going to be better for kids, and every decision is based on whether it is going to make it better for kids.

"Making it better for kids" seemed to mean at least two things in the Lakeview context. It meant finding solutions to grouping and teaching problems that would not result in permanent labeling of students. It also meant making multiple opportunities available to students to learn according to their own particular strengths and weaknesses.

A third core value was treating the school as a family and valuing the self-esteem of teachers and students. Daniels developed a reputation as a caring and compassionate administrator. Speaking about Lakeview's use of cooperative learning [multiple-ability student groups in which students teach each other], Daniels said, "Here are kids who are reaching out to help each other, and not only does it affect how they learn, it also affects the relationships they have with one another. That's one of the things we're supposed to be doing. This is a desegregated school, and we want kids to be working together, not just sitting beside each other. So the things that we're doing not only respond to the academic needs of students but also to their personal needs." A Lakeview teacher said: "I think the teachers really get to know the children; especially with this exchange [teams working with different groups of students], you really feel like you know everybody in the school, so it is more like a family and we all care about each other and we don't hurt any other person. The faculty cares about each other and we all care about the children. I think the children basically care about the faculty and their parents are involved and it is really a nice feeling."

A fourth and final core value in Lakeview's restructuring was individual learning styles. An early staff development session was devoted to a discussion of a detailed framework, developed by an outside consultant, for describing differences in how students approach learning. The framework was an amalgam of several popular psychological theories used to characterize differences in problem-solving approaches among adults, extended to characterize children. The training exercised a powerful influence over the teachers at Lakeview. In our interviews with them, Daniels and all the Lakeview teachers spontaneously referred to learning styles. With time, the idea of learning styles also began to influence the way teachers thought about their approaches to teaching, as well as the way they characterized differences among students. It was common for teachers to use the language of individual learning styles in characterizing differences and complementarities among team members. One teacher, for example, reflected a common style of discourse in the school by referring to herself as "more global and conceptual" and to her teammates as "more linear and sequential." The idea of learning styles was used to justify tolerance for differences in approaches to teaching and learning among students and teachers; differences were, for the most part, characterized not as being "better" or "worse" but simply different.

These core values—opposition to labeling students, promoting collaboration among teachers, creating a sense of family and self-esteem among students, and respect for diversity in learning styles—formed the basis for a strong belief system at Lakeview. While these core values were identified with Daniels's leadership, and were often demonstrated in the way parents and teachers talked about Daniels, they were widely espoused and shared among teachers.

Changes in Teachers' Work at Lakeview

The structural changes initiated at Lakeview during Daniels's tenure had a considerable impact on teachers' work in the school. Teachers worked in teams of three or four during the morning of each day, when reading, math, and language arts were taught. For the most part, teachers in a given team would specialize in a given subject matter and circulate among groups of students to teach that content. In some instances, teachers would teach different subjects in a given morning to different groups of students. Teams of teachers were largely responsible for deciding how to organize themselves, within the broad charge that they were expected to use multi-age groups and to teach designated subjects. One consequence of this structure was that Lakeview teachers experienced—most for the first time—what it was like to collaborate on decisions about what would be taught, to whom, and when.

Students were grouped during the morning into broad, heterogeneous, multi-age groups according to teachers' judgments. This grouping strategy required teachers to consult extensively with each other and to explain and justify their grouping decisions to their colleagues. For the first time, Lakeview teachers found themselves consulting with each other about appropriate placement of students.

Another effect of these changes in structure was that students began to develop close relationships with more than one teacher. According to Daniels, at first parents and teachers were concerned that students, particularly those in the early grades, would find working with more than one teacher confusing. But teachers and parents found that students adjusted readily to working with teams of teachers and to the fact that they were in different classroom environments during the morning and the afternoon. Students seemed to move smoothly from one activity to another and to be engaged in learning, whether they were in multi-age groups, as they were in the morning, or in more traditional age-grade classrooms, as they were in the afternoon.

Coupled with these organizational changes were changes in the structure of curriculum. Each year, teachers decided on a schoolwide theme that would be used to organize various projects at the school, team, and individual teacher levels. In addition, the entire school had a common fifteen-minute writing period each day to stress the importance of having students engage in sustained writing.

Cutting across these organizational and curriculum changes were faculty retreats, workshops, and meetings. Summer retreats were a regular part of the life of the school, often involving detailed work on changes in the structure of the school, development of curriculum themes and units, and the introduction of new curriculum materials. Throughout the year, in-service workshops were held regularly on diverse topics, ranging from curriculum innovations (such as Real Math) to the problems confronting teachers, such as discipline and general teaching strategies. Finally, there were regular faculty meetings, as often as twice a week, in which schoolwide issues were discussed.

These changes significantly increased collegiality and morale among teachers. A common theme in interviews with teachers was the way in which these new structures and processes changed their attitude and outlook toward teaching. One significant change lay in breaking down barriers among teachers. Here is how one teacher characterized it:

> I found in going to work [at Lakeview] that [it's] an environment where people care about one another. You don't have a school [here] where people go into the classroom, shut the door, and you don't see them again until 3:10, but at [Lakeview] you're actually inviting people in. . . . You can go into anybody's class at any time and you will be welcomed. . . . There's a lot of sharing that goes on and it's never . . . "I've got this wonderful project, I won't let you do it because I want to get all the credit for it. . . . " [Instead, it's] encouraging growth in one another.

In addition, greater collaboration among teachers translated into greater use of collaborative learning approaches among students. All teachers used cooperative student learning groups for some portion of the day. Here is how one teacher described her motivation for doing so:

> I have cooperative groups in my homeroom, and I do that in reading and mathematics. I try and get them to work together to cooperate, learn together, and help each other. I think kids learn a little more from each other than they do from me. I also try to let them know that I'm not the keeper of knowledge, you know, and I don't hold the key. There are a lot of things I have to look up and there are many resources they can use to find information.

Collaboration among teachers also created opportunities for teachers to act as mentors for their colleagues. One teacher, who had to leave teaching for nine months because of what she described as burnout, became motivated enough at Lakeview to teach a workshop on multicultural education. "I never wanted to," she said, "but I did it. The support I got was fantastic and the response was great. . . . Being at [Lakeview] has allowed me to initiate a lot of things."

Collaboration opened up new opportunities for teachers, but it also brought problems to light. In being more dependent on each other, teachers formed opinions about each other's practice.

One teacher, for example, was seen by her peers (and saw herself) as having problems maintaining order in her classroom. The collaborative environment helped her to acknowledge this perceived shortcoming. She began to see her peers as helping her understand how to grapple with the problem of maintaining order and to see herself as teaching her peers how to think more globally. Another teacher had a reputation for acting in a "destructive" way with her fellow team members and with other faculty, by being overly critical and personally demeaning in public meetings. While they did not know quite what to do about her, her colleagues felt this was a clear violation of the norms shared by other teachers.

To a person, teachers saw Lakeview as a very different kind of organization than they had ever experienced before. The structural changes at Lakeview gave teachers a new view of their practice, of their relationships with each other, and of their relationships with students. The structure created regular opportunities for interaction among teachers, it provided teachers with opportunities to teach each other, it gave the organization a human face, and it opened up teachers to new views of how students learn.

Dealing with the District, State, and Federal Systems

In the spring of 1986, Daniels's third year at Lakeview, "the staff thought they were in heaven," according to Daniels. "We had small class sizes, we had seen dramatic changes in discipline and student achievement, and we saw differences in our relationships with one another. We felt we had discovered the answer.

> We were feeling like we had created a minor miracle, but we hadn't taken into account that the district was going through major changes—a new superintendent and a lot of instability in the central office. I hadn't anticipated the effects of these changes and hadn't thought about, for example, what it might take to make a financial commitment to stabilizing staff. I also didn't have many allies in the administration. Because of the changes going on in the district, the area superintendent and the assistant superintendent for instruction couldn't advocate for us because they felt threatened.

An August 1987 study of Lakeview by the Clearhaven school district showed that schoolwide average test scores in math and reading moved from below the district average to well above in the two years since the school had moved to its new schedule and structure. White students, who had scored above the district average before the changes, continued to score well above. African American students, who had scored well below the district average before the changes, moved to well above, while overall minority test scores were declining districtwide.

But Lakeview's unconventional structure and strong performance on standardized tests proved to be a liability in its relations with the district. Federal compensatory education policy (at that time, Chapter 1 of the Education Consolidation and Improvement Act) and special education policy (Public Law 94–142), as interpreted by state and local authorities, required that services to eligible students be delivered in ways that were clearly distinguishable from the "regular" educational program of the school. Lakeview's philosophy of not labeling students and its practice of grouping students without regard for their eligibility for federally supported services ran against established practice in the state and local administration of federal programs. In addition, under Chapter 1, local school districts are required to concentrate funding on the neediest schools according to student achievement and socioeconomic status, rather than spreading funds across all schools that happen to have eligible students. The Clearhaven school district used test score performance as one measure of need for allocating Chapter 1 funds to schools. Each year, the district would rank schools with Chapter 1–eligible students, and funds would be allocated to those schools with the highest indexes of need. As Lakeview's test scores increased, its priority within the district for Chapter 1 funds declined.

At Lakeview, losing federal funds meant losing staff. In the spring of 1986, it became clear that Lakeview would pay for its changes in the form of reductions in teachers. Lakeview stood to lose five staff positions. In Daniels's words, "we dropped, over the course of two years, from having eighteen to twenty special education kids to having two, not because the kids were any different, but just because we found a way to teach them without labeling them." Lakeview's strategy of not clearly labeling students had subjected the school to a steadily declining staff.

Also in 1986, the district announced that Lakeview was on a list of schools being considered for closure. The district was facing serious financial problems and declining enrollment. Lakeview's small size and old physical plant made it an attractive target for closing. Parents and staff mobilized, as they had many times before in the school's history. They attended district board meetings and used their contacts in the city's business and philanthropic community to put pressure on the school district to remove Lakeview from the list of schools considered for closure. They succeeded, at least for the time being.

Daniels was not completely surprised by the obstacles that she faced in her dealings with the district, but she was determined to keep the school's innovative program going. "When we first started making changes," Daniels said, "I went to the zone administrator and told him what we were doing. He was a fairly linear, sequential guy, and he said, 'You can't do that.' Then I went to the district special education director, who was a temporary appointment, and he was great. He said, 'Call it a "blended project" and do it.'" After Daniels and her staff had worked through their ideas in the summer between her second and third years, she went to the district's assistant superintendent for curriculum, who said, in Daniels's words, "By all means, go ahead." Daniels sent a letter to parents explaining what the school was doing. And she invited state administrators to visit the school, which they declined to do.

It became clear in 1985–86 (Daniels's third year) that Lakeview was out of compliance with local interpretations of both Chapter 1 and special education regulations. Daniels began to work actively to find a way for Lakeview to maintain its program and still receive federal funding:

> I was president of the [district] elementary principals' association at the time. That gave me a fair amount of access, and I was learning how to manipulate the system. A reporter called me, asking to do a story about the school. I invited him to visit, and he wrote a story that surfaced our situation. Then when it looked like we would lose our eligibility for special education funding, I called [an assistant to the state superintendent] and he said, "Why don't you come down and talk to us?" Before I went, I called [an assistant superintendent in the district], and she said, "Why would you want to do that?" She didn't tell me I couldn't go, but I could tell she was unhappy. We went and we made a presentation. The state special

education people were great. They said they would come up with $25,000 in funding if the district would match it. The district met the match, we got back two of the five positions we had lost, and we were in business for another year.

It was only long after the fact that I realized that there was some lingering hostility at the district level about this episode. I guess their attitude was, "There she goes again, doing inappropriate things." There were a lot of new staff in the district office. They didn't like being pushed. They were irritated that I hadn't gone through channels. I wasn't trying to hurt anybody; I was just trying to get someone to make the decision that was appropriate for the program. That's my job as a principal. It was a pretty dysfunctional system. I know how to work in dysfunctional systems, since I'm a product of a dysfunctional family myself. But some people took it personally. They thought I had taken unfair advantage. In my mind it wasn't unfair at all; we were just getting back what we had lost by doing well. At any rate, we probably carried some negative baggage from that.

The opening of school in Daniels's third year was rough. In her words,

The state gave the district the money in August, but the district didn't work out the match [the state required local matching money] until after the beginning of school. The kids showed up, and there weren't enough teachers. Because the district used the October student count to adjust positions, three of our new staff weren't in position until November. We tried two or three substitute teachers, who were terrible. There was one teacher I really wanted to hire, but we couldn't get her through the district personnel office. She volunteered some time and she really carried the class. The PTA decided to pay her $500. But at midyear she got a job offer in [a suburban district] and left. It was terrible for the school.

As the year progressed, Daniels recalled, "We were doing better with fewer staff and larger class sizes. I had never felt that class size was the important factor, but I fought for it because the teachers thought it was important. Working with fewer staff, though, made us more creative." But Daniels faced the same funding problems in the following year as she had in the previous one:

About the middle of the year I began to talk with the PTA president. She had recently moved [to Clearhaven] from Washington, D.C., where she worked in an education-related job, and she offered to make some calls. We found out that the current year's funding wouldn't work for next year; the state was willing to contribute, but the district wasn't willing to make the match. So we decided, with the PTA president's help, to apply for a grant from the Secretary's Discretionary Fund at the U.S. Department of Education. When we contacted the Department, we found out the application deadline was one week away, and they said they didn't usually give grants to individual schools. We put a proposal together, and I called [a prominent state official with an interest in education] to look it over before we sent it in. We applied for the grant and got it—$125,000—which allowed us to bring our supplementary staff back up to four people, to hire a half-time psychologist, and buy some computers. The following year was a good year for us.

The following year (1987–88), Lakeview applied for and received a grant under a state program designed to recognize exemplary schools. The grant brought about $50,000 per year to the school over three years and was used to increase use of technology, strengthen community involvement, and implement alcohol and drug abuse prevention programs in the school.

Daniels Leaves Lakeview

The first year of this grant, 1988–89, was Daniels's last year at Lakeview. That spring, she accepted a fellowship to study for a doctorate at an eastern university. Today she has become an independent consultant and an advisor to the federal government and foundations.

Reflecting on her experience as principal of Lakeview in the spring of 1989, Daniels said,

I guess I am disappointed at the response of the district to what we've done here. We got all kinds of external recognition—we were written up in [a prominent national education weekly newspaper], the superintendent of a neighboring district sent five of his principals to study our school, several national organizations visited, and [we got] the state and federal grants—but I felt all along that the district saw this as irritating.

I began to hear that people in the district and in other schools were saying, "Of course it's a good school. We could do the same thing if we had all those extra resources from the outside." That really hurt, because I always saw the extra resources as replacing those that the district had taken away because of our success.

The last straw came when I was running a workshop for [a regional school improvement consortium] and I ran into [an upper level administrator from the Clearhaven district]. I asked him why more Clearhaven schools weren't participating in the consortium, and he said, "Did it ever occur to you that the reason they aren't participating might be you?" And then he went on to say that [Lakeview] wasn't any better than any other school in the district, that we had developed our reputation because of good public relations, and that what I was doing was actually hurting other principals. Well, I was just crushed. I thought what I was doing was for the kids in [Clearhaven]."

Clearhaven district administrators declined to be interviewed about Lakeview. Another principal, a long time colleague of Daniels's and an administrator with a similar reputation as an innovator, said:

You have to realize that this is a genuinely pathological system. Once you get that straight, you either choose to work around it, or you leave. A lot of good people leave. Some stay. District administrators for the most part have no idea what's going on in the better schools, no idea what to do if they did know, and no idea how their jobs relate to what goes on in schools. On top of that, they [district administrators] are very easily threatened, so you have to spend a lot of time mollifying them, or you just don't tell them what you're doing. Unfortunately, [Laurel] wasn't good at that style. It just wasn't how she operated. She just did what she thought needed to be done. It didn't surprise me at all that they closed in on her.

Lakeview teachers credited Laurel Daniels with changing the organization and climate of the school, and many saw her as having changed their personal view of teaching. But as it became clear that Daniels was, in fact, leaving, they began to express some ambivalence about her tenure at Lakeview. Many teachers saw her as modeling in her own behavior the norms she wanted students and teachers to follow. "I remember the first day I walked in," one teacher reflected, "[Laurel] said, 'We're so glad.' She didn't [even] know me. 'We're so glad to have you.' And she gave me a big hug. When you see that you feel so much freer to do that yourself because it's infectious, and everybody on staff, instead of holding back feelings, whether it's their anger or their good feelings, . . . it's okay to show those feelings."

As time went on, as pressures on Daniels mounted, and as Lakeview's notoriety spread, teachers began to perceive Daniels as spending less time at Lakeview, although they found her no more distant personally or emotionally. Teachers also felt overloaded at times by the intensity of work in teams and the extra effort required by the retreats, meetings, and workshops. Some teachers saw Daniels's leaving as not altogether bad for Lakeview. As one teacher put it, "[Laurel] was fantastic and you know if it wasn't for her this program wouldn't exist. [When she left] she had instilled in us a confidence that no one would take this program away from us. We had our fears and trepidations, but she said, it's yours, it's been yours for a long time, because she traveled a lot as a facilitator to other school districts. She was gone a lot and we didn't realize [that] we had the best of both possible worlds."

Cheryl Curtis assumed the principalship of Lakeview in the fall of 1989. Curtis had been in the Clearhaven district for eight years and had spent 1988–89 in the district's central office. Asked about her first year at Lakeview, Curtis said, "I called this an implementation year because it was my observation that the teachers [had] had so many new ideas thrown at them that they hadn't had time enough to take them to completion, or to understand fully the new methods that were being presented." She also distinguished herself from Daniels: "I basically tend to be a rule-follower, but I think I'm politically pretty savvy about who I talk to. I'm not as much of a rebel as [Daniels]. I haven't had the kind of problems she did because she wasn't afraid to say, 'The heck with you.'"

Curtis cut back on the number of outside in-service training sessions and on the number of staff meetings in the school, arguing that Lakeview teachers needed fewer new ideas and more time to concentrate on implementing practices to which they had already been introduced. The Lakeview teachers viewed Curtis with cautious respect. One teacher said, "[Cheryl] is giving us things [Laurel] couldn't give us, and she's created a beautiful balance, and she doesn't touch us, she's so confident we're doing something great. She's learning from us and she's magnanimous enough to let us do our thing."

Teachers had felt both energized and a bit overwhelmed by Daniels's leadership and saw Curtis as more focused. As one teacher put it, "We felt exhausted, but we loved working under [Daniels]. . . . We needed [Daniels's] style, because [it] shook everybody up. . . . What [Laurel] did was to say, 'You know, all this stuff is not working and you need to look at what you're doing and look at what's going on out there and then take it back to the classroom and use it.'" As Daniels's tenure went on, teachers felt that she spent less time observing them in classrooms and that the school was increasingly open to external scrutiny by outside observers interested in its innovations. Teachers also grew somewhat weary of Daniels's participatory decision-making style. "I think [Laurel] tries so hard to be fair that sometimes it gets to be taxing because we're not making decisions or headway. . . . [Laurel] is sweet and very wonderful, but sometimes you need her to be a little bit more administrative." Teachers saw Curtis as a less ambitious, less exhausting, more orderly administrator, and generally thought her style was well suited to Lakeview's stage of development.

After a year at Lakeview, Curtis had experienced many of the same problems with the district as Daniels had, even though she was less assertive in dealing with them. She complained about spur-of-the-moment staffing reductions and insensitivity at the district level to the school's successes. "My difficulties are the same that probably everyone else is having," Curtis said at the end of her first year. "I'm upset because of the staffing reductions, and I'm upset about how they assign students to us. And one thing that really bothers me is that . . . the district is really talking school-based management, they are really talking restructuring, and I feel like we have a model here that is [both], and they are spending all this money on consultants, half a million dollars, and we aren't even going to be able to implement our model because we don't have the staff positions. . . . That's goofy!"

Chapter Three

Teams and Themes

There is substantial evidence that Lakeview changed significantly as an organization during Laura Daniels's tenure as principal. Students spent mornings in cross-age groups with broad ability bands for reading, math, and language arts, reverting to the traditional age-grade structure in the afternoon for social studies, art, and science. Teachers' work departed from the traditional egg-crate structure as they worked in teams with collective responsibility for groups of students, and together as a whole faculty on school-side changes. Finally, curriculum was structured differently from the traditional one-subject-per-hour format: teachers constructed curriculum units around broad themes that were designed to challenge students to engage actively in learning and that integrated subject matter.

But we were interested not only in whether Lakeview's organization had changed but also in the degree to which changes in organization influenced teaching practice in the classroom. How did teachers think about the content they were teaching? How did they interact with students? What role did students play in learning? To probe the relationship between structure and teaching practice, we now focus on four teachers and four specific examples of classroom practice.

Two of these examples deal with the use of teams and themes in instruction, and two deal with the teaching of self-esteem and self-expression. Because these examples capture the main structural changes at Lakeview and the core values of the organization, they are central to what the organization was about. The teachers we have chosen to focus on were among six whom we observed and interviewed about their teaching practice at Lakeview. As noted earlier, the original six teachers were selected as representing changes in teaching practice that were taking place at Lakeview. We observed each of these six teachers for a full day on three occasions, and we interviewed each extensively about their views of teaching and learning and about what we had observed in their classrooms. Four are featured here.

Lisa Turner and Trudy Garrett

Among the structural and curricular changes that occurred at Lakeview under Daniels's leadership, two were particularly significant: (1) the use of teams to develop new relationships among teachers and students and (2) the use of instructional themes to integrate content across traditional subjects. Teachers worked together in teams, and students worked together in classrooms. Teachers promoted student learning by integrating ideas and knowledge through the development and use of theme units and hands-on activities and experiences.

We observed Lisa Turner and Trudy Garrett, members of the intermediate team (grades 4 and 5), teaching a curriculum unit on the theme "Animals in Our Immediate Environment." Both teachers used cooperative learning in teaching this unit. The curriculum unit and accompanying activities were written and designed by a professor at a nearby university who had been recruited by the principal to work with the school in the area of environmental science. The goal of the unit was for students to gain an understanding of how animals and their environments are interrelated through observation, hands-on activities, and working individually and in teams. During this unit, each of the three intermediate teachers—Trudy, Lisa, and Kaitlin—taught their homeroom classes and did the same activities, but each class focused on a different animal in the immediate environment: ants, spiders, or snails and slugs.

On one particular day of observation, each class carried out an activity in which the students ventured onto the school playground in teams to find and record the number of animals in various places on the school grounds. In Turner's class, students were to tally the number of ants they found in various sites; in Garrett's class, it was slugs and snails. In both classes, students brainstormed on the number of animals they thought they would find at various places on the playground; then they were to make actual observations and later compare their predictions with their observed findings. As we shall see, some differences emerged between the teachers and classrooms in these common hands-on experiences and cooperative learning activities.

Observing and Recording Ants in Lisa Turner's Class

Lisa Turner's lesson on "Ants" consisted of a sequence of introduction or brainstorming, fieldwork on the playground, and discussion of the results in the survey of ant shelters.

Introduction: Brainstorming

Turner introduced the lesson on ants by announcing to her fourth- and fifth-grade students that they would be conducting surveys of where ants lived. She opened the lesson in this way:

Turner: This is going to be a more accurate survey of what we find on the playground. What I want you to do is brainstorm some of the places. You have already had a chance to go out and see some of the hot spots. I want you to think of some other places. I want you to think of three important things that every animal needs.

Students and Turner: Food, water, and shelter.

Turner: It has to be a place where they can have shelter. If it is in the middle of the asphalt, it is not a place where they can get underground. You have to think about that. If there are cracks in the ground, they can get under the ground, and that is a place where there is shelter, right. So let's think about some of these places.

Turner asked students to brainstorm areas in the playground where they would expect to find ants. Students named about eleven different places on the playground, and Turner wrote on the board such responses as "the big toy," "by the wood chips," and "in the grassy area north of the building." After having students write down the names of the eleven places, Turner told them to count the ants found in a particular place and record that next to the name of the place on their papers. Her directions were as follows:

> *Turner:*   Get out your paper and write down all eleven places, and you will do a count. Then you need to check all eleven spots. You might not check the exact same location as somebody else. We will try to get an approximation of how many ants we find in the grass. We are going to count the ants. If you see 20 ants, count them. If you see one ant, count it. If you see 150, count fast because they will be moving quickly. There are a lot of ants out there.

Students received magnifying glasses to aid their recording of the number of ants and then lined up to go outside.

In introducing the activity, Turner attempted to set the purpose and explain directions for the fieldwork. She seemed to want students to understand that ants needed shelter like other animals and that they would be more likely to seek and find shelter underground rather than on the top of the asphalt. She gave them a clue by suggesting that it was unlikely that as many ants would be found aboveground as below. Turner also encouraged the students to think, welcoming their responses. The purpose of the assignment seemed to be for students to count the number of ants in each area to determine which areas were likely to be the best environments to support ant life. Turner did not tell the students how long they should stay in one place, nor did she explain the overall purpose of the activity. Exactly how to record the number of ants and why was left to the interpretation of individual students. We saw how this introduction played out when we observed students' investigations on the playground.

Fieldwork

Pairs of students spent about twenty-five minutes on the playground counting how many ants appeared in different places. Different pairs approached the task differently. For instance, Joshua and James kept a running record of the total number of ants they saw. Richard and Max kept a systematic record, staying about the same length of time in each place and recording the number of ants counted. Students got together in groups of about six and informally compared with one another the number of ants recorded. Two boys found an unusual ant and decided to capture it and bring it to Turner.

The informality of the fieldwork revealed Turner's openness to inquiry. Because the task was not specified explicitly by the teacher or discussed by students, teams developed their own approaches. Although Turner encouraged students to do the surveys in pairs, they conducted informal comparisons with one another and captured an unusual ant. On the one hand, students' differing approaches suggested that they were unclear about the purpose of the talk and the procedure for collecting their survey data. On the other hand, students' approaches suggested scientific investigation akin to "discovery." The follow-up classroom discussion revealed how Turner treated her students' approaches and their resulting discoveries.

Discussion: Reporting the Results

Back in the classroom, Turner began the session by holding up an ant farm and describing how the worker ants build tunnels and caves to store food.

> *Turner:* These ants have built tunnels through here. There isn't a queen ant, there aren't any males, there are just work ants. All they do is eat and drink a bit of nectar. Sometimes you put droplets of sugar water in here. They will build tunnels and little caves to store food if they happen to have extra food.

Two students then asked questions about the cost of ant farms. Turner responded and moved on to recording students' fieldwork results. She stood at the board and asked students to report the number of ants found at each playground site. At times, students called out their responses, which she recorded. At other times, she called on specific students. Turner kept a running count of the number of the ants in each location. Her only comment as she was recording the information was to indicate that she would collect ants by the big toy and not on the hot asphalt because there were so many by the toy. No discussion of possible interpretations followed the reporting of results by students.

At one point, the principal entered the room to give students letters from the mayor in response to letters they had written earlier. Turner then ended the lesson rather abruptly by saying:

> *Turner:* I know where I am going to collect—by these little hills. I am going to write this down neatly—actually, Josh, why don't you write this down for me neatly [the total number of ants at each site]? I am going to pass out a paper. You guys have fifteen minutes to get started on your poster [a different assignment, unrelated to the ant unit, creating posters for the carnival].

A student then asked if he could see the letters from the mayor, which Turner read aloud. Turner did not return to the fieldwork results.

The classroom discourse about the fieldwork results provides an interesting glimpse into Turner's teaching. During the brief discussion about the observation and recording activity, students told the teacher their counts, which she then recorded on the board. Turner might have queried students about whether certain places on the playground had more ants, and why that might be the case. We wonder: what interpretations did students draw between the surveys and ant habitats? What understandings did students have of the relationship between the number of ants and shelter? Had Turner asked students how they approached recording the number of ants at each site, she might have discovered that teams interpreted the assignment in different ways. For example, Josh and James recorded the total of ants across all sites, while other teams tallied the ants at each site. Because much was left implicit for students to construct on their own, teams of students developed different understandings of the task, and these different understandings were never "unpacked," either during fieldwork in teams or during the later whole-class discussion. After the principal entered the classroom, Turner moved on to a new activity, leaving individual students to make sense for themselves of their observations and recordings of ants for that day.

In Turner's lesson, we see the opportunity for an open-ended, inquiry-oriented approach to learning about ants and their environment. Turner encouraged students to provide ideas about where to gather data, valued their responses, and provided an opportunity for students to be involved in an interesting, field-based activity to view ant habitats for themselves. Yet the lack of conversation relating the purposes of the investigation to the methods and to the results of the actual data-collection activity left students with different discoveries and understandings of their "findings" after conducting their investigations in teams.

The students might have discussed with their teacher any number of themes about the relationship between the environment and the number of ants, the reliability of students' findings, different teams' approaches to data collection, or the relationship of their data collection to the larger ideas of ants and their environment. As it was, students engaged in an exciting hands-on team activity that consisted of counting ants and reporting the numbers, but without written or oral discourse on possible big ideas about either the relationship of animals to their environments or about scientific method. The underlying purposes, assumptions, ideas, and understandings of the students and teacher remained implicit during this lesson, so the teacher and individual students were left to infer and make sense of these for themselves. As observers, we puzzled about how students interpreted the events during this lesson and what ideas and understandings students took away from this activity about the habitats of ants, about environmental science, or about scientific method.

Observing and Recording Slugs and Snails in Trudy Garrett's Class

As the theme unit on "animals in our immediate environment" unfolded in Trudy Garrett's class, students engaged in a sequence of activities similar to those in Lisa Turner's class. On a previous day, Garrett had her fourth- and fifth-grade students "brainstorm all the places they thought they would find snails and slugs around here." She indicated that the students had predicted they would find slugs and snails "in damp and cooler places, rather than out in the sunshine." Each team had brainstormed specific places on the playground where they might find slugs and snails. Then students had worked in teams to make a map of places on the school grounds to look for them. Garrett saw this map-making activity as good "practice" for her students. She originally intended for each team to "use their maps to find out whether or not their predictions were true." But she worried that it would be very difficult for her fourth- and fifth-grade students to make the kind of map she thought they needed, which would include specific areas, such as the drain, where she thought they would find slugs. To deal with this worry, Garrett herself constructed for her students a map of the schoolgrounds to use for their observations, with twenty-six areas circled where the teams were to look for slugs and snails and record the number. The circled areas included the sites where teams had predicted they might find slugs and snails.

In planning for the fieldwork in teams, Garrett also worried that students would not feel "ownership" or "responsibility" and that the groups would not stick together. She dealt with this worry by assigning roles for each member of the group and by having an elaborate system of procedures, directions, recording sheets, and materials. As Garrett construed it: "I'm a believer in prevention, and I don't want to see what would happen if I didn't have assigned roles within each group because there's only one of me and they are roaming all over. If I don't somehow have them responsible for something, I might have some kids working away and others not being involved. I just wanted to make sure that everybody had a job so they all knew they could take part in the project."

Introduction: Assigning Roles and Explaining Procedures

The actual lesson on this day consisted of an introduction and fieldwork. Garrett spent fifty minutes assigning roles and explaining and drilling on the procedures for the fieldwork in teams. Each team received a packet of materials, which included two copies of a white sheet having the map and group directions; a pink sheet to list team members and assigned roles of each team member; a yellow sheet labeled "tally sheet for mathematician," containing the list of the eleven sites where the teams were to look for snails and slugs; a blue sheet labeled "totals," containing the same list of eleven sites and three columns, one each for slugs, snails, and total. The group directions were as follows:

1. Place tally marks by the circles to determine where slugs and snails are found (pg. 1).
   (1 tally = 1 slug or snail)
2. Add up tally marks in each specific area (pg. 2).
3. Place totals on specific area sheet (pg. 3).

Each member of the group chose one of the following roles: map recorder #1 (slug tally); supervisor of #1; map recorder #2 (snail tally); supervisor of #2; mathematician; supervisor of mathematician; recorder of totals; supervisor of recorder of totals. Using the overhead projector, Garrett explained each of these sheets, each of these roles, and the procedures in detail. For example, the role of the mathematician was "to add up the tally marks." When students seemed confused by the elaborate system of procedures, Garrett responded by drilling the students on the procedures:

Garrett: One of you in your group is going to be the recorder of the snails; Now tell me again, what color of tally marks will the recorder of snails be writing in?

Class: [*In unison*] BLUE!

Garrett: Blue. Good job! . . . What color is slugs to be written in, class?

Class: [*In unison*] RED!

Garrett: Red, good job. So if you're going to tally up how many slugs are found, you're going to be marking in which color?

Class: [*In unison*] RED!

Garrett: Red, right. You're going to be going around as a group. Notice these maps are exactly the same, but you have two different jobs because one of you is going to tally in red, and one of you is going to be marking in blue. . . .

Before they left for the playground for their fieldwork, each team created a name and logo for their team. The teams called themselves the "Slug Busters," "Adventurers," "Slimers," "S and S Hunters," and the "Black Panthers."

Fieldwork

The class had time for only twenty minutes of fieldwork. During this time, all the teams conducted their investigations out on the playground with clipboards and tally sheets. Most teams proceeded together from site to site, where each member of the team recorded, tallied, or supervised, according to his or her role. Most of the students' talk had to do with counts of the numbers of snails or slugs found or exclamations about the slugs or snails. One group, the Black Panthers, continued to be confused about the procedures that they were supposed to carry out.

At one point an altercation broke out among the Black Panthers, and David ran up to the teacher saying, "She hit me. She hit me. Dimetria hit me." The following conversation ensued:

Garrett: Dimetria, what's your job, honey? What are you doing in this group?

Dimetria: When I was over there, he keeps hitting me.

Garrett: When you are on the job market, would you want the supervisor to hit you?

Dimetria: But he hits me. He keeps on hitting me so I hit him back.

Garrett: David, David, David. I want you guys to work together. If you try real hard, you can work together, can't you?

Discussion

When the class returned to their room, they had time for only a brief discussion before their next class. Garrett told the class that they would continue to work on the project the following day. Then she queried the class as to whether in doing the "same experiment tomorrow" they would get the "exact numbers" that they found today. Several students responded that they thought the numbers would be different. Garrett then followed up by asking, "Why?" Several students offered reasons. For example, Keith suggested that "it might rain tonight and more slugs would come out." Garrett accepted all these reasons and then queried, "If we continue this tomorrow, how many of you think we'll have an honest true observation? How many of you think we'll have a combined observation?" Then she told the class that she was not going to give them an answer. Garrett left the class "thinking about this—how can we make a clear observation today, what we spotted, and then what we will spot tomorrow?"

In Garrett's class the discussion ended with the posing of a thought-provoking question and a unique opportunity for students to explore ideas of validity and reliability of data gathered in scientific investigations, as well as ideas about the characteristics of habitats of slugs and snails. This last five minutes of the class period was the only time that the students and the teacher engaged in discussion of substantive ideas related to science, scientific inquiry, or the "theme." Most of the class period—more than fifty minutes—was concerned with explaining or implementing procedures for doing the observations and recording in teams.

Teams, Themes, and Teachers' Classroom Practice

Through our observations and interviews with Lisa Turner and Trudy Garrett, we explored how two teachers on the same team at Lakeview School came to interpret, understand, and enact two structural innovations within the school: teamwork and theme units.

The teachers brought very different knowledge and experiences to their teaching of this theme unit. Turner was a young teacher, in her sixth year of teaching. Her undergraduate degree was in natural resources, from a prestigious midwestern university, and she brought to the classroom her interest in science and her concern for the environment. She was an active initiator of ideas in the school and had been responsible for bringing in several grants in the area of science. Turner considered herself a continuous learner who was constantly improving. She took many classes in architecture, Asian studies, and science to increase her general knowledge and to develop her pedagogical skills.

Trudy Garrett was an experienced teacher who had formerly taught special education and had been trained in Distar—a highly structured, teacher-centered instructional model—at a major western university. As a result of the Lakeview restructuring, she felt she had become more flexible and open to change; she saw herself as having made large changes in her teaching practice, toward being significantly less "structured," or more student-centered, than she used to be. Daniels concurred that Garrett's teaching practice had become significantly less structured. Indeed, the discourse pattern in her classroom seemed to have at least the possibility of becoming more open-ended, if only briefly, as evidenced, for example, by her posing the why question at the end of the slugs-and-snails lesson. Yet even a casual observer in Garrett's classroom would see vestiges of the Distar approach, including extensive use of drill, having students repeat and chant in unison, and directly instructing students in skills and procedures. For principal and teacher, Garrett's practice reflected major changes when compared with her former total immersion in the highly structured and scripted Distar approach to teaching. Yet an observer or a fifth-grade student new to her classroom might see chanting in unison and extensive drill and repetition—vestiges of Distar—as even more highly structured, scripted, and teacher-centered than the typical pattern of instruction for an upper elementary public school classroom in the United States.

Both Turner and Garrett said that teacher teams had opened the door for them to the knowledge, expertise, and understandings of their colleagues. Through their participation in the school-wide retreats organized by Daniels, in which teachers examined and discussed their own learning and teaching styles with one another, teachers became aware of the similarities and differences in teaching styles within the school and within their own team. On one level, the value placed on "learning styles" provided a kind of philosophy about teaching and learning. It called attention to the necessity to examine and discuss how teachers and students learned. At a deeper level, however, learning styles served to justify continuing past practices.

When Turner and the other Lakeview teachers completed a learning-style inventory by Bernice McCarthy (1980), Turner found that she was in the minority. While most of the teachers fell into the structured "type one learner," she was a "type four learner," who enjoyed being creative and coming up with her own ideas. She described her teaching as unstructured and creative; she saw the big picture. Her colleagues, on the other hand, were structured, organized, and concerned with details. She viewed these different teaching styles as equal in value, providing opportunities for teachers to complement one another. Although the teachers had differing styles, Turner felt they needed to adapt their styles to different children. Just as teachers have different styles, children learn in different ways: "I think if you think that kids learn in different ways, then you have to see that teachers are going to teach in different ways too, depending on how they learned. . . . You can't just teach to the style you learned. We all have to try to teach to other styles, and that's really important to do." Turner interpreted the idea of learning styles as justifying her own less structured, more student-centered practices, but she also interpreted the idea of learning styles as justifying change for herself toward becoming more "organized." Yet she seemed to be in the minority in attempting to change her "style."

As Lakeview teachers became aware that they differed in learning and teaching styles, most teachers used the learning-style notions to justify their existing practices by labeling these as "strengths." While they claimed to respect the different teaching styles of their colleagues and teammates, they extended this respect inconsistently and often showed less respect for nontraditional teaching approaches, such as that of Lisa Turner. She described herself, and her teammates saw her, as an outgoing innovator who was creative in her lessons. She saw her colleagues, including teammate Trudy Garrett, as having "structured" teaching styles and as "concerned with details," whereas she saw herself as creative and as adept at providing "hands-on learning experiences" for her students. On the other hand, Garrett, who also saw herself as structured, organized, and concerned with details, viewed this as a strength; and Garrett, Ames, and Daniels viewed Turner as having a weakness in classroom organization and management. Turner herself confessed that this was so; she looked to her teammates to help her learn to better organize and manage classroom instruction for her students. She saw her teammates as providing a good complement to her innovation.

What did teaming mean for these teachers? Through meeting together and working in teams, Lakeview teachers had come to understand that each teacher had different knowledge, strengths, and learning styles. They construed teaming to mean that each teacher had his or her own self-selected role, knowledge, and expertise within the team. Since teachers were regarded as having their own unique roles, knowledge, expertise, and individual learning styles, they regarded it as entirely appropriate for individual teachers to teach in different ways.

What did teaming mean for students at the classroom level? The conception of teaming at the school level seems consistent with how Garrett enacted teaming in her own classroom. She thought each student should have a unique role or responsibility on the fieldwork teams. The result was that each student really worked individually within the team, with the "supervisors" working individually to check and monitor calculations. Knowledge was compartmentalized within each individual team member, rather than constructed collaboratively among team members. Each member constructed a piece of knowledge (tally of slugs in a particular site) that was then supposed to be put together to form the whole. This knowledge was never discussed by the group as a whole. A similar, compartmentalized view of knowledge and an individualized view of teaming seemed to underlie Turner's practice as well. When students worked together in pairs in her class, one student would count as fast as he or she could and the other one would write down the tally of ants. The students might as well have done the task individually. As it was, individuals did different parts of the task, and then the different parts were supposed to add up. Knowledge was treated the same way in the whole-class discussion. The assumption was that each group had an accurate count of the ants in a place. Each group did the same task, and then in the whole-class discussion, Turner merely summed the results for each group to get a total. What was meant by the total was not entirely clear.

Although Turner had expressed interest in adapting her teaching style to each student's learning style, within their classrooms both she and Garrett used the same pedagogical approach and the same teaching "style" with all the students in their classes regardless of students' learning styles. Garrett taught the slugs-and-snails lesson to her students with her more structured, detail-oriented teaching style, while Turner taught the ants lesson to her students with her more open, holistically oriented teaching style.

How were theme units enacted in practice? In the case of the theme unit on "animals in the immediate environment," the actual curriculum unit was constructed and written by an external consultant, a professor of environmental science, and not by the Lakeview teachers. Thus the ideas were those of the consultant, and the assumptions and knowledge underlying the activities in the unit were left to be inferred or constructed by the teachers. Each unit itself consisted only of a list of the activities for each day and several pages of information on the animal being studied: ants, slugs and snails, or spiders.

According to the curriculum unit, Turner and Garrett were both supposed to be teaching similar ideas (about relations between an animal and its environment), built around a common theme of inquiry (animals in the immediate environment), using a common scientific method that was built into the curriculum unit. Indeed, these two teachers did have students engage in similar activities, observing and recording the animals in particular sites. But the underlying model of learning, and the conception of knowledge that accompanied it, was very different in the two classrooms. Turner seemed to be taking a discovery approach, assuming that students would construct scientific knowledge on their own. In contrast, Garrett proceduralized the relevant knowledge and also separated the procedures that the teams followed from the substantive ideas of scientific method, so that the roles of recorder and supervisor seemed unrelated to the work of a scientist or to inquiry within a scientific community. Rather, the roles and the way she conceived of accountability, record keeping, and supervision seemed more akin to the roles and procedures of workers in a factory than to scientists within a community of inquiry and knowledge generation.

This lack of relation between the classroom work and knowledge and inquiry in a scientific community seems not surprising in Garrett's case because she did not regard herself as a scientist, and she stated that she was unfamiliar with science and scientific inquiry. She observed that all she knew about slugs and snails was what she had learned from the information sheet provided as part of the curriculum unit by the consultant. The tenuous relationship between classroom work and scientific inquiry seems more surprising in the case of Turner, who had expertise and knowledge in the area of environmental science. But perhaps because she was an expert, she made unwarranted assumptions about what students "understood" from the fieldwork. Perhaps because of this knowledge of science and the scientific method and her ability to fill in between the lines, she assumed that her students could do so as well and could make sense of her oblique comments about "knowing where she would collect ants."

In sum, Turner's and Garrett's previous experiences, their self-perceived "teaching styles," and their assumptions, whether about scientific knowledge and ideas or about classroom work, served as frames within which they taught and created their practices. The school-level interventions seem to have had remarkably little influence on changing these frames, and on the teachers' knowledge, understandings, and enactments of the science theme unit in their classroom practices. Indeed, the school-level learning-style intervention was construed by the teachers to fit within their existing practices and to justify teachers' maintaining their different views of learning and teaching.

Chapter Four

Self-Esteem and Self-Expression

At the center of Lakeview's strong sense of community was the core value of building self-esteem and self-expression among students and faculty. Several teachers described the Lakeview staff as a family. Peg Ernst, a veteran Lakeview teacher, found Lakeview to be a very supportive environment where people really cared about one another. Lisa Turner believed that principal Laurel Daniels had provided her with a wonderful opportunity to be at the school and suggested it was the themes that unified both the staff and students. As Turner said, "[the themes] really unify the whole building and the kids; they're like comrades—they're real close." Several teachers believed that the atmosphere at Lakeview provided them with opportunities to try out new ideas and to grow both personally and professionally. Referring to her hands-on approach to science and her literature-based instruction, Turner believed at Lakeview she could engage in the kinds of teaching she wanted to do, whereas this was not possible in her experiences at previous schools. She added that teaching at Lakeview had provided her with the opportunity to "learn, to grow, and expand and refine [my] skills."

Laurel Daniels was the key figure in providing a supportive environment for two other teachers of the six we observed, who had personal problems affecting their professional lives. In the cases of Peg Ernst and Lynn Horn, Daniels made changes in the

51

organizational structure to accommodate the needs of the teachers. For Ernst, who had suffered from what she called "teacher burnout," Daniels helped negotiate a reduced contract after a leave of absence in order to make a gradual transition back to full-time teaching responsibilities. The reduction allowed Ernst to regain confidence in teaching and to play a renewed role in the school. She credits Daniels with having developed an open, encouraging, and trusting school environment that allowed her to become a successful teacher with a renewed interest in teaching. Ernst attributed changes in her own teaching to Daniels, saying, "We have to give her credit; she's just been a wonderful person to work with. I think a lot of these changes that we've made are due to her."

In the case of Lynn Horn, who suffered from cancer, Daniels adapted her workload and schedule, allowing Horn to teach art in the afternoons and one section each of mathematics and reading in the morning, and relieving her of full-time responsibilities for a self-contained classroom. Horn credited Daniels with having created an adaptive professional work situation that allowed her to express her own special needs, interests, and strengths. Horn also felt that Daniels had attempted to create a feeling among the staff that was like that of a family where individuals cared about one another and individuals' strengths were valued.

Staff members at Lakeview shared a common conviction that it was essential to provide a collegial environment and to develop self-esteem in both teachers and students. The staff believed that a supportive setting promoted risk taking and personal growth for both students and teachers. Teachers' self-esteem, nurtured by a supportive school setting, would then result in the provision of a safe environment where students could take risks in their own learning. Students could learn better in an environment that fostered risk-taking and individual self-expression.

The cases we present here describe these two teachers, Peg Ernst and Lynn Horn, both of whom were considering leaving the profession for health reasons yet found support and confidence at Lakeview School. Because of their own personal experiences, these teachers focused on students' self-esteem and providing students with opportunities for self-expression through the writing curriculum in their classrooms. These cases explore relations between self-esteem at the school level and self-esteem at the classroom level.

Writing in Peg Ernst's Primary Classroom

Peg Ernst had been teaching for fourteen years, the last five at Lakeview School; during the period of our study she taught kindergarten and first grade. She described herself as a shy, reticent person who, prior to coming to Lakeview, was unwilling to take risks. After a period of depression and self-doubt, which she described as burn out, Ernst said that she had experienced personal and professional growth at Lakeview.

On the subject of promoting students' self-esteem, Ernst said, "[I] do things with self-esteem because that's one of the most important things I think that we can help children to learn." The development of self-esteem undergirded much of what Ernst tried to do in her classroom. For an inventions unit, Ernst selected music and dance as the areas for exploration because they provided opportunities for children to take risks and develop self-esteem. Elsewhere, she had students learn sign language for the opportunity to feel good about being able to communicate with others. Preferring to work with individual students, she refused to use ability-based reading groups for fear of hurting children.

The atmosphere in Ernst's K–1 classroom was both lively and comfortable. Students felt free to walk about the room for materials and to ask other students for help. Students often approached Ernst to ask about logistics and to ask for her help on assignments. She dashed around the room, helping students get organized, putting her arms around students, and listening to their stories, problems, and questions. Ernst responded very warmly to student requests, often using endearing terms with her students, and establishing an atmosphere of warmth and activity. The warm atmosphere underscored Ernst's commitment to developing self-esteem in her students.

The following excerpt from Ernst's classroom practice during writing time in January illustrates this commitment to self-esteem. This lesson had two major parts: the whole-group session for generating ideas and the individual writing and conferring time.

Ernst introduced students to the writing topic, balloons, by bringing in a balloon for children to feel and discuss. Gathering students at the back of the room, she explained that she would give everyone a chance to touch the balloon. She asked students to think about how it would feel to be a balloon, or to pretend the balloon had eyes and think about the things it could see, or to imagine what could happen to the balloon as it floated by when the wind came up. Ernst then asked students to provide ideas about what could happen to the balloon then; students responded that "It could float away," "It could pop," and "It could go faster."

After students had touched the balloon, Ernst told them that for their "journaling" (writing or drawing) they were to get a piece of paper, use crayons or felt pens to draw a picture of a balloon, and write about what it would be like to be a balloon or about how a balloon feels. When students began to draw and write on paper, Ernst circulated and talked briefly with individuals. Her style of interaction was a supportive one, in which she praised students, got additional materials such as pens for them, and wrote words on the paper for them. The following excerpt from the classroom dialogue provides an example of how Ernst worked with individual students.

Sammy: I made a balloon.
Ernst: [*Leaning down beside child*] You made a hot air balloon. What a good idea. I didn't think of that. You're so creative.

After she discussed several logistical matters with children and the student teacher, Ernst went over to another child.

Ernst: What happened to it when it popped? What does it do when it pops? This is really good. What are we going to have down here, though? Can you think of something to have down there? Is it in the clouds? Um, is it down towards the ground? Can you think of something to put over here? That's really good, Sarah. Very nice. [*She then speaks to the whole class.*] Okay, we'll let you do your drawing now, and then we'll do some writing on this tomorrow for those of you who haven't had a chance to write yet.
Susan: I'm not making balloons, I'm making string.
Ernst: Oh, that's the string. Oh, I like that. That's great.
Alison: This is, this is Jessie and me.

Ernst: That's Jessie and you, huh? Okay. [*Leans down to another student*] Well, that's beautiful, yeah. Tell me what yours says? I want—

Sean: —to be a balloon.

Ernst: A plane?

Sean: A balloon.

Ernst: Oh, balloon, isn't that neat? Okay.

Ernst talked to several different students briefly. In each exchange she praised the student's work. With the second student she also asked her questions, encouraging her to put additional drawings on the paper. Ernst continued to support students' efforts at drawing and writing stories.

Ernst: Oh, thank you Beth. Wow. That's a lot of string, isn't it?

Beth: The balloon's going crazy 'cause the air's going out.

Ernst: Oh, I can see how you're making the air come out. That's great.

Beth: Make it from here. Make it right here.

Ernst: Okay. That is so good. Are you going to put some balloons over here, or are you going to do some writing, some more writing over here? [*To another student*] This is good, Matt. Okay, now what, are you finished drawing? No, okay, okay.

Ernst talked to many students about their writing in a short period of time. Her questions and responses were brief as she moved around the room continuously from student to student. Ernst's main concern was encouraging the students to write or draw something.

The many endearments that Ernst used with students, the continuous praise of students' work, and her supportive body language are indicators of a teacher who was trying to develop self-esteem. Ernst's interactions in the classroom seemed to reflect her personal concerns with self-esteem and building confidence.

While Ernst's interactions were quite supportive of the individual student and she seemed to care deeply about each child, it was not clear how much substance the dialogue about writing contained. Ernst did not encourage students to compose a story line, for instance. Instead, students drew pictures and told her what they had drawn. She supported students' ideas and acted as a scribe for students who wanted her to form the words for them. Yet she did not seem to be concerned about the story itself or the ideas that children had to communicate. Most of Ernst's talk with children consisted of praise for their efforts or their ideas. Her orientation toward building self-esteem was to accept everything that students wrote without questioning, challenging, or engaging in substantive conversations with children about their work.

Ernst's practice raises the question of the relationship between building self-esteem and promoting substantive changes in practice in the classroom. She saw a direct connection between Lakeview's emphasis upon self-esteem and her own classroom practices to build self-confidence in her students. Her conception of building confidence seemed to be to accept all of the students' ideas. Ernst seemed to see the development of confidence as a necessary step for children's writing development. However, in focusing so heavily on self-esteem, children may have missed opportunities for developing substantive understanding of the writing process or of the ideas they were writing about.

Poetry in Lynn Horn's Classroom

A woman in her fifties, Lynn Horn had been for most of her life, by her own account, "a square peg in a round hole." She saw herself as having been constrained from personal self-expression for much of her life because of the social community in which she lived. She had been a nun and lived in a convent where she was "just bashed and bashed and bashed" until she finally realized that she "could be destroyed." Then she worked for eleven years in a school with a predominantly African American population, where she loved working with the children but "was stressed and traumatized" by the African American male principal who was "very paranoid" and was "either real high and jovial or came down, 'boom'. . . and would carry on this tirade and bang the table and be angry." After these experiences, Horn felt burned out, and even after she came to Lakeview she was just a "little island" unto herself until Laurel Daniels came to the school.

Daniels arranged for Horn to teach art to all students in the school. Horn also taught reading-writing and mathematics to two sections of children on the intermediate team to allow the intermediate team teachers to have a common planning time. Daniels accommodated Horn, who wanted to teach art, by getting her certified by the district to teach art even though Horn did not have a degree or training in art. In this way Daniels matched the needs of the intermediate team for a common planning time with Horn's desires for lower stress and a career change.

Personal Expression and Esteem

Horn felt she was achieving a greater "fit" at Lakeview, although she still saw ways in which she was different and needed to express herself. It was important for her to feel confident about being able to be different and to express those differences. She described herself as a "right brain" person and as having a learning style that was creative and expressive. In this way she saw herself as different from many of her colleagues in the school whom she saw as "left brain" or more linear or structured in their teaching. Also, her recent bout with cancer had influenced her deeply, heightening her concern about living life to its fullest intensity, being in what she characterized as "a continual state of becoming." She saw herself as intensely committed to the reforms at Lakeview.

When Horn described the philosophy of the school, many of her personal themes came through in her portrayal. She talked about achieving balance between development of right-brain and left-brain learning; balance within the context of team teaching and theme teaching; a philosophy of intense working together; and dedication to innovative learning: trying out new practices, being daring, getting away from worn-out stereotypes of teaching. She saw Lakeview's restructuring and the teachers in the school as needing to "stay in process." As Horn put it: "We want to keep this flowing; it's ours now. . . . We don't want it to die. We don't want it to become mediocre. We don't want it to lose its intensity, and that keeps you in a constant state of intensity."

In her art teaching and her language arts teaching, Horn was guided by her belief that her role was to facilitate children's self-expression. As she saw it, children have a freedom of expression that is innate. But as we humans interact with the world, "we get so caught up with the worries, the complexities, and the traumas of living . . . we have a tendency to forget how to express ourselves as children." Horn taught poetry as a means to encourage children's self-expression.

Horn also viewed her poetry teaching as a way of enriching the lives of her students. She volunteered that while some Lakeview children had "enriching experiences," for example, with books and poetry at home, other children did not. LaShaunda was one such child. Until the previous year, LaShaunda had lived with her grandparents. During the current year she lived with her mother, whom Horn described as "cute as a bug's ear, but a space cadet" and "just a kid" herself. Horn felt that nothing would happen to LaShaunda—no enrichment—if it were not for her grandparents. Horn seemed to see enrichment and expression as interwoven for LaShaunda when she said that LaShaunda's grandma "helped things flow from her." But Horn saw LaShaunda as "very stilted, creatively, but not like she was. She's written a lot of darling stories."

A Writing Lesson on Poetry

One day we observed Horn teach poetry to a class of third and fourth graders. During that lesson, the students worked on writing poems at their seats, while Horn worked with individual students to correct the clerihew poems that they had written on a previous day. Horn described the clerihew as a "simple poetry form—a form of couplet." During the poetry lesson, Horn's interactions with individual students were similar in discourse and approach to the editing task. In the example that follows, we focus on one interaction that was representative, and we use the specific case to raise questions about what it meant for students to express themselves and develop confidence in Lynn Horn's classroom.

LaShaunda, the fourth-grade African American girl we spoke of earlier, brought her clerihew to Horn for correcting. On her paper LaShaunda had written:

Annie got some ice

Then she had crossed that out and written:

Little Annie found a dog then
she found a little hog when she
went in her house

Then she had crossed that poem out and written:

Little Annie found a
dog then she found a
little hog, When she went
in her house she fed them a
mouse.

Horn began by reading LaShaunda's clerihew aloud:

Horn: "Little Annie found a dog." All right. Big dog, little dog, puppy dog, describe your dog.

LaShaunda: It's a puppy dog.

Horn: Oh. "Found a little puppy dog." [*On LaShaunda's paper, Horn rewrites the first line of the clerihew to read "Little Annie found a little puppy dog."*] You want it to be smooth. Oh, that's cute, now just a minute. "Then she found a little hog." That's cute, but let's put some cute little words in there with it.

LaShaunda: "Then she found a little hog."

Horn: Well, "then she"—those aren't exciting words. Here—you found this little puppy dog, and you're cuddling it and taking it home, and you heard these little . . . oink, oink, oink, oink, oink, oink, oink, oink. My golly! We're not alone; I not only have a little puppy dog for a pet, but a—

LaShaunda: A cute—

Horn: —piglet hog. We'll call it a piglet hog because it's tiny, huh? Was the piglet following you?

LaShaunda: Yeah.

Horn: Mmm, 'kay.

LaShaunda: I had to carry them home.

Horn: Was it close behind you, or was it a block down the street?

LaShaunda: It was close—

Horn: All right, "then close behind her . . ." [*Writes this on LaShaunda's paper as she says it*] Did she hear it before she saw it?

LaShaunda: Yeah.

Horn: She saw a piglet hog. [*Writes as she says it*] We'll put "piglet hog"; that sort of sounds silly, but we don't want to . . . unless you want a great big one?

LaShaunda: No, not a big one.

Horn: [*Reading*] "Little Annie found a little puppy dog, then close behind her she saw a piglet hog." You don't want to feed her a mouse, they don't eat mice, little doggies. [*Crosses out last line of LaShaunda's poem*] All right, they went home. She . . . away they went to her little . . . is that a house?

LaShaunda: Uh huh.

Horn: What's another name for a house that makes that house very warm to you?

LaShaunda: Mmm?

Horn: You don't want it just to be a house, you want your house to be a . . . where do you go after school? You say, "I'm going to, going house now, Mrs. Holmes?"

LaShaunda: I'm going to my cute little house now.

Horn: You don't say you're going to your house, you're going to your—

LaShaunda: —home?

Horn: Yeah! Home is much warmer than house. A house doesn't have feeling until it becomes your home. And away they went to her little home, hmm?

LaShaunda: Yeah.

Horn: I only have three minutes before I have to get my math ready. "Then away they went. . . . Then away they went to her little home." [*Writes as she says it*] The piglet got what for dinner? What do you feed a pig?

LaShaunda: That rhymes with home?

Horn: No, no, no. What you feed your dog. What rhymes with home for doggie?

LaShaunda: A bone.

> *Horn:* Yes! The piglet got—
>
> *LaShaunda:* —a little bone.
>
> *Horn:* No, no. You don't give a bone to a pig.
>
> *LaShaunda:* Oh.
>
> *Horn:* The pig got . . . blank . . . the puppy, a bone. What are you going to give your pig?
>
> *LaShaunda:* Leftover food.
>
> *Horn:* All right. "The piglet got leftovers." [*Writes as she says it*] How's that?
>
> *LaShaunda:* Yeah.
>
> *Horn:* It's usually what they get. "-O-V-E-R-S comma, the puppy a bone." [*Writes as she says it*] Put that in your booklet and copy it when you come in the morning, rather than reading a library book.
>
> *LaShaunda:* OK.

The final clerihew, as written by Horn, now read:

> Little Annie found a little puppy dog!
> Then close behind her she saw a piglet hog,
> Then away they went to her little home,
> The piglet got leftovers, the puppy a bone.

A "Facilitator" of Students' Expression?

Lynn Horn's stated goals for writing were to teach her students to express themselves and to instill self-confidence. She said that she had to teach herself to express her ideas and "not to plagiarize or be stilted." She wanted to instill in her students the confidence to write in their own styles.

Horn described herself as a "facilitator." As a facilitator, she said that she did not want to push her values on her students or her words. Rather, she would "drop little subtle hints to get the mind working." She wanted to enhance students' vocabulary skills and, for example, to avoid overuse of words like *nice* and *good*. Also, she thought that children had to be "constantly reinforced" so that "they realize that this computer up here [their brains] can do phenomenal things."

Analyzing Horn's interactions with LaShaunda within the framework of her own stated goals, we can see some evidence of Horn's perspective. For example, she began the interaction by questioning LaShaunda about her ideas and her words. Horn asked LaShaunda to describe the piglet, its size, and its location, and then she used LaShaunda's ideas in the subsequent rewriting of the poem. Then she proceeded by giving LaShaunda hints about what words might fit into the poem, such as *home and bone*. Consistent with her perspective on teaching vocabulary skills in context, Horn turned the words *little hog* into the "more exciting words" of *piglet hog*. Further, Horn suggested in an interview after the lesson that if the writing had been a free-form story, she would have encouraged LaShaunda to go and look up *hog* in the dictionary and see what words would make that a more exciting word. In this instance, however, Horn did not encourage LaShaunda to do the thinking but rather supplied the words for her.

If Lynn Horn's interactions with LaShaunda were analyzed from the learner's perspective, we would see a marked lack of consistency among her stated goals, her words, and her actions. There was incongruity between what Horn said she was instilling—self-expression and self-confidence—and what students might have inferred from their teacher's words and actions. For example, Horn took the pen, crossed out LaShaunda's words, and rewrote the poem in her words and in her own writing. Further, without querying LaShaunda about what ideas she was trying to express, Horn suggested that LaShaunda's words and ideas were lacking or insufficient when she said, "Those aren't nice words"; "No, no. You don't give a bone to a pig"; and "You don't want to feed her a mouse." LaShaunda did very little of the talking, and the talking LaShaunda did was directed by Horn. The discourse followed a pattern determined by Horn with scant influence from her student. The teacher did the thinking and the expressing in this speaking-and-writing episode, not the student.

Reflections on Self-Esteem and Self-Expression: The Cases of Peg Ernst and Lynn Horn

Both Ernst and Horn believed they had found a nurturing environment at Lakeview School, where they felt revitalized about their contributions to the school and about their teaching. Their principal had accommodated the personal and professional needs of the teachers by arranging appropriate schedules and classroom settings. These two teachers valued affective learning outcomes such as self-esteem, self-expression, and sensitivity to relations with individual students. While the experiences of the teachers in the school shared common elements, these experiences played out differently for each teacher at the classroom level.

For Ernst, self-esteem was the most important value to develop in young children. Her practice reflected this value as she continuously supported children's writing and encouraged them to express their ideas. From the students' perspective, learners undoubtedly felt supported and confident in their attempts at writing and expressing themselves in Ernst's classroom. Her own experience of collegial support at the school level seemed related to the ways in which she interacted with students in her K–1 classroom. However, the emphasis upon building self-esteem did not seem to lead to her thinking about or interacting with children around academic content in a sustained and serious way.

In Ernst's case, she believed that establishing a safe, risk-free context for writing was the first step before asking children to elaborate upon their ideas or asking questions about their texts. She believed that students learned to write by having many opportunities to write without criticism; her main goal was to "make them comfortable with the writing process." It seems that for Ernst establishing a supportive classroom environment was the most important step in students' learning to write. Ernst's writing practices raise several questions, however:

Is developing self-esteem fundamental to students' learning to write?

Are production of writing and development of self-esteem sufficient goals for K–1 students?

How do teachers facilitate students' moving beyond written production of text to thoughtful analysis and discussion of their writing?

In Horn's case we see something a little different. Although Horn shared Ernst's expressed values of developing students' confidence and expressiveness, Horn's practice seemed less reflective of these values than did Ernst's. While believing teachers ought to encourage students to express their ideas creatively and take risks, Horn subtly undermined the efforts of her students by imposing her own ideas and rewriting their texts to reflect her own interests and standards. Horn thought she saw coherence between what she was facilitating—students' self-expression and self-confidence—and her actual practice; yet her students experienced more mixed messages than Horn seemed to realize.

These two cases suggest that school-level changes relate to classroom changes in complex and interactive ways. In the case of Ernst, school-level values were more obviously reflected in her classroom work: she felt valued in the school, and in turn she strove to support her students' self-esteem. In the case of Horn, school-level changes were reflected less apparently in her classroom practice. Horn was supported by Daniels; she had regained lost morale and self-esteem; and she herself had achieved a greater fit for her own creativity at Lakeview than she had in previous settings. Her own experiences of regained self-esteem and support for individual expression were reflected in the stated goals that she embraced for students: increased confidence and ability and willingness to express themselves. Yet from the students' perspective, Horn's practice did not seem to be designed to inspire confidence on the part of her students or to support their efforts at self-expression. In responding to students' writing, she negated their ideas, rejected their words, and imposed her own ideas and her own "style" upon them.

What might explain the different relations between these teachers' espoused beliefs and their classroom practices? An important difference between Ernst and Horn was apparent in what led them to revise their classroom practice. Although both teachers endorsed the need to change their practices continually, and they provided evidence of having made specific changes in their own practices, they differed in their reflectiveness on their own teaching practice, specifically, in their reports of what led them to revise their classroom practice. Both Ernst and Horn felt that growth was highly valued at Lakeview. But for Peg Ernst, changes in her teaching come about through growth in her own learning, and learning occurred through reflection and analysis of how she was influencing her children through her teaching, particularly in the area of human relations. As Ernst put it: "It's a priority not only that you grow, but the way you grow is to look at what you're doing, and you have to tear it apart. You can't be afraid to look at everything—how you teach reading, how you relate to the kids, how the kids are relating to one another."

Ernst described how she learned by reflecting on her teaching practice, and she focused particularly on her relationships with students and their relationships with one another. She also stressed the importance of analyzing critically her own teaching in terms of its effects on students' self-esteem and on relations among students and herself in the classroom. In her own way, Ernst seemed to have internalized one of the main ideas of Lakeview's reform, that changes in practice should be justified in terms of students' learning. In Ernst's case, she did focus on her students' production of writing, students' self-expression, and their self-esteem as important learning outcomes, and she used her assessment of these to adjust and modify her own practice.

Similarly, Horn viewed changing her practice as important because she did not want "to get in a rut." In contrast to Ernst, however, she described a different process of revising her practice. When asked why she chose to have her students write clerihews, Horn replied initially that she "didn't know." It was just part of her lesson plans; she wanted them to experience different types of poems. When asked whether she would teach the clerihew again next year in her writing class, Horn replied that she did not know and that it would depend on the group of students that she had next year. When queried about how she would decide, Horn said that she would go to the local educational materials store for teachers, Learning World, and search for new materials to teach poetry. She did not keep anything from year to year, she said. She viewed each group of students as "so different," she would not plan intensively until she "got her group." Yet she asserted that she knew she would teach poetry again next year because she wanted to give her students "a chance to express themselves poetically." Also, she said that Cheryl Curtis, the new principal, wanted students to do poetry. "Cheryl has been in poetry groups where adults go and read to each other. . . . Before school is out, my whole room is invited to go to her office, and sit around on the floor, and she is going to have tea. She wants them [the students] to make [poetry] selections. . . read any selections they want to."

Horn's thinking about her practice was activity-based and oriented toward change and experimentation. For example, in reading and writing, she chose from new activities as they became available, and she had an overarching goal that students would "express themselves." Yet in her own teaching of writing, Horn's focus was considerably less on students' abilities and dispositions to express themselves than was Ernst's focus in her classroom. Rather, Horn's focus was on her own expression, and her teaching reflected her own desire to express herself: "I think poetry is a lost art and want to enhance my own expertise by experimenting." Further, the idea that a teacher might engage in deliberate decision making about her teaching did not fit with Horn's self-perceived learning style. She saw her style as creative and spontaneous: "My mind doesn't go: 'Why did I choose this?' I'm very right-brainish. Each group [of students] is different. I am really adventuresome. I just don't have any absolutes."

Although on the surface Horn's classroom practice seemed less consistent with school-level reforms than Ernst's practice, after digging deeper we feel they both appear more consistent. From Horn's point of view, the school was engaged in innovation, growth, and change. This orientation toward experimentation and creativity was consistent with Horn's own learning style and teaching style, she herself was supported by Daniels for her "strengths" of expression and creativity, and Horn saw herself as experimenting and having students express themselves by writing new and different kinds of poetry. Similarly, Ernst saw herself as supporting and encouraging her students to express themselves just as she has been supported in her own self-expression. Ernst had come to feel more personally comfortable at Lakeview; she was able to take risks and to innovate. Both Ernst and Horn saw themselves as having created new classroom practices in response to school-level reforms. For example, both Ernst and Horn said that students were writing much more than they ever had before. On the one hand, they experienced what they regarded as a massive change—having students write when they had not written much before—and written production and fluency of expression were valued in the school as worthy goals. On the other hand, writing and self-expression were not necessarily taught in a way that gave students a clear model of how they could become effective and thoughtful producers of text.

In the final analysis, Lakeview was good for Ernst and Horn, both personally and professionally. The school made them feel good about themselves, gave them an active and vital view of teaching, and caused them to do things that they probably would not have done before. On the other hand, their practice often seemed seriously at odds with the espoused aims of the school and with their own teaching goals.

Chapter Five

Structure and Practice

What can we infer from the Lakeview case about the relationship between school structure and teaching practice?

By any defensible definition of the term, Lakeview was a "restructured" school. The school had made major changes in both the formal structure of the organization and its norms. Under Laurel Daniels's leadership, teachers changed the way they grouped students, and the way content was allocated time during the school day; they learned to work in teams, and they changed their work routines to accommodate more collegial work. The school also changed its social norms. Teachers regarded the school as something like a family, in which they learned to help and support each other. They learned to reinforce and support the self-esteem of students. And they learned to respect individual differences among teachers and students. These new structures and norms had an energizing and empowering effect on teachers, as they learned to look outside the organization for new ideas about how to teach. They valued and acted upon the training that Daniels brought to the school. By any fair reckoning, these were significant changes relative to the way a typical elementary school operates; and the changes were certainly significant relative to what the teachers themselves reported they had experienced in the schools they had worked in prior to Lakeview.

Lakeview's changes were even more significant given the generally unsupportive district environment in which they took place. The changes in structures and norms that Daniels and the Lakeview teachers brought about ran against the grain of local interpretations of federal policy. They also raised the visibility of Lakeview within the Clearhaven school system in ways that displeased district administrators. From the district's point of view, Lakeview seemed to be more a troublesome anomaly than a successful school—a point of view that persisted despite evidence, which the district itself had developed, that Lakeview students were performing well academically. In the absence of district fiscal and political support, Daniels looked to state and federal sources, as well as to her well-developed base of political support at the neighborhood level, to sustain Lakeview. Reaching over and around the district for support, Daniels discovered, only reinforced the district's resistance to her leadership. Daniels left. She was replaced by a principal who, from the district's perspective, was more predictable; but within her first year on the job she too discovered many of the same problems that had dogged Daniels.

The troubled history of relations between Lakeview and Clearhaven district administrators suggests that significant changes in school structures and norms can occur without support from the district level. Whether they can occur with any frequency, or be sustained over time, without district support is more problematical. In the end, most of what happened at Lakeview happened in spite of the Clearhaven district, not because of it.

How did Lakeview's restructuring relate to teachers' classroom practice? On one level, there was significant evidence that the new norms and structures had an effect on how individual teachers and students acted in school. The daily experience of students at Lakeview was, on the face of it, different from the daily routine that students experience in most elementary schools. Students were grouped differently at different times during the day, providing them with diverse contacts with students across a considerable age span, lessening the likelihood that they would see themselves as permanently part of a high- or low-achieving group. The daily experience of teachers was also quite different from that of most elementary school teachers. They taught different groups of students at different times during the day, they worked in teams, and they saw themselves as broadly responsible for the learning of a larger group of students than in the typical elementary classroom.

The norms of group work and family responsibility also exercised considerable influence on the lives of students and teachers. All teachers used cooperative learning groups in one form or another; the use of groups reinforced norms of collective responsibility among teachers and students for everyone's learning. Teachers worked in groups, both in teams and as a whole faculty, again reinforcing the idea of collective responsibility. Throughout, Daniels was credited with creating a positive and productive atmosphere for teachers and students, making it possible for teachers who had written themselves off to take a new view of their work.

So at the level of daily routines, espoused beliefs, and teacher and student morale, the changes in structure and norms at Lakeview seemed to be manifest in the practices of teachers and the lives of students. At a deeper level, though, the connection is murkier.

Our examples of teachers' practice give evidence of the teachers' fundamental lack of understanding of the connection between structures, norms, teaching practices, and student learning. We observed that:

- Lisa Turner's application of the ideas of group work and active student inquiry resulted in an experience for students that was engaging and promising, but in the end it resulted in no visible common learning among students.
- Trudy Garrett's application of the same basic ideas resulted in an experience for students that was largely focused on proceduralized knowledge, heavily influenced by Garrett's earlier training in Distar. At the end of the exercise Garrett did open up the classroom discourse to student inquiry, but only perfunctorily.
- In neither case was there much evidence that either the teachers or the students understood what it would mean to develop a common understanding of a complex subject through joint inquiry.
- In both cases, teachers seemed to be betting that if they applied their own prior, "common sense" notions of learning to the creation of an experience for students, something productive would happen.
- In neither case did teachers go beyond prior notions of learning to construct a new view of how students might learn collectively from their diverse experiences.

- In both cases, teachers were using a sample exercise that had been developed by a university faculty member with little or no explicit adaptation to the specific requirements of the Lakeview setting or their specific instructional needs.
- In neither case did teachers attempt to draw an explicit connection between the externally developed exercise and the specific requirements of the learning experience they wanted students to have.

In other words, these are not simply examples of ragged execution of fundamentally sound ideas about teaching and learning. They are examples of a fundamental lack of understanding about the connection between structure, pedagogy, and student learning.

Peg Ernst's application of the ideas of student-initiated writing, and her support for students' self-esteem, resulted in a literal torrent of positive reinforcement for students, but almost nothing in the way of concrete support for the development of knowledge about the craft of writing. Lynn Horn's application of the same ideas resulted in a heavy-handed substitution of her own ideas for those of the students. Again, new and complex ideas of teaching practice seemed to be filtered through the teachers' existing practices, with idiosyncratic and confused results:

- In neither case was there much evidence that the teachers understood or grappled with the complex connection between student-initiated work and the development of common ideas about written and artistic expression.
- In neither case did the teachers seem to go beyond their own prior ideas about self-esteem and learning to develop concrete ways of drawing students into higher levels of understanding of their own self-expression.
- Both exercises were based on externally developed instructional materials, with no explicit attempt to make a connection between the materials and the specific requirements of what teachers at Lakeview were trying to accomplish. Indeed, in Lynn Horn's case it was not clear whether the exercise had any place in a well-thought-out structure for student learning, since she said she would not know whether she would use it

again next year until she made a determination based on the specific students.

Again, these seem to be examples of something more than faulty practice. They suggest a lack of understanding or interest in the fundamental issues of the relationship between individual self-expression, self-esteem, and the development in students of an understanding of complex cognitive tasks.

While there were abundant examples, then, of the influence of new structures and norms on the operation of Lakeview, our studies of individual teachers did not produce examples of teachers consistently coming to grips with the problems of pedagogy and learning in ways that matched the espoused beliefs of the school. Teaching practice seemed to be an amalgam of teachers' prior ideas and practices with examples of new pedagogy; the whole did not rest on a foundation of knowledge or of thought about how students would learn complex new ideas better under the new pedagogy.

The shakiness of the connection between changes in structures, norms, and operations on the one hand and the development of teaching practice on the other was abetted considerably by the prevailing norm of "learning styles" at Lakeview. At some basic level, teachers' methods were inconsistent with their espoused views of how children learn and how they should be treated in school. Moreover, teachers gave no indication that they were engaged in an effort to better align their own goals with their teaching. They saw classroom practice, and student learning, as matters of "style"—a strategically vague term that was calculated to allow differences among teachers and among students to flourish amid a common set of beliefs about how the organization should be run. Teachers saw differences in pedagogy as matters of style, rather than as matters for serious discussion, reflection, debate, and change. Teachers saw their own differences in teaching style as reflections of differences in the learning styles of students, rather than as occasions to question what common set of cognitive understandings they wanted students to have as a result of their experience at Lakeview. In other words, learning styles provided a more or less airtight guarantee that teachers could change their teaching practices only in ways that they found comfortable and compatible with their previous beliefs and practices.

Was Lakeview a "successful" example of a restructured school? The answer is undoubtedly yes at the level of structures and norms, and even at the level of operations that affect the daily lives of teachers and students in school. For many who study school organization and learning, such changes are enough. Certainly, they represent rather large changes relative to the typical elementary school of self-contained classrooms, ability-grouped students, pull-out programs for children with special needs, limited teacher collegiality, and limited collective responsibility for student learning. Did the changes in structures, norms, and daily operations at Lakeview result in teaching that was more directed by a fundamental understanding of how children learn? The answer is a qualified no. Teachers tried interesting, stimulating, and engaging new practices, but these trials typically did not result in a visibly clearer understanding by either teachers or students of what it means to master complex ideas.

The major lesson that we take away from this case is that there is no necessary connection, in the short run at least, between changes in structures, norms, and operations and teaching practices. Teaching practice, as demonstrated in the examples we developed, is not a direct product of the working conditions that surround teachers. It is much more deeply rooted in the prior ideas and established patterns of practice that teachers bring to the organization. New structures and norms, even when they are translated into changes in the operating routines of organizations, are refracted through these prior ideas and established practices, and in this process of refraction they produce interesting variations. The result, however, is often nothing more than interesting variations—connections to some coherent view of student learning remain illusive. In order to work at the level of teaching practice, then, school restructuring has to confront the difficult process by which teachers' prior ideas and established patterns of practice are formed and changed. Working strictly on an organizational level probably does not have this result.

Part Two

Webster Elementary School

"You're about school change, you're about school reform, you're about school improvement, and you are the people who make a difference."

—STAFF DEVELOPMENT LEADERS, THE MASTERS CENTER

Chapter Six

The Development
of a District's Flagship

The School and Its Community

Webster Elementary School is a low-slung, modern building, sitting in a large open area surrounded by modest single-family houses. Its physical appearance is spare, and clean. Webster's neighborhood is quiet and modest, dominated by the simple family homes. The neighborhood is far from the urban center of Fairchild, a sprawling, medium-sized city in the south-central United States.

The vastness of the district and the relative isolation of Webster are accounted for by the fact that, in the early 1970s, Fairchild was the object of a school desegregation lawsuit that resulted in the consolidation of city and county school systems. Under the plan, students are bused, often long distances, to produce desegregated schools. Most schools in the district, including Webster, enroll a diverse student population. Of Webster's roughly 475 students, about one-quarter are African American, virtually all of them bused; about one-quarter have family incomes that qualify the students for free or reduced-cost lunches. So while Webster is not an "urban" school in the usual sense, it is a school that represents the diversity of a broader urban system.

In the mid-1980s, the Fairchild School District began a major school improvement and restructuring program. With the support of a local foundation, and with the advice of an outside consultant, the district established a large, quasi-independent center. It was to manage districtwide school improvement, including staff development for teachers and principals in curriculum, teaching, and school-site management, as well as to collaborate with a local university to establish training and induction programs for new teachers. The center, which we will call the Masters Center, was staffed largely by practitioners from schools in the Fairchild district who had been leaders in their own right before being recruited to work on districtwide issues.

The superintendent of Fairchild and the leadership of the Masters Center articulated a common reform agenda, focused on school-site decision making, a curriculum that embodied active student learning of ambitious academic content, and increased teamwork among both students and teachers in the daily work of the school. The center ran regular workshops in school-site management for teams from Fairchild schools and staff development in new curricula and teaching methods for teachers. It also provided consultant services, from its own staff and from the local university, for on-site work with teachers in schools.

Cheryl Billings at Webster

Webster was in the first wave of Fairchild schools to become seriously involved in the district's reform effort; it is now considered one of the district's flagship schools. Cheryl Billings was recruited to the principalship—her first—at about the same time the district began its reform initiative. Billings describes her development as a principal as moving in parallel with the district's restructuring efforts and her own work as a principal at Webster. During her first year, Billings and two Webster teachers were invited to attend a series of professional development workshops at the Masters Center, dealing with broad issues of school reform and school-site decision making. During the second year, groups of teachers from Webster attended a series of professional development workshops on new approaches to teaching. These teachers began to experiment with the use of new materials in the classroom.

In the summer after her second year, Billings held a "shared vision" workshop with Webster teachers and support staff, assisted by the staff of the Masters Center. The resulting statement of the school's vision for its students stressed "purposefulness, creativity, self-direction, and respect." The staff considered making "orderliness" a part of the statement but ultimately rejected it because, as

Billings said, "we decided it was understood" as a condition for the other purposes. They also settled on a school slogan, "Expect the best, achieve success." Billings saw this workshop as a pivotal event in the development of teachers' responsibility within the school. "I love the fact that they chose a visionary statement that was not the one that I had put down on my piece of paper," she said.

During the following year, Webster teachers continued to attend professional development sessions at the Masters Center. They also visited schools in other districts with exemplary programs in areas in which they wanted Webster to develop.

With these experiences, Billings's own ideas about school restructuring became more specific. "Before I thought about reform and restructuring," Billings said, "I thought about doing things better for children but using the same methodology. I was thinking the same way: 'We'll do a better job on reading, . . . we'll do a better job on math, . . .' but I never thought of things such as looking at different ways for people to operate in school." As her exposure to new ideas increased, she developed a broader conception of what it meant to improve teaching and learning.

Billings feels a key event in her personal development was attending a summer workshop sponsored by the Principals' Center at the Harvard Graduate School of Education. Billings claims she would never have applied to the Harvard summer program "[i]f I hadn't been part of [the staff development at the Masters Center], and if the [leaders of the center] hadn't said, 'You're about school change, you're about school reform, you're about school improvement, and you are the people who make a difference. . . .' As it was," she said, "I was so embarrassed about making application that I typed my own application. I didn't want my secretary to type it because I didn't want to be embarrassed when they wrote me back and said, 'Who do you think you are?'"

Billings describes her experiences at the Masters Center and the Harvard summer program as giving her confidence and affirmation. "I'm real grateful to those people because they made me feel very significant, and everybody needs to feel significant." She attempted to impart the same feeling to Webster teachers. "I remember one teacher saying in our third year of restructuring, 'Nobody thinks teachers are anything and I'm just a teacher. . . .' I said, 'You're not just a teacher, not just a plan operator, not just a child, not just a student, and you have to be the person who knows that you're not just an ordinary person. You have the responsibility to make things happen.'" Billings saw the process of restructuring at Webster as the unfolding and development of her own knowledge and confidence as well as that of the Webster teachers.

For Billings, school restructuring meant creating "better ways for teachers to teach and students to learn." As a result of their work with the Masters Center, Billings and the Webster teachers settled on a collection of closely related changes in the school's structure and content of its academic program. The structural changes involved the introduction of multi-age grouping and teacher teams. By the 1989–90 school year, just over half the teachers in the school were organized into five teams. The "Snoopy Gang" and the "Tigers" included teachers and children in grades 1, 2, and 3; the "Ducks" came from grades 1 and 2; and the "Thoroughbreds" and "Eagles" from grades 4 and 5. Billings initially saw multi-age teams as an experiment; she did not necessarily intend to generalize the team structure to the whole school. But as experience with teams progressed, she became increasingly committed to them as the major vehicle for restructuring. Her interest in multi-age teams was reinforced by the staff at the Masters Center, who saw teams as one of a small number of restructuring initiatives they were interested in having schools try, and by the emergence of multi-age teams in policy initiatives at the state level.

From Billings's perspective, the team structure had a twofold purpose. First, teams provided a mechanism for teachers to work together on common instructional problems. Teachers in teams were assigned adjacent classrooms to allow free movement among rooms. Teachers were encouraged to develop expertise in a curriculum area, by attending Masters Center workshops and other staff development activities, which they could use to help other teachers in the team. Second, multi-age teams allowed teachers to group students flexibly, according to their academic readiness rather than their chronological age, and to avoid retaining students with learning problems. Billings was proud that the school had a "no retention" policy, largely attributable, she argued, to the flexibility that the multigrade team structure provided to teachers in dealing with differences among students.

The team structure provided the setting for a series of curricular innovations in the school, all of which were designed to engage students more actively in learning. Billings described her vision of teaching and learning as creating an "adventure for children," a "bonding relationship" of the child with the subject matter and the teacher. It was the teacher's job, she argued, to "provide for student success and allow children to grow in whatever direction that they grow in." These goals were to be accomplished by the introduction of hands-on activities in the classroom—"kids actually doing it," by which she meant active engagement of students in understanding and interpreting literature, doing science experiments, and solving mathematics problems. These experiences were to be created by using cooperative learning (multiple-ability student groups engaged in common problem solving) and curricula that involved students in concrete problem solving (literature-based reading and writing, mathematics with manipulatives [blocks, tokens, rods, and shapes used to demonstrate mathematical concepts], and science with experiments and inquiry) rather than recitation of facts.

Billings characterized successful teachers at Webster as "curriculum experts," by which she meant

> they've been able to take a basal curriculum and interpret and enrich it in a new and different way for children, adding to what they already knew. . . . They are having children talk about what they're reading and participating, and then write about it. [In math] Ms. X is handing out those math manipulatives and saying [to students], "Who can show me?" . . . And then she'll have kids exchange information and sit together and work through far more complex problems. . . . It's curricular interpretation and enrichment as opposed to a standard process. . . . [They are like] artists. . . . They have transformed the curriculum.

For Billings, then, active engagement in learning characterized both the situations that teachers create for students in classrooms and the posture of teachers themselves toward the curriculum. Students learn by engaging in active problem solving with each other; teachers learn by transforming the curriculum from inert subject matter into active projects that engage students' interests.

In addition to these changes in curriculum and teaching, the Webster staff undertook to change the district-mandated student report card. According to Billings, the teachers involved in teams became increasingly dissatisfied with the form and content of the report card the more they became immersed in multi-age grouping and curriculum change. The report card, they argued, did not accurately represent the way they were teaching or the goals they had set for students. The teachers proposed an alternative report card and student assessment process to district administrators. The proposed report card provided more extensive teacher narrative descriptions of students' work and more frequent assessments, in some cases as often as once a week. The Fairchild superintendent responded by endorsing the Webster proposal and asking Billings and a group of Webster teachers to present their alternative report card to the district school board. The board acted favorably on their request and the new report card was implemented.

As part of the district's initiative for school-site management, in 1990 Webster began to practice a form of school-site budgeting. The school formed a budget committee, composed of teachers, to review and make recommendations for how the school would use its discretionary funds for supplies and materials. The committee met in the spring of 1990 for the first time to decide on allocations for the following year.

Regarding this mix of activities, Billings argued, "My role is to see that the ship steers the course we set. We got together as a school and we set the course when we determined our vision. . . . I see my role as just keeping us on that course." She described the district's version of school-site management as "a voice, not a vote," meaning that teachers should be directly involved in decisions that affect their ability to perform in the classroom (schedules, curriculum materials, supplies, etc.) but should not be required to participate in decisions that involve things distant from their work (custodial budgets, physical plant decisions, etc.). She noted with approval that in the spring of 1990 the school budget committee devised a new system for allocating money for supplies and materials that gave individual teachers and teams more control over the funds.

That spring, during the major part of our observation at the school, Webster was in a transitional phase. Roughly half the school's teachers had been involved in teams for almost a full school year; the other half were due to be brought into the team structure the following year. Billings was aware that teachers differed in their support for the restructuring ideas she was sponsoring in the school. She was also aware that even those teachers who subscribed to the new structures and methods had varying capacities to implement them. She expressed her beliefs about this variability among teachers as follows:

> Teaching styles can vary depending on the personality and the philosophy of the teacher as long as everyone has the same basic premise, and the premise at Webster is that we are here for success for children; and the strategy we have chosen as a school to implement that success is multi-age teaming. And hopefully teachers will have and are buying that philosophy. . . . Does this provide success for children?

She continued later, in response to questions designed to elicit her views about differences among teachers:

> I think that you will have different teaching styles and that you can't expect all teachers to teach the same way. What is more natural for one teacher than another depends on the teacher's style and it also depends on . . . what she's been exposed to. . . . There are times when kids need to have a teacher lecture or they need to listen to something that's being presented by someone, but not all day and not for a long period of time because their attention spans are not set for that with young children, and they need to move and they need to be involved. I encourage teachers to have activities where kids are involved in the learning. I do that by passing out literature on what is effective teaching of young children, and by having our teachers present at [the Masters Center] and by encouraging others to go hear them, and by talking about it in faculty meetings or in various settings. . . . You don't have to say to somebody "You need to teach like that." I guess that's what I would call a less direct approach.

Billings's management style, then, was a combination of public support for and deference to teachers as individuals, coupled with a persistent push for structural and curricular change. Even teachers who were not enthusiastic about the changes at Webster saw Billings as a supportive colleague. In the final analysis, though, there were limits to how much variation Billings would accommodate. In her first five years at the school, four of the school's approximately twenty teachers had transferred, two in the year before the school converted entirely to teams. Of these transfers, Billings would only say that they were based on "mutual" agreements that the teachers would be more comfortable teaching at other schools.

Billings saw the agenda of reform at Webster as consistent with, and supported by, the Fairchild district superintendent and the district as a whole. Speaking of the superintendent, she said:

> He has sanctioned [supported] the efforts in the building, like our new report card. . . . He could have said no . . . instead of saying, "That's wonderful, yes. Go on and do it. . . . Bring it to the board meeting and let's make a report and let's tell them what we're doing." To get that kind of sanction means you're willing to take risks, so that all of us at Webster are, I think, forever indebted to him for that opportunity. He's given us a piece of [our] lives. . . . He keeps letting us do things. . . . In education, for years we've been told what to do. You know, to suddenly be able to think on your own is a real new experience for a lot of us.

The District's Role

The Masters Center is located in a large building close to the center of Fairchild. It bustled with activity: groups of people from schools in the district entering and leaving the building, staff striding busily from one meeting to another, large sessions and small discussion groups going on in every available space. One sensed quickly that the center was a place that teachers and principals took seriously.

Ted Brandt and Pamela Thompson were leaders in what the district called its restructuring team, a group of staff at the Masters Center who worked with individual schools. The team was organized into a matrix structure, with staff specializing both by level of school (elementary, middle, high) and by districtwide initiatives (cooperative learning, school-site management, curriculum reform, etc.). As with virtually all the other staff of the Masters Center, Brandt and Thompson came from teaching and administrative jobs in the Fairchild schools. Brandt was a high school teacher and middle school principal recognized for his innovative leadership. Thompson was a highly regarded elementary and high school teacher known for her innovation in curriculum and teaching.

A large portion of the Masters staff were "resource teachers," regular teachers on leaves of absence from their regular duties to provide on-site assistance to schools. Thompson, herself a resource teacher before assuming her current job, described the role of a resource teacher as "a broker of resources for [their] school . . . [an] advocate for resources for that school, so they spend a lot of time in their schools and they participate, they listen, they get involved and they help to forge a shared agenda between that school and this central office . . . and they come back in and they become an advocate for that school's shared agenda, and that helps the district meet its restructuring vision, but it makes sure that the school owns that restructuring agenda."

The role of the Masters Center staff embodied a tension between top-down and bottom-up views of change. On the one hand, the staff argued that each school was responsible for developing its own restructuring agenda and that the Masters Center was responsible for providing support for each school's agenda. On the other hand, the district and the Masters Center staff had their own agenda of specific reforms they wanted schools to pursue. As noted above, this agenda included cooperative learning, multi-age grouping, a more hands-on and active curriculum, and greater school-site decision making. The center staff did not see a contradiction between urging schools to develop their own agendas while at the same time pushing a set of reforms from the district level. They slipped easily between describing their role as initiating and prodding on the one hand and eliciting and supporting on the other.

Ted Brandt, for example, described the operation of the district's school-site decision making initiative. He began by noting that the restructuring team faced a problem in the growth of the number of schools participating in the initiative, from twenty-four to ninety-six in three years: "I'm a very big believer that those individual schools have to work out their own restructuring agendas. How do we provide appropriate guidance and technical assistance when the numbers are just kind of blowing [us out of] the water

[and] we have intentionally not increased staff here? . . . We as an organization or as a team within the district have to figure out, you know, how do we deliver what services are needed to that number of schools."

He went on to describe the role of resource teachers in the district's restructuring strategy: "Each of the resource teachers really now play a very prime role in one initiative or another. . . . We're trying to . . . clearly fix prime responsibility for [one aspect] of restructuring on an individual so that if I hold [Pamela Thompson] responsible, then she's holding the resource teachers responsible."

While Brandt saw individual schools developing their own agendas for restructuring, he clearly saw such development as taking place within a prescribed district agenda that specified what restructuring meant, and with a district-centered staff of resource teachers whose responsibility was in part to make sure that schools focused on some aspect of the district's agenda.

Within this district context, Webster occupied an important position. "[Webster] is much further along than our other schools are," Thompson argued. "They have . . . significantly bitten off a lot of curricular and structural change. They've moved to—but not everybody's at the same point within the school—literature-based reading, a lot of experiential science and math. . . . I'm not too sure about the degree of interdisciplinary work that they have done yet. They're emphasizing foreign languages." Thompson saw Webster as an exemplar of district restructuring themes as much as exemplifying school-initiated change. While Billings described her school's restructuring initiatives as largely initiated by her and her staff, those initiatives exactly paralleled the district's and the Masters Center's restructuring initiatives. Hence, there was symmetry between what the district-level staff were sponsoring as restructuring initiatives and what the school staff saw as their own ideas about restructuring.

Among the inducements and rewards that the district offered to schools like Webster was extra faculty. Webster was given an allocation of two extra faculty from the district as it began to undertake multi-age teams. This special attention had a mixed impact on the school. It gave the school additional resources to use in the process of changing its structure and program. Within the school, however, it created modest short-term problems. One outside observer noted that Webster teachers who were not initially involved in teams felt that the extra personnel were used to differentially reward the teachers who were involved in teams. Over time, however, the same observer noted that the effect was to induce more teachers to join teams.

Bureaucratic Tensions in Fairchild

The Fairchild district's strategy of relying on the Masters Center to carry the district's restructuring agenda was not without its costs. For one thing, the staff of the district's central office who were not affiliated directly with the Masters Center sometimes felt that they were excluded from the district's restructuring efforts. On the other hand, Masters Center staff, coming as they did primarily out of schools, sometimes felt that district staff were isolated from schools and not fully sympathetic to the district's restructuring agenda. The superintendent and the district management reflected uncertainty about the relationship between the Masters Center and the curriculum and instruction staff, first giving Ted Brandt at the Masters Center authority over both and then removing the curriculum and instruction office from Brandt's responsibility.

These tensions became particularly evident in our study around the issue of curriculum assistance. In our interviews with Masters Center personnel, we heard a more or less consistent refrain that the district's curriculum specialists (in such subjects as mathematics, reading, and science), who were not part of the Masters Center staff, were too focused on subject matter and not focused enough on the broader aims of restructuring and therefore could not be fully trusted to work with schools in the same way as Masters Center staff. The curriculum specialists, for their part, saw the Masters Center staff as not always providing adequate guidance to teachers on the finer points of curriculum, and they saw themselves as being isolated in unproductive ways from the district's restructuring agenda.

This tension might have come from the Masters Center staff's need to establish an independent identity in the district and their feeling that curriculum specialists represented an outdated view of how to provide assistance to teachers and schools. The tensions might also have arisen from the curriculum specialists' feeling that they had been excluded from an important district initiative and that the district's restructuring activity risked superficiality if it did not deal with specific problems of curriculum development and implementation.

Also at stake was a dramatic difference in perspective between the Masters Center staff and the district curriculum specialists on how to manage the process of changing teaching. For Brandt, the process had to be radically decentralized: "Teachers should provide support and technical assistance to other teachers. The notion of us telling teachers exactly how to get to a certain level of performance I think flies in the face of everything else we're doing. . . . Those teachers have really been anointed to go forth and invent their curriculum as long as they can meet [performance] standards."

He added that, while he thought the curriculum and instruction staff understood the district's philosophy on changing teaching, changes in their approach to curriculum were "probably not as fast and pervasive as they should be." Centralized curriculum assistance to teachers was clearly at odds with the prevailing model of change in the district.

Curriculum specialists, on the other hand, expressed puzzlement at the idea that their expertise was not being used by the district to help teachers develop new ways of teaching. One specialist, a recognized authority in her curriculum area and a former state-award-winning teacher, said she found it ironic that she could collect large consulting fees from other districts in the state for her advice on curriculum and teaching while her own district was not interested in using her expertise "for free."

Whatever the sources of this tension between the Masters Center and the curriculum and instruction staff, its effects reverberated through the Fairchild system, as we shall see later. The notion that curriculum could be more or less invented at the school site, without the direct assistance of subject-matter experts, was influential in determining the effect of restructuring in Fairchild.

Jay Ross: Resource Teacher

A pivotal player in relations between the district and Webster during the 1990–91 school year was Jay Ross, the district resource teacher assigned to Webster. Ross described his assignment from Ted Brandt and the district restructuring team as "pretty broad. . . . It's like 'Kind of go out there and hang out and see what you can do.'" Ross's special interest was literature, reading, and writing. He described his entering Webster as follows:

> When I started at Webster I was coming into a school where they didn't know me and I didn't know them. I feel there is a general suspicion of central office people by most teachers. Sometimes that's well founded. So what I needed to do was to establish some kind of relationship with these folks.
>
> I didn't know Cheryl Billings well. She didn't have any reason to trust me. So what I did, my hook to get into people, was to offer to come in and teach something in their classroom. I'd say . . . "I can teach writing, I can teach it at any level. . . . I'll come in and I'll work with your kids and then let's talk about what you see or what's going on and we'll go from there." So that's what I did.
>
> That gave me entree then to team meetings and that let me establish some credibility, because they knew that I could come and I could teach something, and I think for teachers . . . at any level you've go to establish some kind of credibility with them right away, [so] that they could see that I could do what they could do. . . .
>
> Once I'd established a relationship . . . with them then I began to try and branch out and . . . bring in some other people, and offer myself or my services or my knowledge or whatever to some other groups . . . in the school because what we wanted to try and spread was this whole idea of teaming to other folks.

In keeping with the matrix form of the Masters Center's organization, Ross saw himself at Webster as both a subject-matter consultant and as a reform advocate for multi-age teams. He worked with the Snoopy Gang (part of grades 1 through 3) and the Thoroughbreds (from grades 4 and 5) on writing, but he also observed and coached them on teamwork. He described the Snoopy Gang's approach to teaching reading and writing as "initially . . . pretty traditional," meaning they relied heavily on traditional basal readers rather than literature, offering students relatively few opportunities to express themselves with words and pictures. In Ross's estimation, the Snoopy Gang's progress as a team was enhanced considerably by Julie Brandt (Ted Brandt's wife and a Webster teacher), who "was open in trying some different things." Brandt was admired by her colleagues, and "they followed her leadership a great deal." The Thoroughbreds had no one similar to Brandt, and in Ross's judgment their progress was slower: "I felt like I spent a lot of time doing writing activities with them and I felt like it never caught on as much as it did with" the Snoopy Gang. Likewise, the Snoopy Gang seemed to gel more as a team than the Thoroughbreds. "[The Thoroughbreds] were split more, they were divided more by grade level than I felt was necessary," Ross observed.

Ross described the spread of teams within Webster as a social, rather than a bureaucratic, process. "Over the course of that first year I think a common vision [for the school] did emerge, from each of those groups [the initial teams], then toward the end of that first year other teachers gradually began coming around, began coming to visit. People on the teams got out to other people to talk about what was going on. . . . There was much greater awareness. They did a retreat at the end of that year. . . . It was overnight. . . . [After that], I think there was much more of a kinship among everybody."

There were limits to the effect of this kinship, according to Ross. Asked about agreement among the teachers on the school's vision and pedagogy, Ross observed, "I don't think it runs that deep. I think it's really on the surface. My sense was that not everybody was connected by a common . . . theory. You could go into five, six classrooms and really find a variety of . . . teaching strategies and maybe even teaching philosophies."

At the end of his year as a resource teacher at Webster, Ross was selected to be principal of another elementary school. "I spent two years at the Masters Center helping other people do it, and I needed to see if I could do it myself," he said of his decision to become a principal. Ross was succeeded at Webster in the following the year by another resource teacher who continued to work with teachers on multi-age teams and curriculum.

Webster in a Nutshell

Webster was a school in transition. Cheryl Billings had doggedly nursed the ideas of active learning for students and teachers, multi-age grouping of students, and teacher teams through the initial phase of getting half the teachers at Webster involved. She had developed her own views of leadership in tandem with the development of the school's restructuring strategy. The Fairchild district played a broadly supportive role in helping Webster, by providing access to training and development for teachers and by giving visibility and praise to Webster's achievements. Webster was, for Fairchild, exemplary of their district strategy; but what did the school look like from the inside?

Chapter Seven

Active Learning in Mathematics

At Webster, as at Lakeview, there was substantial, visible evidence that school organization had changed for teachers and students. Teachers were working together in teams; students were grouped more flexibly across grades within teams; and teachers were taking increased responsibility for decisions within the school related to their work, including the nature of the report card and budget matters related to curriculum and teaching. In addition, Jay Ross had entered the school as a resource teacher—a new role for Webster teachers to adapt to.

From several teachers observed at Webster, we have chosen four for detailed analysis here. We are attempting to learn something about how these teachers thought about and acted upon their conceptions of academic content, how they related to students, and how students participated in learning in the classroom. Underlying these questions is a fundamental concern for how the changes in organization at Webster did or did not affect the way teachers were teaching.

A basic tenet of Cheryl Billings's beliefs about curriculum change, as noted earlier, was that teachers should become what she called "curriculum experts." That is, they should become knowledgeable about a particular part of the curriculum, cultivate a broad understanding of how students might be engaged in more active participation in learning that content, and develop new approaches, departures from what Billings called the "basal curriculum." They could then share their new approaches with other teachers and implement them in the classroom. The idea of curriculum experts was intimately connected to structural reform at Webster. Creating teams was supposed to allow teachers to develop distinctive competencies in particular skills and content areas and to bring those competencies to a group of teachers working together with a group of students.

In this chapter and in Chapter Eight, we focus on two pairs of teachers who exemplify the ideals and practices of restructuring at Webster. Melissa Benton and Joanna Griffin specialize in mathematics and are in separate teams. They represent Webster's attempts to come to grips with the issue of what it means to be a curriculum expert. Julie Brandt and Joyce Hancock specialize in reading and writing on the same team, the Snoopy Gang. (Jay Ross, the resource teacher from the Masters Center, was a specialist in reading and writing and spent much of his time at Webster working with Julie Brandt.) Brandt and Hancock represent Webster's attempts to use teams to influence teaching practice, and they offer a perspective on the effects of the district's strategy of using resource teachers to change practice.

With these two pairs of teachers, we have an opportunity to observe how the changing norms and structures of Webster worked their way into the classroom.

Melissa Benton and Joanna Griffin

Melissa Benton and Joanna Griffin were acknowledged as mathematics experts at Webster Elementary School. Griffin, the older, more seasoned, and experienced of these two teachers, was the leader of her upper elementary team, the "Thoroughbreds." Benton, a newer and relatively younger teacher in the school, had made a niche for herself in her primary team, the "Snoopy Gang," as the school's expert in teaching a new activity-based mathematics program called "Box It or Bag It Math" (Burk, Snider, Symonds, 1988). Griffin saw herself as having to be a "math specialist." She said, "You have to know ways to present the material, and you have to find some interesting things to do with them [students] if it they're going to learn it. There are too many kids who have had mental blocks or are turned off to math, and my own daughter is one of them."

A Lesson on "Place Value" in Joanna Griffin's Classroom

Griffin taught two mathematics classes. Her "homeroom" mathematics class met at nine, her second class at 11:05 A.M. Both classes were made up of fourth- and fifth-grade students and were racially diverse. The first class had ten African American and seventeen white students; the makeup of the second was sixteen white, nine African American, and one Hispanic.

As we observed Griffin one day in late September 1990, she began her first class by having her fourth and fifth graders go over their mathematics homework from the previous evening. The homework was an "enrichment worksheet" from *Heath Mathematics Level 8*, a mathematics textbook published by D. C. Heath. The worksheet consisted of two crossword puzzles. In the first puzzle, each "clue" was a Roman numeral. The student was to change the Roman numeral into the appropriate "standard numeral" (Arabic) and write it either across or down in the place indicated by the letter of the clue. In the second puzzle, the standard numeral was the clue, and students were to write the Roman numeral.

As the class went over the homework, Griffin first called on a student to read the answer from his or her worksheet. Then Griffin wrote the answer on the board and proceeded to show the translation process from Roman to Arabic numeral. For example, Griffin called on John to give his answer for the Roman numeral *MDCLXXXIX*. Reading from his worksheet, John replied, "1,689." To this, Griffin responded, "All right. You found the thousandths place. You said it was one." As she said this, Griffin wrote on the board:

M
1

"You found the hundreds place," she continued; "you said it was six." At this, she added to her representation on the board:

M   DC
1   6

Continuing, Griffin said, "You found the tens place." Pointing to the *L*, she said "fifty," and then, pointing to each *X* in turn, "sixty, seventy, eighty." She wrote on the board:

M   DC   LXXX
1   6   8

"And then you found the subtraction [of *X* minus *I*] and worked it out," Griffin said, while completing her representation of the number on the board:

M   DC   LXXX   IX
1   6   8   9

Griffin and the class then went over the other crossword puzzle answers in the same fashion. She wrote the answers on the board in the same format as above, using vertical lines to indicate the "places" in the numeral. When the class moved on to the next puzzle, they converted the Arabic numeral to Roman numeral in similar fashion. For example, Griffin called on Heather to say the Roman numeral for *1,130* and to tell the class how she got it. Heather replied: "M stands for one thousand, and the C is one hundred, and then you've got three X's."

Griffin responded, "That's right!" and wrote the two numerals on the board as follows, complete with vertical lines dividing the "places" in the Roman numeral:

1,130   M|C|XXX

As they went over the answers to the worksheet, the students corrected their homework and then handed it in. For the remainder of the period, the students worked on a hands-on activity that Griffin called the "Roman fold," taken from a worksheet commercially published in 1975. It consisted of folding a piece of paper to make a place to insert a preprinted strip with Arabic numerals next to the corresponding Roman numerals. By inserting the strip into the folded area, the student could then move the strip so that various numbers appeared in the test window in sequence. Students could then test themselves on the Roman numeral that corresponded to the Arabic numeral and vice versa. The Roman fold also allowed the students to "check" their answer by moving the strip up one space so the correct answer appeared in the window.

Students first put together their Roman fold using scissors and crayons. As they did this, they chatted with each other quietly. Most of their talk was unrelated to mathematics, but some of the talk was related to the procedures to be used for putting together the Roman fold. After they had finished, Griffin told the students that they should "buddy up" and use the Roman fold to practice their Roman numerals. Students then began practicing their Roman numerals with a buddy. Because their desks were in long rows facing the front of the room, students tended to partner up with a person sitting next to them.

During the last ten minutes of class, Griffin worked with a small group of four boys at the board while the rest of the class continued practicing with their Roman folds at their desks. On the board, the teacher had posted a "place value" chart with columns for "thousands," "hundreds," "tens," and "ones." The chart contained pegs for each place, where the appropriate Roman numeral could be hung. Griffin then proceeded to quiz the four boys on their knowledge of Roman numerals. For example, she wrote the Arabic numeral *1,515* on the board and asked one of the boys, Michael, to hang the corresponding Roman numerals on the place-value chart. Michael selected and then hung the Roman numerals *M, D, X,* and *V* on the pegs, so that the resulting chart looked liked this:

ROMAN NUMERALS

THOUSANDS	HUNDREDS	TENS	ONES
M	D	X	V

Griffin indicated that Michael's response was correct. She continued by giving another Arabic numeral and calling on another one of the four boys to show the number on the Roman numeral place-value chart. Griffin went on with this procedure for several minutes until she announced that it was time for mathematics class to end. Shortly thereafter, at 10:20, students passed out of the room and on to their next class.

During the next forty minutes, Griffin met in her classroom with the other teachers, student teachers, and aides of the Thoroughbreds. Most of the meeting was consumed by a discussion of problems of students' behavior in the lunchroom. As the team leader, Griffin led the discussion and posed most of the ideas that were considered for solving the problems in the lunchroom.

After the team meeting, Griffin's next mathematics class filed in. She then proceeded to teach this class, using the same activities and procedures that she had employed with her first class. She began by going over the homework on Roman numerals, the crossword puzzle worksheet. Then the students spent the rest of the period making their Roman fold practice sheet and using it to practice Roman numerals. One difference was that while in the first class Mrs. Griffin had told them to buddy up to practice their Roman numerals, in the second class she gave them the choice whether to buddy up or practice on their own. She later said that she did this because although she had wanted them to have "some cooperative learning" and some quiet fun, she felt that she had met with some resistance to that in the first class and that they had been a little noisy, so she decided to give the second class a choice.

How Has Griffin Transformed Her Mathematics Teaching Practice?

Although Griffin is one of the two mathematics teachers on the Thoroughbreds team and is therefore a curriculum expert in Cheryl Billings's terms, she does not see herself as particularly knowledgeable about mathematics. As a child, Griffin says, she enjoyed math and always did well. When she went to college, she did not take math because it was not in the curriculum for her major, which was interior design. Griffin sees herself as a "creative" person and thinks it is hard to be creative with mathematics. She sees mathematics as a structured and organized body of knowledge, so she thinks the other mathematics teacher on her team, Harriet Kelso, is actually better at teaching mathematics because she is a more "structured" teacher. Also, Griffin notes that she tends to get bored teaching the same thing twice each day in mathematics.

Yet Griffin feels that she has definitely changed her mathematics curriculum and teaching in recent years. One way she has changed is by trying "to use more hands-on." When asked what she meant by *hands-on,* Griffin gave the Roman fold activity as an example and she said she also used manipulative materials such as place-value bars, Cuisenaire rods, and fraction wheels. Griffin also said she uses more "cooperative learning" than she did fifteen or so years ago, for example, the cooperative and competitive team learning materials published by the research center at Johns Hopkins University.

Griffin has, by her own account, also changed some of her views of the mathematics curriculum. She admitted that she had "taught for years and years and years . . . and realized how really difficult it is to get place value across to [students]." She had learned recently that "the mathematicians of this country feel the same thing because they are updating their list of math skills that will go from K through high school. They are saying that we might be moving the teaching of place value out of the third grade and moving it up because kids really seem to have a hard time understanding it."

Griffin got this idea from attending presentations by Dr. Peter Tell at the local university that were related to the "new math curriculum." She recalled that Dr. Tell, who was a member of what she called the state-level "mathematics council," had said that place value was "difficult for little ones to understand; people can do things from rote" yet not have "real depth of knowledge." Griffin commented that she agreed because in recent years she had to go over place value and "tug and teach, teach and reteach, and pull out of students a deeper understanding of the place-value system."

Place value was central to Griffin's purposes for teaching this lesson. As she put it, this day's lesson on Roman numerals was a way for her students to get extra practice with place value:

With the Roman numeral system, if students were to write "one thousand nine hundred and fifty-seven," they would have to look at each place-value section. . . . They can't write down 1,957. They have to think about what symbolizes the one thousand. It won't be a one, but since it's a thousand they'll put down one *M,* and then they have to look at what makes up nine hundred and that's a nine, so it's got to be a subtraction, so they'll have to do the *CM* for that and, you know, they have to kind of puzzle it and piece it together, and it ends up being fun, but it also ends up kind of being a skill they can tackle real well, and then it helps with place value but, you know, they have to do it in place value. You just can't write it up without thinking of place value. You or I could because we've been doing it awhile but they have to stop and they have to labor through it, one place at a time, the thousands, the hundreds, the tens, and the ones.

By looking over Griffin's shoulder at the teacher's guide for the D. C. Heath mathematics textbook from which the homework sheets came, one can gain a different perspective. Those authors give the teacher the following directions:

> Review briefly the concept of place value. Tell the students that the ancient Romans had a system for naming numbers that did not use place value. In the Roman system, there are only seven symbols:
>
> | I | V | X | L | C | D | M |
> |---|---|----|----|-----|-----|-------|
> | 1 | 5 | 10 | 50 | 100 | 500 | 1,000 |
>
> Explain that the Romans wrote symbols side by side and often added the values (D. C. Heath, p. 16).

A page in the student text for this lesson also gives this same information and states explicitly for the student that "The Romans did not have a place-value system. They wrote the symbols side by side and usually added the values."

A Lesson on "Place Value" in Melissa Benton's Mathematics Classroom

When we visited Melissa Benton's mathematics class the day after we observed Joanna Griffin's classes, we found that Benton's class was also spending time "working on place value" as their teacher described it. Benton began by writing the following on the board:

MILLIONS   HUNDRED THOUSANDS   TEN THOUSANDS
THOUSANDS   HUNDREDS   TENS   ONES

Benton then asked the whole class if they remembered yesterday when they "were trying to read numbers with words" and to figure out "what was the right way." She announced that because it was "el tough amundo" (very difficult), she had made up a game for them to use today to figure out how "to reason out numbers and to write them the right way." She then asked the class to tell her "the places" that they knew of. Pointing to the words on the board, she had the students read the names of the places in unison. The students yelled out in unison: "Ones, tens, hundreds, thousands, ten thousands, hundred thousands, millions!"

Benton then posed this question to the class: "There are twenty-five people in the class. How many people will be on each team?" As soon became apparent, she was posing this as an authentic problem because she wanted to divide the class of twenty-five second-grade students into two teams for the subsequent activity.

Giving them a clue, Benton then asked, "Is twenty-five even or odd?" Half the students yelled out "even," and half the students called out "odd."

Giving the students another clue, Benton continued: "It ends in five." At that, Andrew called out, "odd." Picking up immediately on Andrew's response, she agreed that five was odd, so twenty-five was also odd. She then told them that one team was going to have one student more than the other, and she asked again how many people were going to be on each team. Charles suggested that there would be thirteen students on one team, and the other team would have fourteen students. Denise volunteered the answer "twelve and thirteen." Picking up on Denise's correct answer, Benton agreed that one team would have thirteen and one would have twelve students. She proceeded to form the class into two teams by taking the two rows on one side of the room to form one team and the two rows on the other side of the room to form the second team. She told them that one team would have twelve, and one team would have thirteen, but that would be "OK." Meanwhile, sitting at her seat, Angela was still figuring out how to divide the twenty-five students into two teams. She looked puzzled and suggested that "they move one girl." Rather than asking Angela what she meant and trying to figure out how Angela was thinking about the problem, Benton asked her, "What's twelve plus twelve?" Angela replied, "twenty." Benton responded, "Let's say one person was absent. Twelve plus twelve would be . . ." Benton left the sentence hanging. After Angela replied correctly, Benton affirmed, "twenty-four," and then added, "We've got one extra—twenty-five." Although Angela still look puzzled, Benton turned to the whole class and began the "game."

Benton announced that two people from each team would come to the board. She would give each team the same number written on a strip of paper. The team members' job was to tell her "the right way to write the number." The first team to write the number correctly in numerals on the board would get a point. She then pronounced the first number as she gave the number to the teams written on strips of paper: "seven hundred forty-two thousand."

On the board, team one wrote *700,4200* and team two wrote *742,000*. Turning to the class, Benton asked the students which one was right. Most of the children put up two fingers indicating they thought team two was correct. After a two-second pause, she concurred with the class by saying, "Team two's right, and let me show you why."

Benton then corrected team one's number on the board by adding a comma as follows: *7,004,200*. She then had the class read it aloud with her. A student began, "seven hundred," but was quickly corrected by other students who called out, "seven million." Benton added, "four . . ." A student picked that up and said, "hundred," but she corrected him, saying, "thousand," and concluding with "two hundred."

Benton then read team two's number, saying, "Seven hundred forty-two thousand, and there's no hundreds and there's no tens. Okay? Look what it looks like. Everyone read this number."

At her command, the class read the number, chanting in unison: "seven hundred, forty-two thousand."

Benton then read the next number for the teams and told the rest of the class to write the number on their papers. She pronounced, "five hundred fifty thousand." Team one wrote *5,0050*, and team two wrote *55,000*. She announced that they were "both wrong" and they should "go back" to the board.

She gave them a clue that they should have six numbers. The teams returned to the board and pondered some more. Finally, Benton repeated, "five hundred fifty thousand," adding: "There's no hundreds, there's no tens; there's no ones. Five hundred fifty thousand," she repeated yet again. After a pause, she commented, "This is a tough one. This one we got stumped on yesterday. It is straight from the book."

This time, team one wrote *500,000* and then erased it. Both teams then wrote *500,500*.

Turning to the class, Benton asked them what both teams had written up there. One student replied, "five hundred and five hundred." She corrected him by saying, "five hundred thousand, five hundred." But she added, "I want it to be five hundred *fifty* thousand."

Team one then wrote *500,5,000.*

At this point, except for the four students at the board, the others in the class were squirming in their seats and appeared disengaged from the task. Benton admonished them: "Sh! Boys and girls, be patient!" Turning to the teams, she then encouraged the four students at the board by saying, "You're all gettin' close. Team one's gettin' close." The teams continued to write and erase what they had on the board. Finally, team one wrote *550,000.* She immediately called out, "Congratulations!" indicating that team one was correct. Then she added, "That was a tough one!"

Benton then went to the board herself and covered a part of the number so that only *550* was showing. She told the class that "if there were no zeros, it would say 'five hundred fifty.' But because it's in the thousands place, we say 'five hundred fifty . . .'" She allowed the students to complete her sentence by chorusing in unison: "thousands!" Benton then told the students again that "that was a tough one" and cautioned them that she might "pick this one again" for them to do. A few minutes later, after team two had correctly written *three hundred thousand* as *300,000,* she did indeed give them the same one again, asking the teams to write "five hundred fifty thousand."

Quickly both teams wrote *550,000* on the board. They did it so rapidly that it was difficult to determine who got it right first. She declared that they both were right, but that team one got it right "by a hair."

Benton continued the game for another several minutes. Soon all the children sitting at the desks were talking and paying scant attention while the four team members at the board struggled to write the correct number. Finally, all students on each team had taken a turn at the board, and team one was declared the winner.

Benton then passed out the "general materials boxes" to each student. The boxes contained cups, beans, and a sock. She had each student take the sock, which was to be used as an eraser. Then she handed each student a small blackboard and a piece of chalk. For the remainder of the period, Benton read numbers aloud to the students, and each student was to write the numeral for the number on their chalkboard. Then the student was to "check with their neighbor and see if they got it right. If not, the neighbor [should] tell them how to do it."

Matthew, a blonde boy wearing a Bart Simpson shirt, helped Isaiah, an African American boy, telling him how to write the number. Isaiah appeared to continue to have trouble throughout this activity. For example, Isaiah wrote *380000* for the number *thirty thousand eight hundred;* he later erased it and wrote *30,800* when he saw what everyone else had written. When Benton had the students put their materials away, she stopped by Isaiah's desk and talked with him about his inattentive behavior during class that day.

The class concluded for the day with the playing of a music tape on which the singer sang aloud the multiplication facts. Everybody, including Benton, sang along. At the end of the tape, the singer sang a quiz. As each multiplication fact was posed, the students sang out the answers with gusto.

How Has Benton Transformed Her Mathematics Teaching Practice?

Melissa Benton saw herself as having transformed her practice considerably over the last few years. She described her math teaching as "fun and exciting" because she herself now saw math as "fun and exciting." Why was math more exciting for her? As Benton saw it, it was because she was doing different things each day and because she was playing games with the students. She attributed her love of teaching math to the new program she had chosen, "Box It or Bag It Math," which provided directions for how to make and use the activities that she was now doing in math and the games that she was now using. When asked what subject she thought she was best at teaching, Benton replied "math" because she had "been newly

trained and the kids love it, and they understand it, and it's satis-
fying" for her. She judged that her children understood math better because they were "actively involved."

With this new activity-based mathematics program, Benton felt
that her children were more actively involved in mathematics
because "they can touch it, feel it, see it, and do it." Benton
believed that children learn math better this way than when she
used to have them work from a mathematics book four days a
week, which she said was boring for them because they were not
actively involved. When asked why children learn mathematics better this way, she replied by comparing learning mathematics to
learning to cook: "If you had to learn how to cook, if you read a
book about it, it's not going to be as effective as if you're in the
kitchen taking one tablespoon and putting it in, and mixing it up
with, what, a spoon or a blender. You know [that] actively doing it
is going to be a lot better. I wish I could remember the saying,
'Show me and I'll learn; tell me and I'll—' Especially for children,
especially for skills, if they're actively doing it, it makes more sense
to them."

A second significant way that Benton felt she had transformed
her practice involved teaching mathematics to her primary children entirely within the context of activities: some related to the
calendar, some using manipulative materials, and some gamelike
activities.

For example, she described a game called "To Fifty and Back,"
which she has the children play to teach borrowing and place
value. In this game each child uses place-value mats, beans, cups,
and dice from his or her general materials box. A white mat represents the ones place; a purple mat represents the tens side. The
child roles the dice. If they come up nine, the child counts out
nine beans, puts them on the white mat, and then roles again. If
the child gets a six, six more beans are added to the white mat. As
Benton told it, "The rule is when you get ten beans on the white
side, you have to put them in a 'portion cup' and move them to
the purple side. . . . Then they keep rolling the dice until they get
to fifty, so eventually they have five portion cups over here [on the
purple mat], and zero on the ones side."

Benton is similar to Mrs. O., described by David Cohen in "A
Revolution in One Classroom: The case of Mrs. Oublier." Both use

an activity-based mathematics program, and both assume "appropriate materials and activities alone will do the trick" and "simply working with the proper activities and materials assures that math will be understood" (Cohen, 1991, p. 317). Of course, Mrs. O. teaches in another school district far across the country from Benton and the two have never met, but they share similar assumptions about teaching with an activity-based curriculum. The materials and activities themselves, rather than the teacher's understanding of the underlying concepts, are thought to differentiate "new" from "old" teaching. To teach differently, it appears by this reasoning, is to engage in different kinds of classroom activities, rather than to transform the teacher's—much less the students'—understanding of the content.

The Curriculum: Old and New Mathematical Knowledge

In each case, we see attempts to transform mathematical knowledge from the old to the new and, less wittingly, from the new to the old. In Joanna Griffin's classroom, we see "old" mathematics from her perspective, which puts a "new" twist on the relationship between place value and Roman numerals. We observe Griffin teaching her fourth- and fifth-grade classes a lesson on Roman numerals that she had developed ten years previously, using information that she identifies as coming from her textbook and from the classroom encyclopedia that she still had on her shelf. When asked what she hopes her students will get out of the day's lesson, Griffin replies, "With Roman numerals . . . students are looking at what appears to be a code . . . it really does match up with what the place-value system is, so then they get extra practice with place value." Griffin's perspective is puzzling in light of her textbook's assertion that "The Romans did not use a place-value system."

Indeed, mathematicians and mathematics educators generally agree with the perspective of the authors of the D. C. Heath textbook. For example, Fendel (1987) contrasted Roman numerals with "a whole family of numeration systems, called *base numeration systems,* . . . [which] includes our own familiar 'decimal' system. Our 'ordinary' system of numerals is, in fact, the base ten numeration system. The different column headings are traditionally called 'place values,' with each column having ten times the value of the column to its right" (p. 133). Fendel continues: "there are other systems for representing numbers . . . and these have historical and cultural interest." He pointed out that "one of them— Roman numerals—is used frequently today, and therefore has practical significance," but he argued that these other systems "are not related to understanding basic number concepts" (p. 125).

In Melissa Benton's classroom we find that the "new" mathematics has been transformed through the power of old pedagogies. Benton is considered by her colleagues to be the school's math expert, and she sees her practice as having been transformed by a new activity-based math program. Benton describes herself, prior to adopting this new program, as having hated math; now she sees math as fun because her students are having fun playing games in math class and using hands-on materials.

Although children in Benton's class were using manipulatives and playing games, the pedagogy that Benton used transforms this activity-based mathematics into something more like a curriculum based on right answers and relatively static knowledge. As the teacher, Benton is still the one who has the right answer, and she is the one who checks to make sure that each child has it. The activities serve to reinforce this role, rather than to move the responsibility for understanding in the students' direction. In her classroom, place value becomes synonymous with learning names or labels for numbers, for example, writing the appropriate numerals (550,000) to match certain words (five hundred fifty thousand). While the relationship between written marks and spoken words is an important part of place value, mathematics educators see place value as involving much more than this (Fuson, 1990a). It involves understanding and communicating the underlying logic by which quantity is expressed.

Because Benton and Griffin have had little contact with other members of the larger mathematics-education reform communities, they have had few opportunities to develop their understandings of place value in particular and mathematics in general. Neither teacher has had opportunities for sustained conversations with other teachers or subject-matter experts who are actively working on similar reform activities that might cause these teachers to question the relationship between the activities they employ in their classrooms, their teaching strategies, and the underlying ideas that students are supposed to understand. Benton's and Griffin's experiences stand in contrast to the relationship between Julie Brandt (described shortly) and Jay Ross from the resource center—a relationship that allowed Brandt to learn about new ways of understanding and teaching literacy.

In her only recent contact with the larger mathematics-education community, Griffin listened to a presentation by Dr. Tell, the mathematics-education professor at a nearby university. In this presentation Griffin "heard" the professor say that elementary students have been found to have a difficult time understanding place value. This idea fit neatly with Griffin's existing belief that her students were having a hard time understanding place value. But what she also understood from the professor's representation of mathematics reform was that place value should not be taught until later, when the child could understand it; she did not take in that there were more and less effective ways to deal with place value in the classroom. Tell may actually have said that children have a difficult time understanding place value. Indeed, as results show from the fourth National Assessment of Educational Progress (NAEP) in 1989: "Approximately two-thirds of third-grade students appear to have mastered place-value notions involving tens; fewer than half were successful with tasks involving place-value notions beyond tens" (Kouba, Carpenter, and Swafford, 1989, p. 65).

Yet place value is central to understanding the number concepts in our base-ten system. The National Council of Teachers of Mathematics (NCTM) in their National Curriculum Standards (1989) states clearly that K–4 children should "understand our numeration system by relating counting, grouping, and place-value concepts" (National Council of Teachers of Mathematics, 1989, p. 38). Further, the authors of the NCTM's standards discuss the need to teach place value for understanding.

Like Griffin and Benton, members of the larger educational research community are grappling with this question of how and when place value should be taught, and how to teach it with understanding (Baroody, 1990; Fuson, 1990b; Tom Carpenter, personal communication, Jan. 4, 1994). For example, during this same year of Benton's and Griffin's struggles with teaching place value in their classrooms, the mathematics-education research community was heatedly debating whether teachers should teach place-value concepts in isolation or integrate them into the teaching of multi-digit addition and subtraction.

The issue of how to teach place value with understanding continues to be problematic for both local communities of mathematics teachers, such as those at Webster, and the national community of mathematics-education researchers. The two communities continue to grapple with this issue, but independently, and the problems of each community remain relatively invisible to the other. Even within the community of mathematics teachers at Webster, one teacher's successes and struggles with teaching mathematics were largely unseen by other teachers; thus Griffin and Benton, who were on different teams, knew little about what the other was doing in her mathematics teaching. This isolation occurred, furthermore, in a school committed to structural reforms specifically designed to break down isolation, and in a district committed to similar reforms designed to introduce new teaching practices.

Neither Griffin nor Benton had access to opportunities to learn while actively teaching the content. For example, Benton drew most of her new knowledge and information from "Box It or Bag It Math"—a program that, by itself, seems to constitute a somewhat impoverished context for teachers' learning. As the title of the program implies, much of what Benton has learned to do in implementing the program is to make and do new activities, such as the myriad calendar activities displayed on the board and the general materials box used by each student. Learning to do "Box It or Bag It Math" provided Benton with scant opportunities to learn new mathematics, to increase the depth of her own mathematical knowledge and understanding, or to explore the depth of her students' mathematical knowledge and understanding.

Student Involvement, Practice, and Responsibility for Learning: Embracing the Old and the New

The authors of "Box It or Bag It Math" assert a "constructivist" view of students' knowledge: "Young children learn best when they are actively involved in hands-on experiences with a variety of materials. Understanding takes a lot of time. Children need multiple opportunities and experiences in a variety of contexts to construct knowledge" (Burk, Snider, and Symonds, 1988, pp. 1–2).

Through their activities at the Masters Center and through Cheryl Billings's leadership, both Griffin and Benton were influenced by this new view of their students' learning that said that students learn through active engagement. They came to believe that one way students become actively engaged is through using hands-on materials and through playing games. In these episodes, we saw Griffin's class use the "hands-on" Roman fold to practice changing Arabic numerals to Roman numerals and back again; Benton's class played a game in which teams competed to see which one could correctly write in digits a number that was written out in words.

But others hold constructivist views that differ from Benton's and Griffin's. For example, Benton's own team colleague, Julie Brandt, as we shall see, views knowledge as more fluid, less codified, and more located in students' understanding than in the materials and activities of the curriculum. Brandt focuses on students' ideas and understandings of texts, providing multiple opportunities for students to converse about texts and to co-construct their own knowledge. Learning from her own students and exploring the amazing knowledge and understanding of children is an important way in which Brandt learns and increases her own knowledge and understanding.

Similarly, listening, conversing, and attempting to understand their own students' mathematical knowledge and thinking might serve as an important impetus for both Benton and Griffin to teach more consistently with the premises of constructivist pedagogy. Paying attention to students' thinking has been a significant influence on other elementary mathematics teachers who have been involved in constructivist approaches designed to facilitate teacher change in teaching mathematics (Peterson, Fennema, and Carpenter, 1991; Wood, Cobb, and Yackel, 1991; Heaton and Lampert, 1993). Neither Benton nor Griffin probed students' understanding through questioning. Taken from a constructivist perspective, both teachers missed multiple opportunities to find out what their students knew and understood about place value and how students were developing their own understanding. Further, when she identified "place" for the students while reviewing their homework, Griffin did the thinking for those students, and she missed an important opportunity to encourage the student to do the thinking for himself (see Peterson and others, 1989).

In addition to their new views of learning, both Benton and Griffin still hold the age-old view that learning occurs through practice. In this lesson we saw Benton respond to a student's struggles with writing the number *five hundred fifty thousand* by having the student practice writing the number. When students finally "got it," she believed that it was because of "seeing it [the number] so many different times and perhaps so many different ways." In earlier lessons, Benton had students learn place value through doing "belly place-value numbers." Each of several students received a number to hold in front of his or her belly. Then a group of students would stand up in the ones, tens, hundreds, or thousands places, and form a number that the other students then "read." Through this activity, Benton believed that "belly numbers" gave students practice. "I won't just do it once," she asserted. "I'll do that again" so students will have "seen the numbers in the right spaces; and they actually step in front of words on the floor that say *ones, tens, hundreds, thousands,* so they know what place they're standing in."

Benton used learning to bake a cake as a metaphor for learning mathematics. As she put it: "If I had to learn to bake a cake, and you said, 'Melissa, you do this and this and this.' Unless I really did it, I don't think I would understand it. And then after I did it a couple of times, I could do it without looking at the recipe. It's the same for math." Through this metaphor, Benton neatly fit together her ideas about engaging in hands-on activities and sustained practice as a basis for developing understanding.

In addition, Benton and Griffin were influenced by the school's new vision that all students could learn and succeed at school. Griffin strove to have her students experience a high rate of success in their responding during lecture-recitation in mathematics. To avoid possible embarrassment and negative effects on her students' self-esteem, Griffin said she often supplied answers for students who could not do so with repeated prompting. Benton also taught by giving students "clues" until they succeeded in getting the answer, sometimes through a process of trial and error.

In the end, both Benton and Griffin saw themselves as the ones who were primarily responsible for students' learning, not the students themselves, nor the teacher and the students together. These teachers believed that as teachers they needed to give to students the mathematical skills, facts, and information they would need to function in society. As Benton put it:

> At the very beginning of school, I tell them that 'they pay me to teach you. . . . If you don't understand, they pay me to sit there and explain it to you 500 times if I have to. . . . How did you learn two plus two? You didn't know that at one time or another. How did you learn it? You just know it because you've practiced, and that's what we have to do now. We have to practice. We have to learn different ways. . . .' And they'll get it. They know that I'm going to see to it that they get it. That's why they pay me to do this. Isn't that great?

Chapter Eight

Developing Teams

Teachers at Webster were divided into three- or four-member teams, depending on the personnel needs of the school. During the first year of our study, the Snoopy Gang was a four-member team responsible for first, second, and third graders. In the second year the team had only three members: Julie Brandt, who taught writing, reading, and science; Joyce Hancock, who taught reading, writing, and social studies; and Melissa Benton, who taught mathematics and writing. The teachers decided within their team who would be responsible for what subject areas and how to arrange their schedule. The following sections describe the reading and writing practices of two of these team members, Julie Brandt and Joyce Hancock.

Julie Brandt: Building a Literate Community

Julie Brandt was an experienced teacher who had taught in a variety of situations, full-time or else part-time while raising her own children, over the course of about 20 years. She had taught both elementary and middle school, gifted students in Saturday classes, life science, and the traditional elementary curriculum. Brandt was married to one of the key members of the district restructuring team, Ted Brandt. In the Snoopy team, she taught one group beginning reading, writing to two groups, and science in two groups.

Having been at Webster School for four years, Brandt was part of the primary team and had assumed the role of leader for the first pilot team when the school began restructuring. She described her teaching prior to restructuring as traditional, using workbooks and basal readers, although she acknowledged that when she was a middle school science teacher she had used many discovery-oriented materials. We looked inside Brandt's classroom to view her efforts to build a literate community.

The classroom was organized for students to meet both in small groups and the large group. Students' desks were arranged in two large clusters facing one another. Students' work was displayed throughout the room, including writing and paper bag puppets.

Brandt had designated one corner near the back of the classroom as "a special place to write," with small carpet pieces spread out for students to sit on while writing or reading. Bulletin boards decorated the literacy corner, with writing-related themes such as "author of the week," in which one student's work was highlighted, and "writing process," with its list of some steps involved in learning to write. Student-written stories hung from a clothesline under the heading, "What's happening?" In the corner opposite the literacy space, a round table provided another place for students to write. A rocking chair labeled "author's chair" was centered before this space. The atmosphere suggested that literacy was a valued activity in this classroom.

The Reading Curriculum

Brandt's reading curriculum was based entirely on children's literature; she did not use a basal reader at all. She read aloud to students, students read in twos or alone, and opportunities to discuss books abounded. She taught basic reading skills, from finding the main idea in a story to sound-symbol relationships, within the context of literature.

Brandt began her reading lessons by reading aloud to students. She welcomed students' responses during the reading. She often asked students questions related to their own experiences, asked them to make predictions, or directed them to look for something particular in the story. After reading several books aloud, she asked students to compare them, or she involved them in a quick activity related to the vocabulary in the story, such as acting like a bear who was hibernating. She led the students in "shared reading," where she and the students read aloud two books (*Color Zoo, I'll Build a Zoo*) as she pointed to the words. She asked students to notice how the sounds and letters were related, pointing to individual words and giving hints about the meaning of the words (for example, pointing to a zebra she said, "I have stripes."). With their own copies of the book *I'll Build a Zoo,* students then read to partners and had to write one or more words in their "reading logs."

The Writing Lesson

We observed sessions that Brandt held in September 1990 with her primary-grade classes. She described her students as "of mixed abilities. I have some children that are writing on a very advanced level, and then I have other children that are beginning children to the program." Despite her concern that some of the very young children might not want to share their writing when they listened to the older students' stories, she found that all the students were willing to share their writing after all.

Selecting a Topic

Brandt introduced the writing topic by explaining to students that many of them had discussed their fears during "teacher based guidance" (a time each day where students and the teacher discussed important issues in their lives). She then wrote *fear* on the board and asked students to close their eyes and think of a time they had felt frightened. She asked them to generate other feelings; they offered ideas such as *furious, left out, worried, amazed,* and *happy.* After each idea, the students closed their eyes and remembered some incident in their own lives where they experienced that feeling. Brandt then told students that they could use these ideas to generate stories for their writing. She told students they could go anywhere in the room and write alone or with a partner.

When asked why she had students write about "feelings" as a topic, Brandt explained that she wanted students to write from their own experiences:

What I've tried to do is [have them] write from their experiences, things that they know. They've written about themselves and they've written about their family and they've written about things that they've done with a friend. . . . I think they have a wealth of experiences that they bring to school. . . . I mean, you give them a story starter and it's not within their experience. They haven't been to the circus and they don't want to write about the circus or they never want to go to the circus, or whatever experience that you have given them. So many things that they have done that they don't get a chance to write about. I like to build on that, so that's why I try to write within the realm of what they've done.

Conferences

After students participated in the whole-group generation of ideas and visualization of feelings, they dispersed to write their stories on the floor, in the special writing area, or at tables. Brandt circulated around the room, assisting individuals or partners. She seemed to respond to students according to where they were in their own writing development, focusing on different aspects of their writing including getting an idea, story development, or mechanics such as punctuation. For instance, Matt was having difficulty getting started, saying that he had no fears.

Matt: I had no fears.

Brandt: You had no fears?

Matt: No.

Brandt: Oh, don't write about fears, then; go to another one. What else could you write about? Have you ever been angry with someone? Have you? Tell me, about . . . what happened. What made you angry? Something that she did or said?

Matt: No.

Brandt: What happened?

Matt: It was yesterday.

Brandt: It was yesterday, oh, you should remember that story very well then, if it just happened yesterday. Why don't you write it down? Was it when you got home from school yesterday?

Matt: No.

Brandt: Last night?

 Matt: No.

Brandt: When was it?

 Matt: Eight o'clock.

Brandt: It was at eight o'clock. Start your story that way; tell me what happened at eight o'clock last night. I'll probably be back to pick up yours first because I'm very curious to see what happened at eight o'clock last night.

  Brandt showed interest in Matt's story and kept trying to elicit information from him. Even though he was not forthcoming, she asked him questions to get him started. She described her role as "a facilitator to encourage them to write."

  When another student wrote about a television show that scared him, Brandt acknowledged what he had written and the parts she liked, but she also asked him to relate it back to his own feelings.

 Joe: There is [*unintelligible*] accident that has happened, they have to call the hospital and the paramedics to come.

Brandt: That's a good story. I like the way you wrote, "based on a true story too," that sounds good. Does it make you feel like a part of that story when you watch it? Do you feel like it's really happening? How did you feel when you read the story? Or when you watched the story?

 Joe: I feel scared.

Brandt: OK.

 Joe: [*Unintelligible*]

Brandt: Did they really? I watched it one time. Write that at the end now; tell me how this show makes you feel. I'd be interested in that, why you chose that show to write about. . . . Tell me 'This show makes me feel . . .,' just what you told me; like you said to me, write it down. I'd love for you to read it to me.

  Brandt focused on encouraging students in their writing. With Matt, she was trying to get him started and letting him know that he could write about a topic other than his fears. Her questions, even though quite focused and close-ended, seemed to serve the function of eliciting information and finding a starting point for his writing. In Joe's case, she focused on his feelings and encouraged elaboration at the same time.

Depending on their prior writing experiences and where they were in the composing of a piece, Brandt focused on different aspects of writing with different students. For instance, she tended to focus on content and elaboration of ideas at the drafting stage and mechanics such as capital letters at the editing stage. When asked how she made decisions about what to discuss in conference with students and how she selected the skills she emphasized, Brandt responded: "When I look at their writing folders I try to see what overall they need rather than going by my textbook. This comes first and that comes first. I think it's more meaningful for them if it's something that they need in their writing. Just by flipping through the folders and looking at the stories, I can see overall that they don't know how to use quotation marks. The ones that do can be a great help to me in teaching little groups of children how to use quotation marks."

Rather than the writing skills that come from a textbook or an outside source, Brandt believed it was important to use the children's own writing. She selected some aspects of each student's writing to emphasize, such as capitalization, punctuation, or quotation marks, and involved students in proofreading other's work: "Then those are the particular things that they proofread for. Hopefully, as the year goes on that list will grow and they'll be able to proofread for a great many things. At this particular time it's just three or four different things. At times we'll take a crayon and we'll all go together to look at our stories together and check the first letter in each sentence. They'll do it with partners. . . . What I'm trying to do is get them independently proofreading each other's work."

Not only did students work together by proofreading each other's work, but many students chose to collaborate by writing stories together. Brandt described how two girls in a former class had formed an important friendship first by talking together about similar family situations, where both sets of parents frequently fought, and then through writing about their experiences collaboratively. Brandt said: "I think it's really important to give them a chance to talk and find somebody with a similar idea. . . . I never force a child to write with a partner if they don't want to, but [most] do. They really love to choose a partner."

While we were observing, two girls composed a story together about their bikes by taking turns writing sentences. They explained that this was fair, and that one person's arm would not get too tired. They continuously negotiated not only the content but mechanics and word choice with one another. For instance, after Amanda had written "We got our bikes on our birthdays," Lucy said, "We *have*." Lucy then asked how to spell *our*, and when Amanda told her "a-r-e" Lucy knew it was wrong and corrected her. Lucy often played the role of editor and considered their audience. When Amanda wrote, "Our bikes have the same colors" after she had written, "And they have a lot of colors," Lucy told her not to start sentences with "and" and said, "They already know that because you wrote they were the same."

Later on in the interview Brandt expressed how pleased she was at this partnership, explaining that one girl was a very bright girl and the other had a learning disability, yet they had chosen each other: "That combination was a wonderful combination, and they had chosen it themselves because they were good with each other. It was interesting to me to see them have equal input into that story."

Students had opportunities to work together throughout the writing process. Brandt encouraged them to talk to each other to get ideas, compose collaboratively, and peer edit each other's work. Each action represents a different form of social interaction during writing (McCarthey & McMahon, 1992).

Author's Chair

After students had been writing independently or together for about forty minutes, Brandt called students together for "author's chair." Author's chair, a term coined by Graves (1983), is an opportunity for students to read their work aloud to other students, who then respond. In Brandt's class, the designated students sat in the rocking chair and read their work aloud. First, the two girls who had written about their bikes sat in the chair together and took turns reading their story. Brandt responded: "Is there anything else that you can tell me? That's a wonderful story; that describes the bike. Could you tell something that you do? Tell me where you go with them, and where you arrived. Is there anything else that you can tell us about the bikes?"

When Lucy described more about the bikes, Brandt said: "OK, that would be wonderful, that would be a wonderful ending. A good story, we talked about that, and that's a wonderful story; but when you end your story, give it some kind of ending. Tell us what you do; tell us what finally happened. I've asked so many people as I walked around, 'And then what happened?' Make sure your story tells me 'and then what happened.' Give it a good ending."

Three other students had the opportunity to read their pieces aloud. Brandt encouraged each piece and remarked about something in particular. For instance, when Clay read his story about something under his bed, Brandt responded, "I like the way you put action in it. It was like a mystery story." After the sharing session, students were dismissed for their next class.

Brandt believed that author's chair was an important way to build a classroom community even when the topics were of a personal nature. She described, for instance, a boy sharing a story about his father killing his mother. The other students responded by asking him questions about how and why it happened, and for his birthday the following week they made cards for him and gave him small gifts. She said, "They became more protective of him, and they watched out for him and they made sure that he had what he needed." Brandt believed that the students felt close to one another and cared about one another. She attributed this empathy to the teaming structure, where students got to know one another well throughout their three years on a team.

Making Sense of Brandt's Classroom

Brandt's classroom was filled with activity and a sense of community. She developed this community by providing students with opportunities to hear each others' ideas and to work together in a variety of formats. Writing time and author's chair were two places where students were encouraged to listen to one another. During writing time students could choose to write with partners, as in the case of Lucy and Amanda, or they could talk to peers to get ideas or proofread work. In author's chair students read their work aloud, thus having an opportunity for a larger audience than the teacher. Brandt seemed to have valued these communal norms by encouraging students to talk to one another.

While Brandt's goals focused on encouraging students to write, she also provided instruction in her comments during the conferences and author's chair. Rather than just applauding students' efforts, she also tried to focus them, as evidenced in the case of Matt; encourage them to elaborate, as with Joe; and structure their pieces with an ending, as she did with Amanda and Lucy. Brandt provided direction, but she was not authoritative. Her choice of the topic of feelings seemed to come indirectly from the students; she noticed that students had expressed fear in the teacher-based guidance and seized that opportunity to let them write about their feelings. However, for most students this was only a start. They wrote about a variety of incidents, not necessarily directly connected to feelings, which pleased Brandt. Her purpose was to engage students in writing, and in sustained thinking about writing, not just to express their feelings.

Brandt provided students opportunities to participate as readers and writers in a particular community. In writing, the skills she taught came from students' own writing; she emphasized student expression primarily and then had students focus on particular aspects, such as mechanics, within the context of their own writing. She started with their experiences and built on that, rather than beginning with an outside curriculum.

Joyce Hancock: Combining the New with the Old

Joyce Hancock, a primary-grade teacher, had been part of the Snoopy Gang from its beginning. Her responsibilities within the team included reading, writing, and social studies. Hancock had been teaching at Webster since it opened twenty-one years previously. She described herself as the prototypical "basal teacher" before restructuring, meaning she had used the basal reader as her only text, followed the teacher's manual carefully, and focused on skills instruction. For the last two years, however, she saw herself as a convert to literature-based instruction and said she could never return to her old ways of teaching. Referring to literature-based reading, she said: "It is just . . . it is a great way to teach reading. I hated teaching reading, I had gotten to the point I just despised it. It was my least favorite thing to do. . . . I wasn't happy with what I was doing, but I really didn't know better. I'm totally changed now. I love teaching it, I don't think I could ever go back to the way I used to do it."

Hancock believed that students enjoyed reading in this new way, and she enjoyed teaching it much more. When we observed Hancock's classroom, we saw a teacher in the midst of change. Filled with excitement and commitment to her new view of literacy teaching, spurred by Brandt's example, Hancock sought to foster critical thinking and children's self-expression.

Inside Hancock's Classroom

Hancock's classroom was arranged in five clusters of four to six desks around the room. Teacher-made bulletin boards with inspirational sayings, such as "Show your team spirit with good work" and "Make reading your target" decorated the room. A board describing the three main parts of a book—beginning, middle, and end—took up part of one wall, while another board describing the steps of the writing process—prewrite, write, revise, proofread, and publish—decorated the other. Students' writing on the topic "If I had a magic penny . . ." hung from a clothesline at the back of the classroom.

Reading Practices

Hancock was pleased with her reading program. She did not group children by ability in reading; each week she introduced three books to the whole class and allowed students to select from those. Book selection often related to the new school themes or other activities they were doing. Hancock brought in many activity sheets to promote critical thinking skills that she developed or that she obtained from the Masters Center.

In September, Hancock introduced three books in the "Miss Nelson" series. Each group had a different worksheet to accompany each book: one had a "detective map" consisting of features to be filled in, such as characters, setting, problem, ending; a second group had an "activity sheet" of questions: "You are walking to school. Suddenly a dog runs up and pulls your lunch box out of your hand. What would you do?"; and a third had a sheet to list characteristics of Miss Nelson.

By May, students chose among more difficult books, such as *How to Eat Fried Worms* (a story about a boy daring others to eat fried worms), which related to a camping trip they had taken together; *Little House in the Big Woods* (set in pioneer days), which related to a "Wood Wonders" theme; and *From the Mixed-Up Files of Mrs. Basil E. Frankweiler,* which followed from *Whipping Boy,* both containing characters who had run away from home. Activity sheets accompanied each book. For instance, for *Fried Worms* students separated lists of words into edible and inedible foods; for *Mixed-Up Files,* they generated ideas about foods they would bring and what they would pack if they were to be away for a week; and for *Little House* students generated ideas about chores and responsibilities in pioneer days. Hancock believed that cooperative grouping of students by diverse abilities was important, so she often allowed them to work on these activity sheets in small groups or with partners.

Writing Practices

In late September, Hancock was establishing her writing program with the kindergarten and first and second graders. To introduce students to the idea of selecting a topic, Hancock used "story starters." She provided an outline of a tall hat, with "One day I found in my tall hat . . ." written at the top of the page. The students wrote ideas inside the outline of the hat. Hancock also used patterns such as "I see . . . ," which students completed with "creative" ideas such as "a dog flying to the moon," "a dog meowing," or "a cat barking." She circulated and talked informally with students as they wrote. Finally, students had the opportunity to read their work to one another in author's chair.

Preparation for Writing

As a preface to the actual writing in September, Hancock began her lesson with a mystery bag containing an object containing the "long i sound." To narrow the possibilities, students were allowed to ask questions, such as "Can you play with it?" "Can you eat it?" or "Can you find it outside?" After the teacher gave some clues, a student guessed it was a tie. Hancock held up the tie and asked students if they could hear the "long i" sound.

When later that day Hancock explained her practices, she suggested that she was very pleased with the students' questioning during the mystery game: "I cannot tell you the difference I see in their questioning. It is so important that children learn the technique of asking good questions. When we first started, it was like,

'Is it a bank? Is it a pig?' and we quickly said you can't ask that, you have to ask questions about the object that is in the bag. We are coming up with some really fantastic answers."

After the mystery game, Hancock pulled Jerry's name out of a hat, giving him the chance to wear the puppet High Hat as Hancock read a story that contained many "long i" words. She pointed to the "sound finder," a chart with all of the vowel sounds listed, to show students the "long i" sound. Students then provided examples of words beginning with the "long i" sound, such as *spy* and *ice*. She wrote the words on the board and discussed the differences between the "long i" in *spy* and *ice*. In reflecting about her practice, Hancock expressed her beliefs that students need work on phonics: "I have beginning readers, and I also have second graders in there too, that I felt needed some extra work on phonics. We're really building hard on a phonics program for them, some word attack skills. . . . It gives them something to work with, when they come to unfamiliar words, besides context clues."

After the mystery bag and High Hat events, Hancock then introduced the "capital I" to indicate first person. She expressed in an interview that "it is a skill they will be tested on, that's a skill they need to know—that the *I* stands in place of their name." She chose this particular skill from an English book and believed it was a good time to introduce it, especially since students often wrote sentences that start with *I*.

Conferences

To extend this concept, Hancock precut paper ice cream scoops for each student and wrote one of her story starters, "I like," on the blackboard. First, students glued a premade capital *I* onto a picture of themselves; then they completed the sentence with their own ideas. For instance, Jerry wrote "I like Mom" on one scoop, "I like Dad" on the second scoop, and "I like God" on his third scoop.

As students wrote on their scoops, Hancock circulated, helped students focus, and encouraged their work.

Hancock: How you doing?
  Adam: Can I draw a picture?
Hancock: Adam, you have to write it first and if you would like to
          put a little picture with your writing when you finish,

you may. Okay, what do you put after your *K*? Good. Let's see. Point to what you like.

Adam: I like playing kick ball.

Hancock: You're very good at kick ball too. Jamey, Kelly, what do you need? Oh, you have a nice sentence.

Kelly: I like to go to my gymnastic class and my favorite part is aerials.

Hancock: Oh, I bet you're good at them.

Kelly: Not really.

Hancock: Oh, you're just learning.

Kelly: Yeah.

Hancock: Oh, Chris, what do you like? You like cats; do you have a cat?

Chris: Two.

Hancock: You got two of them? What's your cats', what's their names?

Chris: I have a big one and a little one.

Hancock: What are they named?

Chris: Tammie and Ke-Ke.

Hancock: Ke-Ke. Okay. You guys, can you think of something you like?

Lori: Yeah, ice cream.

Students were allowed to talk to one another during their writing, but each student worked on individual projects. More formal social interaction occurred when students read their pieces aloud.

Author's Chair

Students worked on their ice cream scoops until it was time for author's chair. At this point, Hancock called students together, saying "Let's share our ice cream cones." She pulled a name from a hat, and Graham sat in the author's chair and read aloud his "scoop." At the end of the student's reading, she said "That was good," and allowed Graham to select the name of the next reader from the hat.

Hancock showed an interest in what students liked, often asking a student a question related to what was read. For instance, when Michelle read that she liked gymnastics, Hancock asked how long she had been taking lessons. This continued until all the students had read and it was the end of the period. Hancock ended the lesson by asking "What was our sound?" to which students replied "i."

Hancock explained that what occurred that day was consistent with her goals and usual practices: "We try to use a lot of story starters. We do the phonics programs like High Hat. We try to pull out a story starter or something that will go with that sound that we are working on that day. We are trying to pull it all together and really give them a good dose of . . . that sound for the day."

Hancock wanted students to have both phonics skills and opportunities to write. She seemed to want to connect the sounds students were working on with their writing, thus combining skill instruction with student expression. Her goals reflected these dual purposes as she sought to include students' self-expression—"I'm trying to get them to open up and feel free"—while providing a structure: "You turn them loose with too much, I mean, they just sit there and stare at the paper." Referring to her practice of giving them an idea as "sentence building," Hancock commented that the ice cream scoop activity was appropriate to many ability levels; more able students could write more complete stories on their scoops if they chose.

Making Sense of Hancock's Practice

Committed to literature-based instruction, Hancock embraced new ideas and practices while holding on to some of the old. She removed the basal reader from her classroom, introduced literature, allowed students to work together, and provided students with opportunities to write and share their writing through author's chair. At the same time, she continued more traditional practices such as the use of story starters. Hancock believed she made traditional skills instruction such as learning the "long i" sound more exciting for students through the use of a puppet and encouraging students to suggest their own "long i" words.

Hancock's use of story starters seemed to be a step away from teacher-assigned topics, toward students' choosing their own topics. Few students developed a story or created any number of disconnected thoughts, but Hancock believed this was a first step with young writers. While author's chair allowed students to share their work with peers, only the teacher asked questions or provided comments about students' writing. This too may have been a first step toward students' commenting on each other's stories.

Perhaps Hancock's most significant shift was away from isolated skills instruction toward more contextualized, connected use of phonics and "main ideas." She was no longer driven by lists and sequences of skills from the basal reader. Instead, she selected skills from the writing development list that the team had produced together, and she connected those to the writing she wanted students to do. Her use of the puppet High Hat and the mystery game probably made learning "long i" sounds more enjoyable for students than isolated drills and practice.

As Hancock described the changes in her own teaching, she suggested that her most significant changes were no longer using the basal reader, introducing creative activities to develop critical thinking, and giving students more opportunities for self-expression so they would love reading and writing. While she no longer relied on the basal reader, she still made significant use of outside sources for her ideas. High Hat, for example, was for her "a teaching kit" she had checked out from the Masters Center. Activity sheets related to literature often came from publishers. This sourcing of materials was indicative of where she was in her own development. She did not see the skills she was teaching as coming from the literature that the students were reading or from students' own stories. Nor did she see it as important for students to generate their own topics for writing. She was, however, beginning to recognize the importance of looking to her students, determining their needs, and designing instruction around them.

Hancock seemed to be at a transitional point. She was expressing new ideas and trying them out in the classroom, while experiencing a new sense of success and enjoyment of teaching. Yet, she was not quite ready to give up some of her traditional practices nor change her role in the classroom. Manifested in her practices of selecting topics, controlling the discourse during author's chair, and assigning activities for her students, she was not ready to fully negotiate with them. But in only two years of multi-age grouping and literature-based instruction and one year of process writing, Hancock had come a very long way in her own estimation. She attributed her changes to her connections to her colleague, Julie Brandt, and her mentor, Jay Ross.

Differing Stages of Development Within One Team

Because Julie Brandt was the team leader and viewed by her peers as the source of innovation within the school, it is not surprising that she appears to be further along in the development of a distinctively different teaching practice than her teammate, Joyce Hancock. The two teachers had much in common: they provided a literature-based reading program; believed that students could work together; and established similar features in their writing programs, such as providing some direction in topic selection, opportunities to write, and opportunities for students to share their work through author's chair. However, there were subtle differences between their practices and their understandings of literature-based programs and process approaches to writing.

Brandt provided a general idea (feelings) for students to develop as a topic and asked students to generate ideas orally. In contrast, Hancock used a very specific "story starter" of "I like" and had students place it on a precut paper ice cream scoop. Brandt's approach suggested more comfort with student-generated ideas and an emphasis upon student elaboration in any number of directions. Hancock's approach, on the other hand, suggested she was not yet ready to allow students to generate their own topics or elaborate on them without providing a clear structure to follow.

While Brandt's students were encouraged to talk together at all the stages of writing, Hancock's students were allowed to talk to the person sitting nearest. The result in Brandt's class was that students seized the opportunity to bounce ideas off one another as well as to proofread each other's work, thereby increasing their access to ideas and other examples of written text. Several pairs of children, such as Amanda and Lucy, actually co-constructed text, producing something different from a single-authored paper. Hancock's students, on the other hand, created their own scoops and interacted with one another but did not really help each other to develop their ideas.

The nature of the teacher's talk also differed in the two classrooms. While conferring with students and conducting author's chair, both Brandt and Hancock expressed interest in students' ideas, encouraged them, and acknowledged their contributions. However, Brandt provided more instruction than Hancock and responded more substantively to students' writing. For example,

Brandt selected only three students to read aloud, providing more opportunity for comment focused on a single student's work. Hancock had all the students read, thus limiting opportunities for extended discourse about one story. Whereas Hancock focused on asking the author a single question about the scoop, Brandt assisted students by building on their ideas and providing ways to improve or expand the stories.

Brandt and Hancock had different ideas about how to use skills in their reading and writing programs. Brandt examined students' work to find out what they needed in their writing and designed her lessons around those needs. For example, she chose topics that came out of the "teacher based guidance" or allowed students to choose their own topics. Writing skills such as capitalization and punctuation came from the students' work. In contrast, Hancock did not look specifically at students' work but examined materials she found interesting, selected topics she thought the students might like, and used the lists of skills the team had developed. Brandt seemed more comfortable taking her cues from the students, whereas Hancock looked to outside authorities or to her teammates. Her instruction seemed less developed and less coherent than Brandt's, perhaps because she was depending on outside authorities rather than on a close reading of what students seemed to need.

The Role of the Team in Teacher Change

What role did the teams play in teachers' changes? How did teachers interact with one another? How had the teams developed over time?

Brandt and Hancock believed that the team organization at Webster was the essential ingredient in success for both the children and the teachers. Students felt themselves part of a larger group, and because they stayed in a team for two or three years the teachers believed they got to know the students very well. The team also provided opportunities for teachers to discuss ideas and specialize in a particular subject. As Brandt expressed it:

> In a team situation, you have people to share ideas—somebody to help you analyze this child, somebody to share your problems, and

then, in our case not to teach every subject is really good, too. Your goal always is, number one, to have the children be more successful and to eliminate failure and those type things. But it really does help to know that if you have a particular problem child, that child gets a chance to move to another classroom and get a fresh start. . . . [In a team situation] you work as hard and maybe you work harder, but you work more effectively. You spend more time on task, I think.

Team meetings, held once a week during shared planning time, consisted of discussions about scheduling, placement of children, curricular ideas, field trips, specific children, or issues such as evaluation and report cards. Teachers in the Snoopy Gang also often met with parents as a group. Throughout the three years the team had been meeting, the content of their meetings changed somewhat, according to Brandt. She described the first years as filled with talk about logistics and scheduling, whereas in the last year there had been more focus on "social development and curriculum." While Brandt believed that teachers needed to have shared goals if they were to succeed as a team, she also believed that teams should not infringe upon teachers' "personal styles":

> I think as you begin that you have to have goals. That was one of the first things we did when we started our team was talking about what our goals were—what we thought children should know, how we thought children should learn. . . What are your expectations for the children? Are they going to come in and sit at desks in rows? I think that's something you work out as a team, and I think you have to come to somewhat of an agreement there. But I don't think you have to sacrifice your total personal style. When we started our team we had one teacher that was really not comfortable with the literature-based [reading]. She said, "I cannot give up this basal reader; we have to have this." And she could still do that within her reading class, and she did supplement with literature-based, and eventually went completely to literature-based.

Brandt went on to suggest that although she would not want "three identical people on the team," it needed to agree on certain important issues such as discipline. How did the teams develop agreement on key issues? Brandt and Hancock believed it took time and effort by the team members, but that an outside person had also been important to their development as a team and to the changes in their practices.

Jay Ross's Role as a Resource Teacher in the Snoopy Gang

As noted earlier, as a resource teacher assigned to Webster from the Masters Center Jay Ross played an important role in linking district, school, and classroom restructuring. Drawing on his own philosophy of learning, which included engaging students in authentic writing tasks and having students use their own experiences as writing topics, Ross modeled writing with students in classrooms where he was invited. Reluctant to impose programs on teachers, he described his approach to staff development as "invitations to learn." During his year at Webster, he spent many hours demonstrating teaching practices in Julie Brandt's room and occasionally taught in Hancock's classroom—always at their invitation.

Brandt reported that Ross was the most influential person in changing her teaching practice. By demonstrating new practices with children, by giving her materials such as a book about how to teach spelling, and by talking with her about specific problems in the classroom, Brandt saw Ross as exercising considerable influence over her teaching of writing. Hancock was most influenced by the general support that Ross provided:

> Anytime we needed Jay, he was there. He helped us with doing a new writing program, and he is the one that got us to go camping. He said, "Well, have you ever thought about taking your kids camping?" and so we went out to Possum Creek and I mean I was ready to kill him when I saw the cabins, they were the pits. I'm not a camper and I said, "I'm going to kill Jay Ross when I see him," but I had a marvelous time. It was great, the kids, oh it was so good for team building. And so we went camping [again] this year, and it was Jay who has really gotten us to do things, to do some different types of things that I probably wouldn't have had the courage to do otherwise.

It was activities done in common, such as camping together, that Brandt and Hancock identified as important contributors to team building and communication in the Snoopy Gang. Ross further developed the communication within the team by exchanging ideas with them and being available for consultation. Many of the exchanges were informal, in the lunch room or in the hallway; Ross often followed up by placing articles or materials in teachers' mailboxes.

Not only did Ross play a key role in introducing new ideas to the teachers, but he played a role in their development as a team. Teachers seemed to be knowledgeable about their teammates' approaches to teaching and underlying philosophies. For instance, Brandt explained that she believed that Hancock was more comfortable using skill cards than depending on having skills emerge from students' writing. She further explained that she respected Hancock's not setting up her classroom just like Brandt's. Hancock also was able to describe Brandt's teaching. Both teachers suggested that their perceptions of each other were based on quick visits into one another's classrooms and on discussions in their team meetings.

Although they knew about each other's styles of teaching, Brandt and Hancock clearly respected one another's practices and did not want to impose their own beliefs about teaching. This working together while maintaining a respectful distance accounts for why they manifested different versions of the same curricular ideas in their practice and seemed to be at two quite different stages in the development practice. While they shared ideas, Brandt was clearly the leader in innovation, whereas Hancock was less developed and still dependent upon some of her more traditional skill-oriented practices. Yet the sharing of ideas within the team seemed to be a significant factor in both teachers' changing practices.

Chapter Nine

A Model of School Restructuring?

The Vision at Webster

Few schools represent the conventional wisdom about how school restructuring should occur better than Webster. The principal, Cheryl Billings, had an ambitious vision for what the school should be. This vision was based on the convictions that learning should challenge children; that teaching should create a strong bond between teacher, student, and content; and that these goals could be accomplished by a curriculum encouraging active engagement of students in hands-on learning activities. The vision was embodied in a specific set of changes in structure and content: multi-age teams, new curricula stressing active learning, and increased school-site decision making. These changes resulted from an elaborate process of consultation, extending over several years, in which teachers actively participated in the construction of the vision. The structural changes were phased in over a period of time, allowing teachers to choose voluntarily whether and when they would participate. Through this process, teachers began to take increasing responsibility for school-site decisions, including major changes in the district-mandated report card and influence over the school's budget.

These changes all occurred in an actively supportive district environment. The changes in structure and content at Webster exactly mirrored the district's priorities. Indeed, district-level restructuring staff saw Webster as implementing the district's agenda as much as the school's own. Furthermore, the district provided resources to the principal and faculty of Webster that few districts currently provide: access to district-sponsored professional development, access to exemplary schools and training activities outside the district, extra staff, and opportunities for teachers to meet and work together within the school site. In addition, the district provided resource teachers to work with the school's faculty on developing curriculum and teaching practices that reflected the priorities of the school and the districts.

Variability at Webster

Webster is in some senses a "best case" of restructuring: a school and a district working in tandem on a common restructuring agenda with significant resources. Yet within this best case one can see evidence of the extraordinarily complex and slippery relationship between changes in school structure and changes in teaching practice. In our analysis of a sample of teachers working in classrooms, the dominant themes are variability in how teachers respond, the resilience of past patterns of practice, and a considerable gap between the aspirations represented by the school's vision (as well as the teachers' own aspirations of what they want their practice to look like) and the actual teaching of specific content to students.

Multi-age teams were designed in part to let teachers specialize in a specific content area, deepen their knowledge of pedagogy in that area, enhance collaboration among teachers around content and pedagogy, and introduce students to more active approaches to learning in those areas. The teachers in our study participated voluntarily and enthusiastically in teams and formed an identity based on their special interests. They saw teams as significantly and positively influencing their teaching. But beneath this active support for multi-age teams lay considerable variation in teaching practice.

Webster teachers differed enormously in their attitudes toward and their knowledge of the content they were teaching. Julie Brandt and Joyce Hancock expressed delight in reading and writing and seemed to understand how to engage students in ways consistent with the school's vision. Brandt's ideas about practice were heavily influenced by her interaction with Jay Ross, the district resource teacher, and by her own investigations. Hancock's ideas were influenced mainly by her relationship with Brandt.

In contrast, Melissa Benton and Joanna Griffin seemed not to be particularly comfortable with or fluent in mathematics as a subject, despite their being considered specialists in mathematics within the Webster team structure. Benton confessed, "I actually hate math," by which she said she meant "higher math," such as algebra and geometry. She said that her elementary education degree required her to take only one mathematics course, a course in elementary math methods. Still, she seemed to like the specific math curriculum that the school had chosen, "Box It or Bag It Math," because it made mathematics accessible both to her and her students. She did think of herself as a mathematics specialist, and she thought her ideas about mathematics and her practice had both been transformed by Webster's restructuring. Her classroom practice, however, represented a combination of new curriculum and old pedagogy: use of new materials and manipulatives coupled with a relatively teacher-centered view of knowledge and teaching. Griffin likewise saw herself as having been heavily influenced by new ideas about teaching and curriculum. But while she was sympathetic to the curriculum, she seemed to lack the mathematical knowledge necessary to make good on the school's broader objective of engaging students in understanding basic mathematical knowledge. Faced with the problem of how to teach place value, she reverted to a lesson that she had developed from a textbook and encyclopedia ten years earlier, a lesson whose use of Roman numerals was clearly at odds with both conventional mathematical thinking and with the curriculum she was using.

Teachers' views of knowledge also varied considerably. Brandt seemed to view knowledge as fluid and socially constructed. She focused on students' ideas and their understandings of text, while allowing them opportunities to participate actively in constructing meaning from what they were doing. Hancock's views seemed less well formed, and she seemed less inclined to see students as active participants in the construction of knowledge. Benton and Griffin, by contrast, seemed to regard mathematics as relatively static and codified knowledge that students could learn by doing certain kinds of teacher-prescribed activities. But by this view, students were recipients of the knowledge embodied in the exercises, rather than active participants in its creation.

At a basic level, these teachers at Webster were not fundamentally different from teachers in most elementary schools in the United States. The enthusiasm of Brandt and Hancock for reading and writing mirrors the general sympathy that elementary teachers have for those subjects. The discomfort and lack of fluency with mathematics represented by Benton and Griffin is also characteristic of most elementary teachers. What makes Webster Elementary School different, though, is that the team structure—at least in principle—was supposed to compensate for these common patterns, by allowing teachers to develop a deeper knowledge and competency in a single content area, and therefore to become more expert. Changing the structure of work at Webster turned out at least in the short run to have only weak and variable influences on teachers' knowledge of content and their capacity to teach differently within a specialized subject. Structural change did seem to have a positive effect on teachers' attitudes toward content, and it opened up their views of curriculum and teaching to outside influences. Over the longer run, these attitudinal changes could percolate into teachers' classroom practice and their views of knowledge. But it is hard to glean from the Webster case exactly how this longer-term influence is supposed to occur. There appears to be relatively little in the environment of Benton and Griffin that would lead them to change their view of mathematics as a subject or of teacher-centered instruction as an approach to learning. Their exposure to outside experts, teamwork at Webster, and new curricula did not have much influence on their practice. Jay Ross's work with Brandt did seem to have a considerable influence on her practice, and indirectly on Hancock through Brandt, but this type of intensive assistance seems not to have been widely available to teachers at Webster. While structural change at Webster seems to have had a significant effect on the design of teachers' work and on their attitudes toward their work, there is little in the Webster case to lead us to be optimistic about the possibility of sustained change in teaching practice over time.

Teams were also supposed to provide teachers with the opportunity to interact around content and teaching with groups of teachers who have a common stake in a group of students. This advantage of teaming is difficult to realize in practice. Brandt and Hancock had many opportunities to work together because they were on the same team. Griffin and Benton, on the other hand, probably could have benefited from more interaction with each other and with outside experts, but they were isolated by being the specialists on their respective teams.

Connections to Professional Communities

Reform in the Fairchild school district and in Webster Elementary School was about more than simply changing the structure of work for teachers in schools. It was also about bringing new knowledge to teachers and administrators by making professional development available to them and connecting them to professional communities through resource teachers and other contacts outside the school. At the level of Webster, the story again seems to be essentially one of variability among teachers.

Outside connections seemed to work best for Brandt. She worked actively with Ross, she actively sought out new knowledge through her contacts at the local university, and she was closely connected to the district restructuring team through her husband. She thought of herself as an active participant in a community engaged in professional discourse about reading and writing. She brought Hancock into this community.

Ross's intensive work in Brandt's classroom played a large role in linking her to these external communities. Ross drew upon his own knowledge and expertise to demonstrate a new kind of pedagogy in Brandt's and Hancock's classrooms. His basic method of working with teachers was to build trust and do what was immediately useful to teachers that also demonstrated new approaches to content and teaching.

In contrast, Benton and Griffin did not have the benefit of a close working relationship with an outside consultant in mathematics. They had access to workshops and to new curriculum materials, but this access did not influence their views of knowledge in the same way as Brandt's relationship with Ross. They did not have a personal identification with an individual who represented an alternative view of content and teaching, nor did they feel that they were connected with professional discourse in the same way that Brandt was.

The district's overall strategy of relying on resource teachers to connect teachers to a broader professional community seemed to work in Brandt's and Hancock's case, but it did not provide Benton and Griffin with the kind of support they needed to transform their mathematics teaching. So while the district recognized that changing teaching requires new knowledge, its strategy did not deal comprehensively with this issue.

Furthermore, the internal politics of the district may have gotten in the way of delivering useful knowledge to teachers. The Fairchild district mathematics curriculum expert was knowledgeable about changing conceptions of mathematics teaching, thanks to her participation in state and national networks of mathematics educators. In fact, she was serving as state president of the National Council of Teachers of Mathematics and was actively involved in professional development within the district. However, because the restructuring team in the Masters Center regarded the curriculum and instruction division within the Fairchild district as not representing the district's current thinking about school restructuring, the district's curriculum experts were not part of the district's overall strategy of school improvement. Hence, teachers such as Benton and Griffin were purposely disconnected from the expertise that might have brought them into the larger professional community of discourse on mathematics.

At least in the short run, changing the structure of teachers' work at Webster seemed to have only modest and variable effects on classroom teaching practice. The main barrier or constraints to changing practice seemed to be teachers' deep-seated ideas about content and pedagogy and their limited access to experiences and external contacts that would help them develop alternative conceptions of knowledge and pedagogy. The district tried to organize itself to deliver this knowledge and experience. For at least one teacher, the district structure seemed to work as it was intended to work. In others, it seemed not to.

Part Three

Northeastern Elementary School

"There should be at least one school that is right for each child."

—Antonio Amada, chief administrator of schools in Northeastern Elementary School's district

Chapter Ten

An Alternative School Is Born

The School and Its Community

Northeastern Elementary School sits on the corner of two wide and busy streets in a crowded inner-city neighborhood, one of a handful of the city's poorest neighborhoods and possibly one of the dozen or so poorest in the nation. Forbidding from the outside, as are many inner-city schools, Northeastern's building dates to the 1950s and has the characteristic brick and metal-window-frame construction of that period. The building, while generally clean and free of graffiti, looks forlorn and tired. Inside, it is another matter: spotless, active, and inviting. Students of all ages, from kindergarten through high school, move through the halls, their work seems displayed on every available surface, and adults and children relate to each other easily and familiarly.

Northeastern shares its building with three other alternative schools. One is an alternative secondary school, grades 7–12, deliberately designed to extend Northeastern's philosophy and pedagogy into the upper grades. The two schools have a symbiotic relationship. Some students from the secondary school fulfill part of their community service requirement by working as aides and tutors in Northeastern. Many of the students in the elementary school advance to the secondary school. The teachers in the two schools share a common educational philosophy and mingle informally in the hallways.

Northeastern's neighborhood has played a deep and important role in the history of the city. On the fringes of the city's more affluent neighborhoods and far from its original core, the neighborhood became a gathering place for working-class Jews and

Italians in the early 1900s. During and after World War II, as the citywide population of African Americans increased dramatically, the neighborhood became increasingly black. Then in the 1950s, with a large wave of immigration from Puerto Rico, the neighborhood became increasingly Hispanic. The schools in Northeastern's neighborhood have educated large numbers of first- and second-generation immigrants to America along with new arrivals to the city from other parts of the country. Many students from the neighborhood's schools have become leaders in the city and nation. Over the past twenty-five years, however, the neighborhood has become progressively poorer and more isolated from its affluent neighbors.

Northeastern's neighborhood is an active and vital place. The streets are lined with small stores, their merchandise often spilling onto tables on the sidewalks; street vendors sell food on the corners. The neighborhood has a more human scale than many other parts of the city, and people of all ages can be seen on the streets during the daytime. Several massive public housing projects occupy blocks of the neighborhood. One of these projects is immediately adjacent to Northeastern. In the past, teachers recall, drugs were sold openly on the street in front of Northeastern and on the grounds of the housing project next to the school. This sort of activity is less visible now, at least in the immediate vicinity of the school, but teachers observe that it has simply moved to other places.

Most of Northeastern's roughly 280 students come from its neighborhood, and a good number of those come from the housing projects. As with all other alternative schools in its district, Northeastern is a school of choice, meaning that parents must deliberately apply to the school, rather than having their children assigned on the basis of attendance area. Because the school attracts many more applicants than it has places for, most children are admitted to the school by lottery, with neighborhood children given first preference in the selection process. Siblings of children already admitted to the school and children of faculty members bypass the lottery. The result is that Northeastern's students are predominantly minority and low-income, mostly Hispanic and African American. The school also attracts some middle-class, non-minority students from outside the neighborhood. With Northeastern's growing reputation for educational success, its capacity to attract middle-class, nonminority students has increased, causing some critics to argue that it no longer represents the community in which it resides. Those familiar with Northeastern's history and its admissions process regard this criticism as ironic, observing that it is a major victory both for the city and the school that middle-class white parents are willing to send their children to Northeastern's neighborhood in pursuit of high-quality education.

Northeastern Emerges

In the mid-1970s, a young and ambitious educator, Antonio Amada, became the chief administrator of the schools in the neighborhood. The citywide school system delegates major responsibility to neighborhood-based school districts, which have their own elected boards. Amada's selection by the neighborhood board was seen as a clear endorsement of reform. A product of the neighborhood's schools himself and an outspoken critic of their failure to serve minority students well, Amada told the neighborhood board that he intended to take drastic action to improve its schools. One part of his ambitious agenda was to offer teachers within the neighborhood the opportunity to organize new schools focused on the needs of disadvantaged students. No teachers accepted his offer. Prior to the beginning of his second year in the neighborhood, Amada recruited an outsider to the district, Diana Mandel, to organize a new elementary school. Mandel came from a network of teachers interested in the "open education" reforms of the 1960s; she had considerable experience as a teacher and promoter of open education in a nearby neighborhood.

Mandel proposed to start the school with two grades, kindergarten and first, and to build the program one grade at a time. Amada found space in a large elementary school building in the neighborhood and gave Mandel the go-ahead. She recruited teachers out of the open-education network in the city and started Northeastern.

The founding of Northeastern was part of a more general strategy that Amada had for the neighborhood district. He wanted to open a number of small alternative schools and eventually to offer parents in the neighborhood the opportunity to choose among many high-quality educational programs. He also saw alternative schools as a way of diversifying the educational offerings of the district to respond to differences among children. "Not every school is, or should be, right for every child," Amada said, "but there should be at least one school that is right for each child."

Early enrollment at Northeastern reflected these district priorities. Some children came to Northeastern because their parents were actively involved in their children's education and had heard about Northeastern's program through the city's open-education grapevine or from other parents. Other children were referred to Northeastern by teachers in other neighborhood schools because they were not doing well in traditional programs.

According to Mandel, Northeastern's educational philosophy grew out of a few core beliefs about education and schooling: that children should be allowed to develop and learn individually in a supportive environment, that teachers should exercise a major influence over curriculum and teaching in classrooms and in the school, and that parents should be treated as partners in their children's learning. These beliefs came from Mandel's and her colleagues' immersion in the open-education movement prior to starting Northeastern. They were tested strongly in the first few years of the school's existence.

Initially, Mandel, the teachers, and parents saw the school as a radical alternative to the traditional bureaucratic structure of the public schools. The school's internal structure was deliberately and dramatically simplified. There were no full-time administrators or support staff; Mandel herself taught and at one point in the second year was a full-time teacher. Mandel took the title of director, rather than principal, and did not become certified as an administrator. The district adopted this precedent for other head administrators in its alternative schools. Teachers were organized into cross-grade teams of two and three teachers; the teams assumed virtually full responsibility for defining the curriculum in their classrooms. Teachers also assumed responsibility for administrative paperwork and relations with parents. The school staff met regularly in schoolwide meetings to discuss and decide organizational issues.

At first this structure was invigorating and engaging for teachers, since it gave them a sense of considerable influence over their work. As the work grew more complex, however, the teachers began to find the structure less manageable. Schoolwide meetings tended to wander across a wide range of topics, as one teacher characterized it, from "what kind of toilet paper to buy to how to teach reading." Furthermore, teachers found that dealing with administrative paperwork, parent complaints, and logistical details, as well as their classroom work, drained energy away from teaching.

Northeastern also confronted some significant organizational and political problems in its second year. Because of the school's lean staffing, teacher absences and illnesses created major staffing and morale problems in the school. During the year, Mandel herself took over a full-time teaching position for a teacher who left after becoming ill. A few teachers took exception to the district's slow processing of payroll requests for newly hired teachers, which precipitated a threatened walk out; Mandel intervened, threatening to fire the teachers who left. She took this position, she said, "because I thought it was understood that as teachers our first responsibility was to the children." Parents, sensing factionalism and disorder within the school, began to take sides between opposing teacher groups. As the conflict deepened, the issues were pushed up to the district level, where Amada and his assistant for alternative programs intervened to calm things down.

Northeastern Evolves

At the end of the second year, two of the school's seven teachers left, a small number of parents withdrew their children from the school, and Mandel retreated to reconsider her role and the school's organization. In her words, "I learned that a school is a very fragile thing, and it has to be nurtured very carefully and continuously changed in subtle and not-so-subtle ways to make it work. I also learned that I had to take more responsibility for holding the school together and keeping it focused on its central purposes."

At the opening of the school's third year, Mandel redefined her own role. In a departure from the school's past practice, she became a full-time administrator, but hardly in the conventional sense. She defined her role mainly as supporting teachers in their classroom work. She also assumed more responsibility for dealings with district administrators and parents. The teachers began to focus more on classroom work, and on collegial interaction to support that work, and less on organizational and external issues. Mandel remained in this role for about ten years, playing an important part in the continuing development of Northeastern and in starting two more elementary schools in the district that reflected Northeastern's philosophy. In the mid-1980s, she left the directorship of Northeastern to develop the new secondary school that extends Northeastern's philosophy to the later grades and shares the same building.

Mandel's successor as director was Luisa Montoya, a veteran teacher at both Northeastern and one of the new elementary schools it spawned, as well as a native of Northeastern's neighborhood and a graduate of its schools. Her succession to the leadership of Northeastern was an important event in the school's development. Her roots in the neighborhood gave increased credibility to the school. But of equal importance was the fact that she was steeped in the philosophy of Northeastern and had played a leadership role as a teacher which signaled to the other teachers and the community that there would be continuity in the philosophy of the school. In effect, Northeastern had taken control of its own destiny, grooming new leadership from within, thus providing an important source of stability over time.

Montoya's philosophy of leadership is practical and teacher-centered:

> I meet with teachers on a regular basis individually to address their concerns about kids, about curriculum. I did it originally when I came here, having been in the classroom for seventeen years and not having had administrative experience, but thinking that my perspective from the classroom . . . was that oftentimes teachers' needs were not always addressed because the business of running a school is such a complex one. . . . I had to keep strong to this belief about making sure that teachers feel supported, and that teachers have an opportunity to share, to vent, to agonize. They need to do it with each other, but they also need someone at the leadership level to do it with.

Montoya makes a point of consulting with individual teachers at least twice each week. She calls these visits "rounds." She also makes clear that she is available to work in teachers' classrooms, which she also does regularly, either to supplement an existing lesson or to fill in for a teacher who has something to do outside of class.

Montoya also makes a point of knowing something about each student. Teachers prepare narrative descriptions of students in lieu of grades. Montoya reads all of these narratives, which allows her to engage teachers not just on the level of general teaching practice but also on the level of how they are doing with individual children. "I know every single student by their first name; I know usually at least three things about them because I've read their reports; I'm in contact with their families; I know the parents."

Montoya also takes her formal administrative responsibilities seriously. As with Mandel before her, she recognizes that there are situations where she must play the role of lead administrator.

> I'm [sometimes] in a position where I have to say—it doesn't happen often because of the nature of how we work together as a staff—but where I have to, after listening to everybody and everybody making their contributions, [I have to say], "Well, this is the way it has to be." That doesn't happen too often. . . . It's not that I'm afraid to make decisions or that I'm wishy-washy about it, but I think that one of the luxuries we don't have in schools [is] time and patience to work through things. . . . My role is to decide what are the things we prioritize.

Among the issues in which Montoya plays a strong role are guiding decisions about how the faculty uses its staff development time and how the school responds to district requests for teachers to participate in various committees. In the spring of each academic year, the faculty decides as a group how they will focus the use of staff development time during the coming year, and Montoya guides the selection of specific activities that focus on those priorities. She also screens requests for teachers to participate in district committees, sometimes talking the district out of what she regards as unproductive uses of teacher time and sometimes guiding a teacher into a particular committee.

Montoya's pedagogical beliefs are clear and universally shared by teachers within the school.

We approach the learner by saying it's exciting to learn and we're going to provide an environment that's going to naturally have the inclination for learning, and we're going to give you some leads, but we're also going to take your lead as a learner. . . . To the family we're saying that we can't do this by ourselves and this is such an exciting, complex process that we need family participation. . . . It's more that just coming to a family conference. It's being actively involved with the teacher about their child's learning. . . . We spend time teaching parents how to ask questions about their child as a learner. . . . It's our responsibility to set up an atmosphere that includes parents and makes them feel that they are participating with their child in the learning process. . . . We are creating habits of mind. . . . We have to be consistent with kids, and we can't ask of children what we don't follow up on ourselves.

Politics around schools in the neighborhood are often turbulent, but because of the strong ties that Mandel and Montoya have established with district-level administrators and with parents, these political currents seem to have little direct effect on Northeastern. The issues of whether the district should have alternative schools and whether the ground rules for admitting students to alternative schools are fair recur with some frequency. A majority of the neighborhood board favor the existing system, which is important to the future of Northeastern, but a vocal minority in the board and in the community criticize the system. So far, these conflicts have not had a substantial impact on Northeastern, but Montoya and Mandel view their role as exercising constant vigilance over the preservation of Northeastern's autonomy and its educational mission.

How Northeastern Works: Norms and Structures

While Northeastern became a less radically restructured school in its early years, it also developed a set of deeply seated norms that would persist in later years and be reinforced in the transition from Mandel to Montoya. One of these norms has to do with collective decision making. As collective decision making around the details of the organization declined in the early years of the school's development, it was replaced by norms of collaboration that reinforced teachers' commitment to teaching and learning.

One structural feature that exemplifies these norms is faculty meetings. While the specific form and content of these meetings have changed over time, the basic principle behind them has remained the same. An ongoing meeting typically held on alternate Mondays deals explicitly with educational matters. It is often a discussion of a specific student who presents a particular set of problems for a teacher. Less often, it is a discussion of a curricular issue or a problem of teaching practice. The content of these meetings has varied week-to-week and year-to-year. When the meetings begin to drift away from a primary focus on student learning issues and into a general discussion of educational philosophy and school problems, teachers question the drift and bring things back to a clearer focus on student learning.

The other type of meeting, typically held every Wednesday, deals with organizational issues. At one such meeting, for example, the discussion focused on plans for a faculty retreat, while others dealt with more general issues at the school. The Monday meetings often last as long as two hours, the Wednesday meetings rarely more than an hour. In both types, the tone is at once relaxed and highly professional. Discussions typically proceed by one teacher presenting a description of a particular student or problem in the school, and then each of the roughly ten teachers speaks in turn. Most of the discourse in the meetings takes place among teachers around a common problem, rather than between individual teachers and the school director. Montoya participates mainly as a colleague, except in the small number of instances where it is clear that as director she must decide a schoolwide issue, in which case the teachers generally defer to her judgment.

The outward structure of Northeastern looks fairly conventional in some ways, but the structure works according to norms that are quite unusual for elementary schools. The school adheres to its original philosophy of broad, cross-age grouping for classes. Children are grouped into four broad grades (kindergarten, first and second, third and fourth, and fifth and sixth), with a kindergarten student typically moving on to spend periods of two years each with a single teacher. But with two teachers at each grade level, children can move from one teacher to another within a given grade level if circumstances dictate. This cross-age grouping structure reflects a belief among Northeastern teachers that students develop in very different ways and at very different rates, and that teachers need to have deep personal knowledge of students from close contact over a long period of time to understand how students learn best. Consistent with this belief, teachers keep detailed narrative accounts of their observations of students' emotional, social, and cognitive development. These narrative accounts usually stay with teachers, but they are often used as the basis for discussion among teachers about the problems, strengths, and weaknesses of a student.

Within this structure of cross-age grouping, the school is organized around self-contained classrooms. A single teacher has primary responsibility for a single group of students for most of the school day. The school has full-time music and art teachers, as well as two "resource room" teachers and a part-time school psychologist. The latter provide support for regular classroom teachers in working with students with special learning problems, and their presence allows flexibility in scheduling time for classroom teachers to consult with each other during the school day.

Northeastern's self-contained classrooms do not result in the egg-crate structure in which teachers essentially operate in isolation from one another with little or no knowledge of each other's practice. A visitor to Northeastern almost immediately senses a high degree of consensus among teachers on how classrooms should be organized, what constitutes good learning, and what kinds of interactions promote learning. This consensus is manifested most visibly in that every classroom has essentially the same structure. Part of the room is set aside for small-group work, organized with tables where students can sit facing each other. Part of the room is set aside for individual work, with cushions, small chairs, and rugs where students can sit and read or work on individual projects. Part of each room is set aside for cooking—an activity that serves both educational and social purposes. Students never sit in rows facing in one direction; their attention is virtually always focused either on their own work or on the work of another student and almost never focused on the teacher performing work for students.

There is an explicit structure to each day, presented in a schedule on the blackboard. But the nature of the work is often quite different from what students do in the typical elementary school. Students might spend as much as two or three hours in the morning or afternoon working on a project, individually or in small groups, designed around theme writing, constructing models, doing research, drawing, and so forth. Interspersed with these periods of work on projects is time spent focused on academic content, typically reading, math, and science. Students work individually or in small groups, whether on silent reading, writing in journals, writing stories, working on math problems, or other activities. One afternoon, for example, a fifth-and-sixth-grade class was organized into three groups, each designing items for a test on a particular set of mathematics concepts. Individuals in each group developed test items, wrote them on note cards, and administered them to other members of the group, recording the number of correct and incorrect responses to each item. Then the items were organized according to difficulty, based on the number of correct and incorrect responses, and students in the groups discussed how they would construct a test to determine how well they understood the concepts. They discussed the differences between the more and less difficult items and made judgments about which items they might include in a test. The teacher explained the purpose of the exercise by saying that students should be familiar not just with basic mathematical ideas but also with the processes by which tests are constructed. Working in groups, actively using knowledge to produce a tangible product, and reflecting on what knowledge means characterizes much of the student work we observed at Northeastern.

Resource room teachers (teachers responsibile for attending to students with special needs) typically move in and out of classrooms, assisting teachers with specific children in need of help; less frequently, students leave their rooms for individual or small-group instruction. Art and music are interspersed throughout the week, leaving regular classroom teachers free to do their own work, meet with other teachers, or observe in other classrooms. Montoya, the director, keeps a regular schedule of consultations with teachers each week, moving in and out of classrooms, as well as meeting with teachers during their free periods.

Very little whole-group instruction occurs during the day. Occasionally, a teacher convenes the whole class to explain or discuss some important issue. More typically, students meet as a whole class at the beginning, middle, and end of the day to discuss issues affecting the whole class, or to plan work for the coming day. Breakfast and lunch are served for the whole school, which allows students to socialize outside of their normal classes.

An outside observer sees little variation in organization and interactions from one classroom to another at Northeastern. Yet Northeastern teachers disagree strongly with this observation; they perceive significant differences among classrooms. Teachers acknowledge that they essentially agree on what good teaching is, but they see nuances in how their colleagues act on these views. Some teachers, for example, are seen by their colleagues as being much more accomplished at designing and getting students involved in projects, at working with students on reading and writing, at developing students' capacities to represent their knowledge in drawings and models, and so forth. Other teachers are seen as having important subject-matter expertise, in a particular culture or historical period related to student projects, as well as in math and science. These nuances play an important role in how teachers and the director of the school think about their roles. They see the differences resulting in increased interdependence among teachers, since some teachers are more knowledgeable in certain areas than others. It is not unusual for a teacher or the director to take over another teacher's class for a short period of time; nor is it unusual for one teacher to consult with another about the details of designing a particular project or a lesson for students. While outsiders might see a high degree of uniformity in how Northeastern's classrooms are organized and teachers teach, the teachers themselves perceive significant variation and teacher interdependence.

A high level of agreement on basic norms of teaching practice, with variation in details, leads to a norm of interdependence and collaboration among teachers. Northeastern teachers speak of "their" classrooms and "their" students in much the same way that teachers in more conventional schools might. The maintenance of self-contained classrooms reinforces this norm. But the norms of privacy that exist in more conventional schools—the norm of one teacher not intruding on another's classroom or students—are virtually nonexistent at Northeastern. Northeastern teachers freely interact around content, pedagogy, and students' needs in a number of structured and unstructured ways. As noted, there are formal staff reviews of students, which involve all teachers in the school. There are also weekly meetings of teachers that involve discussions of schoolwide issues of content and pedagogy. Beneath this formal structure is a more complex informal structure in which teachers more or less freely interact over lunch, in the hallways, after school, and during regular school hours around the daily issues of students and teaching. Teachers often meet in each other's classrooms and freely observe each other teaching. Hence, while the formal organization of the school maintains self-contained classrooms, the informal structure of the school reinforces a high level of interaction among teachers around students and teaching.

The norm of free movement in and out of classrooms applies not only to regular classroom teachers but to others as well. One morning, for example, in a fifth-and-sixth-grade classroom, the regular teacher was working with a group of students on reading and journal writing, a secondary school student was working as a community service intern tutoring a group of students in reading, a resource room teacher was observing a student who the regular classroom teacher thought needed help, a parent volunteer was helping to manage the independent work of students who were not working with the regular teacher, and two outside observers were doing research in the classroom. Despite the presence of all these "outsiders," the teacher in charge of the classroom seemed focused, undistracted, and low-key in her work with students. Northeastern teachers seem comfortable with routine outside involvement and scrutiny of their practice in ways that would make most classroom teachers uncomfortable.

Another norm at Northeastern is attention to the families and communities from which students come. As noted above, all Northeastern students are in the school by choice, and most of them come from the community in which the school is located. Choosing Northeastern requires some degree of commitment on the part of parents. They have to apply to the school. The school requests that they visit, observe classes (the school provides a simple protocol for observers to use in understanding what they are observing), and meet with school personnel before they decide.

Because of Northeastern's reputation, it is oversubscribed by a substantial amount, so not all who apply can get in. The school's students and families are deliberately chosen to maximize diversity, but also to focus on students and parents who are comfortable with Northeastern's philosophy. Critics of Northeastern argue that the school's selection practices mean that it is "elitist" and that it does not reflect the diversity of the community in which it resides. Northeastern staff argue that they have a student body that is diverse in as many elements as possible, but that it is important for both their purposes and those of families that parents and students be comfortable with the basic philosophy of the school. Once students are admitted, the school tries to establish a close working relationship with parents. Parents play an active part in the life of the school, as aides and volunteers. The school conducts regular parent meetings, including one at the beginning of the year in which teachers speak individually with parents about what they will do over the coming year.

Northeastern also has a school-family coordinator, whose main responsibility is to run an ambitious intervention program designed to assure families and others that students needing special attention receive it. When a student is having serious problems in school, the coordinator convenes a team, consisting of the student's teacher, the school's director, a parent or family member, and the student. The team discusses the student's problem and decides on a course of action, which may include focusing on referral to an outside agency or special help with the school. This course of action is formally represented in a contract among the members of the team, and the school-family coordinator oversees the actions that are supposed to take place. Asked about the range of issues that arise through this mechanism, the school-family coordinator replied, "the whole range of things, from serious classroom discipline problems, to academic failure stemming from serious emotional problems, to deaths in the family, to issues stemming from things like drug use and abusive behavior in families."

In addition to establishing links with students' families, the school tries to construct ties with the neighborhood and the city. Students and faculty participate in important events in the community. Teachers construct projects that draw students into the cultural institutions of the neighborhood and the city. And the school organizes cultural events of its own to recognize important events and holidays in the community. On one occasion, for example, students wrote and produced a play commemorating Martin Luther King's birthday, drawing the school together for the occasion.

Yet another norm at Northeastern is involvement of teachers in serious intellectual pursuits outside the classroom and the school. All teachers at Northeastern have some serious intellectual interest outside their routine work life that bears on their work. As noted above, the school has its intellectual roots in the open-education movement that emerged in the United States during the 1950s and 1960s. Diane Mandel, the school's first director, is seen as a major figure in educational reform and is connected with a number of networks of people with similar interests. Northeastern maintains an informal affiliation with a private school in New England that serves as a major source of new ideas for Northeastern teachers, who visit the school regularly. Individual teachers' interests outside of school span literature, biography, biology, art, and music. They pursue these interests with independent work: taking courses at nearby universities, taking summer study trips, and working independently on their own projects. The school-family coordinator is affiliated with a local institute of family therapy, in which she regularly participates as a student and practitioner. A number of Northeastern teachers have published articles in journals and magazines.

In some instances, teachers' outside interests have a direct pay-off for the school's curriculum, for example when teachers design student projects around their interests. But in most cases teachers' outside interests are simply part of the pattern of general intellectual growth and inquisitiveness at the school. Northeastern teachers subscribe to the idea that they are trying to develop in students an innate inquisitiveness that will cause them to take charge of their own learning over time. The teachers themselves embody this commitment to sustained learning.

These basic norms—agreement on teaching practice, collegiality within a structure of self-contained classrooms, links to family and community, and sustained lifelong learning—represent the central core of beliefs around which the structure of Northeastern has evolved. The organization of the school supports these norms in a number of ways. The basic structure of the school, while not revolutionary by any definition, fits well with the underlying beliefs that the school has evolved as to how children learn and how teachers support that learning.

One of the most important devices for sustaining deep agreement on these norms is that Northeastern teachers play the determining role in hiring their own colleagues, and they hire only people whose views are compatible with their own. With a faculty of only ten full-timers and low turnover from year-to-year, there seems to be little disruption but also few opportunities to hire new teachers at the school. As a result, the school asserts strong influence over who gets to teach there. One teacher, for example, had been an administrator in charge of alternative programs elsewhere in the city but left education altogether because she did not want to continue being an administrator. Then she heard through the grapevine that Northeastern needed an art teacher. She had an interest in teaching art, but no formal qualifications or certification. Mandel, Northeastern's director at that time, arranged for her to do an internship with an art teacher at an elite private school in the city, and she served as a volunteer at Northeastern before she was finally hired as the school's only art teacher. Another teacher was hired after he was recruited as a student teacher in Northeastern's partner secondary school. In other words, Northeastern teachers are carefully screened, recruited, and selected based on the compatibility of their views with the norms of the school. The school has actively shaped its own culture by recruiting teachers whose values are consistent with its norms.

Northeastern in a Nutshell

At the time we began our research at Northeastern, the school had been in existence for nearly fifteen years, on a more or less steady path of evolution toward the school we describe in these chapters. Unlike the other schools in our study, then, Northeastern was less in the process of restructuring than in the process of maintaining a particular structure, a set of norms, and a view of teaching practice that it had evolved over a considerable period of time. Northeastern arrived at this point essentially by taking control of its own fate in ways that few public elementary schools do in this country. Formed initially at the encouragement of district administrator Antonio Amada from a group of parents and teachers with a common view of education; nurtured through its early crises by a leader who was willing to change her own views of leadership in order to preserve the school; shored up by a system that encouraged parents to choose the school for their children; and maintained by a process in which teachers played the deciding role in recruiting and hiring their new colleagues, Northeastern became a community of people with a strong bond of common interests and values. What did teaching look like within this community?

| **Reading and Writing**

Teachers at Northeastern inhabited a world defined by high agreement on what good teaching should look like and a set of informal norms and structures that reinforced that agreement. Frequent visits by director Luisa Montoya on her "rounds," frequent meetings of the whole faculty in which individual children and more general issues of pedagogy were discussed, and a steady and routine movement of people in various roles in and out of classrooms all reinforced the idea that Northeastern teachers knew what good practice was and were willing to have their teaching subjected to external scrutiny.

While the formal organizational structure of Northeastern was relatively conventional (self-contained classrooms in which a single teacher was more or less fully responsible for a single group of students), the internal organization of classrooms was quite similar throughout Northeastern while quite distinctive from traditional elementary school rooms. The emphasis here was always on providing space for students to work independently and collaborate with the teacher, rather than focusing attention on the teacher as the center of activity. Children spent most of their time working with each other, or independently on their own projects, rather than as a group with the teacher.

Our interviews with teachers also revealed that they made continual reference to the intellectual basis of their teaching practice, either in research on teaching or in their own academic interests outside the school. They viewed certain scholars, books, and experiences as touchstones for their own views of teaching practice, and they were eager that we should understand where these ideas about practice came from. Hence in our accounts of teaching practice at Northeastern, we try to represent some of these touchstones.

As at Lakeview and Webster, we observed several teachers at Northeastern and selected two pairs for close analysis here.

Brian Kramer and Alexis Brezinski were two upper-grade teachers (fifth and sixth grades). Kramer was in his thirties and had been a teacher at Northeastern for nine years at the time of our study. Brezinski was a veteran at Northeastern, there since its inception about fifteen years previously, and had been involved in teaching many years before that.

Dede Patterson and Dan Rollins were two middle-grade teachers (third and fourth grades). Patterson was a relative newcomer to Northeastern, having been there for three years at the time of our study. Rollins was a veteran with eight years at the school.

These teachers represent a range of experience and interests. Northeastern teachers do not think of themselves as "specialists," because they do not take lead responsibility for any particular subject within a particular team; but they do think of themselves informally as having particular competencies and interests that other teachers might not have. Consequently we focus our analysis here on Kramer's and Brezinski's teaching of writing and on Patterson and Rollins as teachers of science.

We did not find the range or variation of teaching practice at Northeastern that we found at other schools—a subject that we will return to in greater detail later. In choosing these four teachers, however, we have tried to give some idea of the range even if it is quite narrow. With the other schools in our study, we have focused on teachers thought by principals and colleagues to exemplify the kind of teaching practice they were trying to attain; with Northeastern we have deliberately tried to represent variability in practice, insofar as it can be said to exist there.

Brian Kramer and Alexis Brezinski

In writing, not only can we create worlds, but we can change them at will. Writing enables us to explore and change the worlds of ideas and experiences that the brain creates. . . . The power of writing is not initially lost upon many children. A child who writes "The dog died" is astounded at what has been accomplished. The child has put a dog into the world that did not exist before—created a world that would not otherwise have existed—and then has killed the dog. None of this can be done in any other way. . . . This is the enormous power and attraction of writing, especially for children—until something happens to persuade them that writing does not have this power at all. . . . They may be subjected to drills and homilies that teach them that literacy is work, punitive, and a bore. Even if they do "learn to write," what they will learn is that the purpose of reading and writing is the shunting of information (Smith, 1983, pp. 129, 133).

Frank Smith's ideas were cited by all the teachers at Northeastern as influencing their thinking about reading and writing. The two upper-grade teachers in the school, Brian Kramer and Alexis Brezinski, both saw reading and writing as interrelated subjects and taught them in this way in their classrooms. To them, writing and reading are means of opening up new worlds for their students, whose own worlds were fraught with the uncertainties and complexities of life in the inner city.

Brian Kramer: Negotiating Reading and Writing

Brian Kramer's classroom appeared chaotic on the surface, a large room full of boxes, rugs, computers, bookshelves, a VCR, refrigerator, toaster, maps, globes, and a few tables. Most prominent were the many animals: guinea pigs, frogs, hamsters, and fish housed in an array of environments from cages to aquariums. From underneath the chaos, however, order emerged: shelves were grouped together, kitchen items were next to one another, and the rug defined a prominent place on one side of the room. Kramer moved among students most of whom were Latino, African American, Asian, and others of color, with a few European Americans, including Kramer himself.

Small and muscular, Kramer kept in shape, often running to school. He lived nearby, although not in the immediate neighborhood of the school. His African American wife also taught at Northeastern, and their children attended the school. He set up his classroom to provide resources for his students; he described his role as facilitator. He was continually negotiating with students, providing ideas for curriculum, projects, or writing topics; yet he welcomed student initiation.

Kramer's Perspective on Reading and Writing

Kramer embraced a philosophy of reading consistent with that of many whole-language and process-writing proponents. He cited both Frank Smith (1971) and Lucy Calkins (1986) as influencing his literacy teaching. He explained his view of reading as "a process of getting meaning from the printed page, but it's also a process of bringing a lot of knowledge about how the student reaches out to the printed page. . . . Very little is taken from the printed page. So much more is supplied by the reader." This approach to reading has been characterized as a "top-down perspective," in which the reader supplies more of the meaning than does the print on the page (Smith, 1971). Kramer believed that students learn to read by being immersed in a literate environment in which they discuss literature and read to themselves. He drew from Smith's (1988) notion of a literacy club, saying that "learning to read is like joining a club. It involves a set of expectations, and there's initiation into it. You're joining with others who are literate. You are surrounded by that kind of thing, and you will learn to read."

Kramer considered writing a natural process. He believed in helping "kids to express their own ideas in different ways." Students had free choice of topics; his role was to "build on the individual's own writing." Besides believing students should select their own topics, Kramer also did group lessons on writing. He would suggest that they write class poems or discuss the structure of a particular poem, or he would "read a particularly scary story to them and ask them, 'How did the author develop the sense of suspense?'" Kramer did not believe in teaching the whole class a grammar lesson, but he did support the idea of pulling together a group of students who were making the same error in their own writing to show them how to master some specific point of grammar or punctuation. These ideas were consistent with Calkins (1986) and other process-writing proponents' beliefs about how students learn to write.

Reading and Writing in Kramer's Class

In Kramer's class students did "quiet reading" every day, choosing their own texts to read alone. He saw his role as assisting students in finding appropriate books both in terms of their interest and reading levels. He also wanted to "be there at that really critical time" when the "child makes their breakthroughs in the way they read. For those who are just beginning to read, to understand the flow of words, to talk about what this means and why does it mean. Why does the author choose to write it that way? For kids who are more accomplished readers, to talk about it the way a writer would read it. How did they develop this thing they're reading? Why did they tell it this way? Are there other ways they could have told it?"

Kramer met with about five or six students daily about their reading. To understand students' interests, reading levels, and thinking, he made notes on the topics the students read, the kinds of questions students were asking, and their reading skills: "Do they prefer fantasy? What kinds of fantasy? What authors do they like? What kinds of questions do they ask when they're reading? How do they approach words that they don't know? What kinds of sight vocabulary do we need to work on?" Besides meeting with individuals, he also met in literature groups once a week. In these groups students took turns reading aloud and then they discussed the story.

Writing occurred both at a separate time of the day and throughout the day as it related to other projects. This writing throughout the day supported Kramer's belief that there were various kinds of writing for different purposes. Students kept journals where they "created their own stories" and met together in self-selected peer response groups: "They read them to each other and we try to encourage kids to make suggestions, read over each other's stories, offer direction for it. When you're stuck, you can discuss it with someone else." He also met with the students individually to assist them in their writing.

At times, Kramer focused on research and on presenting that research in varied ways, including written reports or plays. He emphasized "going to the source. If you want to find out how things worked forty years ago, you can go to someone who lived through them." Writing was integrated into many of the theme units as well. For example, prior to going to Vermont, students had corresponded with pen pals who lived there. They integrated writing into their study of the community, the inner-city surrounding Northeastern, and described their community to their pen pals. Kramer saw writing both as a separate entity and as integrated into other content throughout the day.

Students Initiate Conversations About Texts

The atmosphere in Kramer's room during writing was casual. Students found places in the room at tables, under tables, on pillows, or on the floor to write or share their writing. Kramer moved around the room getting students settled and then talking to students individually. They wrote about varied topics and used a variety of forms. In one instance, a boy was constructing a joke book while another was writing a story about being a radio announcer. A student, Fabian, explained that sometimes they read their stories to each other, "gave their opinion of the story and if the kid liked their opinion he would put that part in the story or change the story." Spread out around the room, small groups of students exchanged opinions while others worked alone.

As an example of these informal peer groups, Erin and Gloria were reading their stories to one another and responding. In the conversation, they took the initiative in responding to each other's work. At Gloria's request, Erin read aloud to her chapter one of the book she was writing entitled *Life and Problems.* The story included dialogue between a mother and her daughter, who was called Spike because of her spiked hair. The conversation was about a baby that Spike was going to have. Expressed through the dialogue between the mother and the child, the story contained some details about the anger and confusion the character felt toward her pregnancy. At the end of what Erin had written, Gloria responded, "That's good. I like it. So you want me to read my story?" Then Gloria realized she had not completed her own story and did not want to read it. Erin urged her to, and in the end Gloria deferred, letting Erin read Gloria's story aloud until she mispronounced a word, at which point Gloria took over and read as much of the story as she had composed thus far. Written in the first person, the story was about a girl, her boyfriend, and her twin sister.

After Gloria read her story, the girls continued their conversation:

Erin: It's good. What is going to happen next?
Gloria: Well she's telling all the girls that she's going to try to get Virginia's boyfriend away from Virginia, right. I don't know, I'm just—

Erin: It's just good. She's sort of like, but then she's her sister, and go out with her boyfriend?

Gloria: Well, it's not like that. Just forget it.

Erin: No, come on. What else should we say?

Erin continued to encourage Gloria despite Gloria's reluctance to tell more about the story at this point. The girls then turned back to Erin's story. Erin constructed the continuation of the story orally with a little help from Gloria. Gloria's role was to express interest, ask questions of clarification, and add additional comments about the story line.

Erin's story described how the character continued to have babies:

Erin: She's still fat. She sticks out there for almost like half a year, and then she starts feeling pains again in her stomach. She goes to the doctor and she's having another baby.

Gloria: [*Laughs*] Oh, my God!

Erin: She keeps on having other babies. This time it's two, they're twins, it's two boys. So it's three boys and two girls, that's five kids. The nanny wants $100 each day, right. She has a right too—five kids and they're all babies. Well, she had her baby—

Gloria: How old is she?

Erin: She's fourteen. . . .

Erin continued to describe the babies and how the character needed to put them up for adoption. When Erin described the character now being older and finishing high school, Gloria inserted, "So that means she can keep them." Erin acknowledged this comment and explained how the character met a friend who also had a baby. Gloria then commented, "God, this story is getting full of babies, it seems." The girls continued their conversation with Erin providing details about the apartment that the main character and her friend shared. Erin continued to construct the story aloud while Gloria asked questions to clarify the story content.

Erin: Then they get married. No, they start going out with this boy.

Gloria: But the boy knows it?

  Erin: No. The boy sees two girls at the same time.

Gloria: But the boy doesn't know that they're friends and they
live together?

  Erin: Right. The boy doesn't know that they know each other.
So then he asks Spike to marry him. . . .

Of interest here was how the two girls sustained the conversation over most of the class period. Erin constructed her narrative orally, as a way of rehearsing the text she was going to write. Gloria was clearly engaged in the story, asking questions and occasionally pointing out places where the logic might not have been clear. The girls were so engaged in the story that they did not want to be interrupted even when the teacher needed to make a couple of announcements to the whole class. Gloria and Erin initiated and sustained the written and oral story construction without help from the teacher. Gloria did not focus on explicitly helping Erin revise or, as is often the case in process-writing classrooms, merely edit her written work. Rather, she acted as an audience very involved in the story itself. In so doing, Gloria may have helped Erin implicitly by asking questions in places where she did not understand the narrative.

Students in Kramer's class were able to respond to each other's work in "authentic" natural ways without focusing explicitly on changing the content or editing the mechanics of their work. Out of interest or friendship, students felt free to initiate conversations about writing. These conversations fit with Kramer's ideas about writing as a natural process where students could express their ideas freely and converse with classmates of their choice. His approach to writing is supported by process-writing advocates, such as Calkins (1986) and Graves (1983), who believe that students need multiple opportunities to rehearse, draft, and revise their writing alone or with peers.

Helping a Student Identify a Topic

While many students were involved in peer conferences, Kramer discussed students' writing with some of them individually. In the following example, he approached Latoya to help her find a topic of interest; they had a ten-minute exchange about her writing. Latoya explained that she did not know what to write about. He responded that the story he liked in her journal was about a bully. He tried to reconstruct the story and then asked Latoya to find it in her journal. When she was unable to find the story, Kramer read to her from his own notes about a story she had written about a sixteen-year-old girl who fell in love.

Kramer: I like those [two] because they seem to be pretty real. [*Long pause*] A couple of people in class are writing about going to Vermont and feeling nervous. One person was writing a story about going to Vermont and getting stuck in an avalanche and surviving after.
Latoya: What's an avalanche?

Kramer explained in detail what an avalanche was and then retold briefly the story the boy had written. When Latoya did not seem to respond to that, he continued probing:

Kramer: How do you think you are going to get along with your pen pal?
Latoya: I don't know.
Kramer: Is it easy for you to make friends?
Latoya: [*No audible response*]
Kramer: Some of the things that I am thinking about starting to write this time are getting along with other people, meeting new people, clashes between the way they do things, and the way I do things.
Latoya: But I can't write anything about that yet.
Kramer: Well, you can anticipate. For instance, we come from the city. You've lived in the city all your life, haven't you?
Latoya: Yeah.
Kramer: And they come from a rural town.
Latoya: A what?
Kramer: A rural town. It's not a city town. It is really out there. Have you thought about that? What things would be different?
Latoya: I've been to Vermont.
Kramer: So then you have a good hint about how things might be up there?
Latoya: I don't know.

Kramer: That doesn't help. Let's make a list of some story ideas. Vermont is out, you don't want to write about that?

Latoya indicates nonverbally that it is not out. He writes down ideas.

Kramer: Vermont is a maybe. What about it? [*Pause*] Can you picture yourself up there?
Latoya: No.
Kramer: Can you picture some of the things you might be doing up there? [*Pause*] Other ideas? How about winter?
Latoya: Boring.
Kramer: How about summer?
Latoya: Boring.
Kramer: How about life?
Latoya: Boring.
Kramer: Winter, summer, life are out. Think of something that is not boring to you. Something you feel excited about.

He wrote something down and when there was still no response from Latoya, he continued:

Kramer: Start with this. Describe a person you know very well. It could be an older person or a younger person. Don't tell me who it is. I may know the person and I may not know the person. Okay. Not just the way the person looks but the way the person is, acts, feels, and so on. Think about that because you do know people. Think about it and then show me.

Several features of Kramer's conversational style with students emerged in this conference with Latoya. Kramer was continually negotiating with her, finding a topic that might be of interest, prompting her to think of new possibilities, occasionally suggesting ideas if she did not respond. He started with stories that Latoya had written and pointed out that he was attracted to their realistic qualities. When Latoya did not respond to this, Kramer tried to connect her writing to the experience that the class was going to have in going to Vermont. He provided examples from other students' stories and related his own thinking and the concerns he had about the upcoming trip. He then tried to elicit Latoya's feelings about the trip. When this failed to spark her interest, he suggested they make a list of possible writing topics. After several attempts at eliciting her thinking about suggested topics, he provided a more specific structure for a topic she could write about. Despite her resistance in the form of saying the topics he suggested were boring, Kramer did not give up. His tone remained supportive and gentle as he suggested ideas. Since Latoya neither initiated her own ideas nor picked up on his, Kramer provided a kind of assignment, to write about a person she knew, in hopes that giving her a specific topic might encourage her to write.

Through these conversations, Kramer revealed his approach to the teaching of writing: allowing students to choose their own topics and then developing them. However, when he met with lack of interest, he provided several alternatives before suggesting a more specific task. Each time he tried to start with the student's own experience. Even when he resorted to a kind of assignment, in Latoya's case by telling her to do a character sketch, he wanted her to begin with her own experience of writing about someone she knew well.

Using Students' Experiences for Theme Units

Beginning with the students' own experiences was a coherent pattern in Kramer's teaching throughout the curriculum. He told us, "I wanted to use their, the kids own, work as the starting point, their interactions with other children." What developed was an entire curriculum evolved out of the students' having pen pals in Vermont. From the letters to pen pals, the curriculum went in several directions. A student found out that one of the pen pals in Vermont had cancer, was undergoing chemotherapy, and had lost hair. Cancer became a major topic. Students raised many questions about the nature and consequences of cancer that they then studied together.

The previous year, Kramer's students had pen pals in Long Island and visited a power plant and the pen pals' school. The Northeastern students offered reciprocity, inviting those students to their school and neighborhood. At first the Northeastern students felt that their pen pals would not want to come to their community because it was filled with poverty, junkies, and ugly buildings. Kramer wanted to reverse students' negative perceptions of their own communities by having students look beyond the ugliness:

> The first thing I want them to do is to discover the power of their own knowledge—their power to get knowledge and the power that knowledge provides, equally, that lack of knowledge or misinformation can be very dangerous—rather than negative conflicts that they have toward the community, and try to look at where did they come from. Then try to look at the fact that there are many different sides to the things they see. In other words, there are obvious things in front of them, like the junkies, drug addicts, and whatever. But what's beyond that? Look beyond the obvious to see what's really there and to see the forces at work. I want them to learn respect and tolerance for people, especially nationally suppressed people.

As part of their efforts to understand the community, students took walking tours, went to the museums and less-well-known historic sites, and developed relationships with senior citizens over an extended period of time. Students also did projects related to the study of the community. For example, two boys created a three-dimensional map with particular buildings from the community. Other students drew a picture of a nearby park; one student explained it was his ideal vision of the park once it was cleaned up. Three students had created a map of the community that highlighted the historical places by connecting them with electrical circuits.

In his use of themes, Kramer put into practice his philosophy, the one that also permeated teaching at Northeastern. He started with students' ideas, concerns, and experiences and expanded them by providing units of study, field trips, activities to build community relationships, and student projects. Many traditional subjects of the curriculum were combined through this integrated-theme approach. Although he started with students' experiences, Kramer directed them into coherent domains of study. He built on his own values of wanting to develop respect and tolerance for other people, but he negotiated with students in the process. Students had many choices over the topics they explored as well as within individual projects they chose.

Coherence of Philosophy and Practice

These glimpses into Kramer's teaching reveal the coherence between his beliefs about reading and writing and his classroom practices. Not only did he believe that students need opportunities to write within a variety of genres for a variety of purposes, but he enacted these beliefs in practice within the context of his classroom. Students wrote personal, expressive pieces often linked to their own experiences, but they also wrote letters to real audiences of pen pals. From these letters evolved an entire curriculum based on students' interests and experiences. Kramer offered students opportunities to make choices about what they wrote, the topics of units of study, and individual projects. However, when students had difficulties making choices, as was the case with Latoya, he stepped in to make suggestions and guide the child. He used the language of constructivism, such as "building on students' ideas," and made his practice cohere with his philosophy by starting from students' experiences and developing curriculum around them. While developing students' ideas, Kramer was explicit about his own values, and he directed projects to result in the kinds of learning that he thought were important (such as understanding and appreciating one's own community).

Kramer's coherence of philosophy and practice was also reflected in how he represented subject matter to students, not as isolated parts of the curriculum but rather as integrated domains of knowledge. Reading, writing, and mathematics had particular time periods allotted to them each day, yet they were used throughout the school day as they related to larger themes such as community. Reading and writing were functional, serving the needs of students who had real audiences with whom to communicate, such as pen pals or senior citizens. This integration was an organizing principle for the curriculum in his classroom.

Another organizing principle of Kramer's practice was the opportunity for students to interact with each other. Students usually wrote individual pieces, but they shared them with each other frequently, as Gloria and Erin did. Likewise, students collaborated during their theme projects by doing projects together. These opportunities to work together reflected his emphasis upon collaboration:

I think collaboration is a given part of the day. For instance, kids write their stories—"I'm stuck for an idea." What do we say to them? "Read it to so-and-so and ask them what they think about it." That kind of thing. "Get some feedback—well, let's bring it into the circle and we'll read it to the class and see what they think." That's collaboration, I think, when someone doesn't know how to—like, Saline was showing someone how to load up and save a program on the computer. Ben was trying to help people in his group figure out how to do some of the math work. Favian, I could see over there, was getting a lot of help in doing the kind of administrative work he had to do as secretary of the class. Clean-up is a collaborative process.

These ideas of working together, integrating curriculum, and building coherence in philosophy and practice that were apparent in Kramer's class played out in similar yet somewhat different ways in Alexis Brezinski's classroom.

Alexis Brezinski: Creating Literacy Among Diverse Learners

Like Brian Kramer and other Northeastern teachers, Alexis Brezinski had filled her classroom with a multitude of materials and resources, some of which changed as projects and pursuits waxed and waned over the course of the year. For example, in the spring a jar appeared containing tadpoles that the children had gotten from Dan Rollins, the third-grade teacher across the hall. Students spent some days observing the tadpoles, estimating and predicting their growth. When the tadpoles died one day, the children and Alexis initiated a discussion of possible causes of their deaths, during which they hypothesized about the effects of pollution within the small jar in which the creatures had lived. They planned to ask Rollins for more tadpoles, deciding to predict and observe the tadpoles' development and life once again, but this time to add to their study the monitoring of the effects of clean water. Arriving anew to Brezinski's classroom and eavesdropping on that class conversation, an observer might conjecture that learning here was not the result of the materials and texts themselves but rather of how the children and their teacher related to the materials and how they jointly constructed meaning from them.

During the class's thematic unit on ancient Greece, various half-finished projects of children were arrayed on tables and shelves around the room, including three-dimensional models of the Parthenon and the Temple of Zeus. What the casual observer might fail to see is the learning involved in their creation. These three-dimensional models had emerged from extended discussions among their student creators, as the children interacted with pictures, graph paper, and drawings and struggled to build these models to scale, wrestling with significant mathematical and architectural ideas as they did so.

These examples illustrate what it meant to be literate and to learn in Alexis Brezinski's classroom. She provided further insight into these issues: "We genuinely respect the kids as being learners, and learners are people who engage in these enterprises of making models of temples, and fractions, and arguing with each other. . . . All children are learners, and it's our responsibility to figure out the ways to help them learn."

While these goals are espoused by many teachers and schools, they are extremely difficult to realize. More often than not, as we have seen in the other schools, they are not completely represented in teaching practice. What happened in Brezinski's classroom?

Reading, Writing, Speaking, and Understanding Texts

An important aspect of how literacy was created in Brezinski's classroom involved the relationships among reading, writing, speaking, and understanding. In her words and deeds, she explicitly connected reading, writing, speaking, and listening. For example, when asked if she used any particular approach to teach writing, she responded that she read aloud a lot. She read what she considered to be good literature, and then she would point out to the children why she found particular passages moving or exciting. She saw reading aloud as a deliberate part of becoming literate and a way of helping children develop their own stories and themes. Sometimes she and the students would read to each other. Or, they might sit together and write poems. Brezinski wrote poems along with the students, and they read them to each other and exchanged ideas about them. She also integrated reading, writing, speaking, and listening throughout the rest of her curriculum. For example, during the theme unit on ancient Greece, she led literature groups among children who were reading the *Iliad* or books on mythology.

By creating a context without boundaries among reading, writing, speaking, and listening, Brezinski's philosophy deliberately echoed that of Frank Smith, whom she cited as influential to her thinking and practice. Smith noted that the categories of reading, writing, speaking, and understanding speech are "useful perhaps in the way we want to organize our schools, but they are not a reflection of a categorization in the learner's mind." He stated that the question for the teacher was not how these should be brought together, "but why they should ever be separated. To a child, language and the world must be indivisible" (Smith, 1983, p. 80).

Reading as Constructing Meaning from Text

Brezinski wanted reading and writing to be integral parts of her students' worlds. She said her most important goal was for students to read freely. She wanted to develop their desire to read on their own. A focal point in her room was a cozy area set aside for reading. Filled with books and padded with carpeting, the reading area invited children to come and sit together and read. Buckets of books and shelves stacked with books surrounded the reading area. Some buckets of books were unlabeled, while others carried such categories as "animal stories," "time travel and history," "biography," "not too easy and not too hard," and "favorite stories." These categories seemed aimed at helping students choose books that appealed to their interests.

Like her Northeastern colleagues, Brezinski viewed reading as a process of constructing meaning from text. She explained that readers bring with them to the text their own understandings from their own worlds, and they make sense differently of the same text. She was intrigued by her students' alternative interpretations of text. She pursued her children's understandings of texts through individual conversations with them during quiet reading time or during the literature groups. During one such conversation, she talked with Chudney, an African American girl in her class, about a book that she was reading. Quoting from a passage in the book about why the mother in the story left her family, Brezinski asked

Chudney what it meant: "She had to find herself, and she was still working on it."

Chudney: She had to get away for awhile, and she had to fix herself.

Brezinski: Do you have any idea from reading the story what was wrong with her or what she was troubled by?

Chudney: I think she was in control of herself. She probably didn't yell at the kids, but she had to fix herself up. I think that's why she went away.

The conversation continued with Brezinski querying Chudney further about her understanding of the relationships among characters in the story. In an annotation of this conversation, Brezinski later wrote:

> This is how Chudney translates or paraphrases "find herself"—reading into it her own understanding of the mother's behavior. She's also clear about the various relationships among characters and the sources of tension or dramatic conflict, e.g., the children's love for their absent mother whose place the housekeeper is usurping. (All of this is very close to home as far as Chudney's own family relationships are concerned.)

In this case, Chudney was reading a book of her own choice, and she easily related the story to her world and her own experiences. Indeed, Brezinski believed that the best way to motivate students to read was to allow them to choose their own books and to read them during silent reading time, as Chudney had. She then described the case of Nicole, an African American girl in her class. As a reluctant reader, Nicole would have chosen to read a "Babysitters' Club" book before struggling through the required reading of the *Iliad*. However, after reading a version of the *Iliad* at her teacher's behest, Nicole wanted to read other stories with such mythic qualities; she chose freely to read another book like that on her own. Brezinski was pleased by Nicole's choice and her developing interest in this new genre of literature.

Chudney and Nicole show us how Brezinski worked with reluctant learners in reading. In the case of Jason, we see how she worked with another reluctant learner, this time in writing.

Writing in Alexis Brezinski's Classroom: The Case of Jason

During the first month of school, Brezinski wrote the following comments in her journal about Jason, a Hispanic boy, as part of her "notes on individual students":

> Jason (Week 1, Sept. 14): During table group, Jason didn't participate, but put his head on the table. Was a little belligerent when I asked him why (because he couldn't understand what others were saying).

> Jason (Week 2, Sept. 26): Confirmed my description of making hard-to-interpret statements. Worked with Francisco [the student teacher who is Latino] on structures and forces [in science], but much work was desultory. Writing minimal—hard for him to talk about details, though he observes them, I think.

> Jason (Week 3, Oct. 3): Began working with Walter [the librarian] and likes it. Also likes the computer. Maybe borrow Walter's [computer] keyboard tutorial for Jason. When he had to write a summary of some . . . ideas, he wrote practically nothing. I told him it was like outright refusal.

In Brezinski's classroom, explicit attention to writing occurred during a period of time in the morning in which the children also did reading. During this time, children were free to choose reading, writing, or both, and all the children seemed actively engaged in both. One thing that students did every day was write in their journals, which were conceived as a dialogue between Brezinski and her students. Each child wrote in his or her journal; then every two weeks, Brezinski read the journal and wrote back to the child about what he or she had been thinking and writing about. The only time she "corrected" a child's journal was if she saw some value in the child "revising" a piece that he or she had written. Then she helped the child revise by pointing out ways of expanding or extending what he or she had written. When she found a particularly useful piece of writing in a student's journal, she suggested that he or she rewrite it and "make it a formal thing." Then the student put the piece on the classroom computer, revised it, and printed it out. This written work would be formally acknowledged by putting it up on the bulletin board, sharing it with other children, or reading it aloud to the teacher and class next door.

Brezinski's comments on Jason at the beginning of the year provide an interesting context in which to consider an episode that occurred at the end of the year. She was working one-on-one with him around turning a draft of his story into a "formal" piece that would be shared with others.

Brezinski annotated a transcription of a discussion with Jason from a particular writing episode in May 1989. The bracketed comments are her later reflections on notes she had made about her practice and her children's learning. She began by filling in some of the context of what was happening:

> The context is sustained, silent reading for all the kids; I'm with Jason at the computer, helping him revise the story he's been working on in his journal. Writing time is usually about 45 minutes, every day. I get to work individually (not always at the computer) with two or three children a couple of times a week. A long, uninterrupted writing time with a single student, like this one with Jason, is atypical. Though I do try to give this kind of attention regularly to kids who are struggling, it tends to be a 15–20 minute session, generally, with not as much detailed work on a particular text.
>
> Jason is not an enthusiastic writer, and the whole process is a struggle for him. He has real problems with spelling—many of the words he writes aren't even close approximations, beyond the first and last letter. His handwriting is small, with letters tightly squeezed together and very difficult to read. In general his ideas outstrip his skills, so that he tends, I think, to oversimplify rather than grapple continuously with words he can't spell and linguistic structures he can't manage. Often, in his writing, he moves from one idea to another omitting crucial transitional ideas; the bridges from one thought to another are often missing. My intentions in working with him at this point, were the following:
>
> 1. Get the actual recopying (from his handwritten version to the computer) done more quickly.
> 2. Help him identify those missing bridges, confusing transitions, awkward phrases, etc.
> 3. Provide some practice with mechanics of punctuation [I had been working with him on and off, on punctuating dialogue].

Brezinski began by having Jason read aloud to her what he had written. The story was entitled "The Boy Who Wanted to Fly."

Jason: [*Begins reading from his text*] Once upon a time there
             was a boy that wanted to learn how to fly. His name was
             Roy. He watched birds and how they land.
Brezinski: He watched birds do what? [I want to point out the
             awkwardness of ". . . how they land."]
Jason: He watched birds land. [Jason self-corrects.]
Brezinski: That's all? [I want a more elaborated statement—more
             description.]
Jason: And he also watched how they fly.
Brezinski: OK, so describe that a little bit. Let's fill the ideas in.
             [Here I restate and expand my "That's all?"] "He
             watched birds—"
Jason: —fly and glide in the air and—
Brezinski: [*Reading from the handwritten version of Jason's journal*]
             He wanted to know—
Jason: [*Makes several different tries at articulating his ideas before
             he puts them in this form*] He wanted to know how come
             the birds could fly, and he can't. . . . He even got a
             book on flying.
Brezinski: He even got a book on flying. Now I think there's
             something confusing about this. When you say, "there
             was a boy who wanted to learn how to fly," it sounds as
             if it's about learning how to fly an airplane. That's what
             it usually means—you know, they take flying lessons,
             and they go to flying school. That isn't flying like a
             bird. That's flying like an airplane, so how could we
             make this first sentence a little clearer? [There's a lot
             here about how Jason thinks and how he expresses
             ideas in language. He means 'learn to fly' *literally,* and
             getting 'a book on flying' presumably means a book
             about how birds fly, not how to fly an airplane. In other
             words, the boy wanted to teach himself how to fly the
             way birds do. So a lot of meaning is packed into very
             few words, but not stated clearly.]
Jason: Without any machine, any machinery?
Brezinski: Okay.

This dialogue with Brezinski's reflections gives us a window
into how she helped her children elaborate and develop ideas in

their writing, and how she saw her role in that process. She viewed her role as helping Jason articulate and elaborate his ideas. The text was not hers, but Jason's. Working with students, she elaborated and developed her understanding of them and their ideas and used this understanding in her interactions with students about their work.

She and Jason talked for a few minutes more in the same fashion, working to elaborate his story. After a time, she asked him again to read his text aloud because she thought he would realize when he had "left something out," and he would "recognize what's wrong" if he continued to read the text back to himself as he wrote. Jason read aloud the revision he had written so far, and the dialogue about his text continued:

> *Jason:* Once upon a time there was a boy who wanted to learn how to fly without machinery. His name was Roy. He watched the birds fly and glide in the air, and he wanted to know how they land. He even got a book on flying. Once he even tried to fly, but it didn't work because he didn't have any wings or enough strength to get off the ground.
>
> *Brezinski:* OK, now what's the next sentence you want to put in?
>
> *Jason:* I should say he jumped off a tree.
>
> *Brezinski:* Yes.
>
> *Jason:* And fell and broke his arm.
>
> *Brezinski:* OK. "Once he even tried to fly, but it didn't work. He jumped off a tree." That's right, Jason. OK. His parents said, "Listen honey, you've got to stop trying to fly—"
>
> *Jason:* [*Works on his story*]
>
> *Brezinski:* OK, wait a second. Let's go to a new paragraph. His parents said, comma, quotation marks. I want you to tell me that too—all the punctuation.

At this point Brezinski began to focus on punctuation of Jason's text in addition to the ideas that he has been developing. She asked Jason to read the punctuation aloud along with the words in his text. Through conversation around the text, Brezinski and Jason rather painlessly worked through some corrections in punctuation of his text.

In her conversation with Jason, Brezinski revealed a coherence between her thoughts and actions, between her pedagogical beliefs and practice. She indicated that in writing, her most important goal was for her children to "write freely." While she was aware of the "process approaches" to writing of Lucy Calkins and Donald Graves, she said she did not use any specific approach to writing. She felt that if her students were comfortable putting words on paper, then she could help "fill in mechanics" at some point. For Brezinski, mechanics meant punctuation and form, such as periods, capital letters, quotation marks, and indenting paragraphs. While she did not see mechanics as unimportant, she did see them as "absolutely secondary to content and ideas and how children express these ideas." In the case of Jason, she successfully enacted these ideas in practice so that he moved from being a reluctant writer and "resistant" student at the beginning of the year to one who, at the end of the year, was conversing fluently with his teacher about his writing and was thoughtfully struggling with expressing his ideas orally and in writing.

Alexis Brezinski: The Teacher as Knowledgeable Learner

How was Brezinski able to carry off this connection between principle and practice? One reason may be that like Brian Kramer, she had a great deal of subject-matter knowledge, pedagogical knowledge, and knowledge of the specific students in her class. In addition, she saw herself as a learner who was continuing to develop her own knowledge in the same way her students did.

Brezinski herself was a serious reader and a learner of literature. At the time of this study, she was taking a course in English literature at a nearby university, having decided to do so for her own benefit. She was getting no special credit from the school or district for taking such a course. As part of this literature course, she participated in discussions of literature with other adults. She had her children engage in similar literature groups with their peers in the classroom.

Brezinski also saw herself as a writer. She was as comfortable and articulate with writing as she was with speaking and reading. She had written and published two articles on her own teaching. She knew what it meant to struggle with putting one's ideas into writing, exactly as Jason was doing.

One of her articles appeared in a national weekly publication and described her perspective on school, teaching, and children. The other appeared in a publication of the National Council of Teachers of Social Studies. In this latter piece she described her project-based social studies curriculum, a major part of which involves studying ancient Greece. Every year Brezinski chose to do a theme unit on ancient Greece because she was very interested in and knowledgeable about it. She had been to Greece several times and had developed numerous resources and materials on this theme. During this "humanities study," she brought in her own personal library of books on ancient Greece for the children to read, study, and explore, and she had her students develop and work on projects of their own choice related to ancient Greece.

Every summer Brezinski went for a weeklong seminar with her colleagues at the Vermont school with which Northeastern was affiliated. She used that time to renew her ties and friendships with her peers who returned every summer, but also to learn more about teaching with like-minded colleagues.

Like her constructivist colleagues, Brezinski was able to teach the way she did in part because of the in-depth knowledge and understanding she had of her students. She kept track of much of this knowledge in her head, but she also kept a written record and talked with her Northeastern colleagues about individual students during regular faculty meetings. Brezinski kept a journal, as her students did. In it she wrote her ideas about each student and reflections on her own practice. At the beginning of the year she made daily and weekly notes on what had happened in class, and she wrote descriptions of her developing knowledge of each individual student.

Brezinski saw the learning in her class primarily through the lens of individual students' developing knowledge. Yet she acknowledged that there was a lot going on socially in her class. Students helped one another frequently and conversed about their work.

During the time of this study, Brezinski was struggling with the idea of having students work more collaboratively, but she was uncomfortable with the idea of "cooperative learning," or peer tutoring, which she was trying to do that year for the first time. She said she decided to try "cooperative learning" because a private foundation interested in supporting reform had sent her to California to give a talk. While there, she went to a workshop conducted by a woman who was a specialist in cooperative learning.

Her discomfort with the idea stemmed, she said, from putting a group of children together and telling them that "You are obliged to teach them [the other students in your group] so that at the end, everybody knows it." She admitted she could not help feeling that it put a tremendous burden on students to say to them "that person [in your group] really knows this, and that person is going to be responsible for your learning it, and the evidence of the success of your group will be that you've learned it." She felt that it also called attention to the differences among students and made it more likely that they would compare themselves unfavorably to other students.

In some ways the social aspects of learning seemed more prominent in Brian Kramer's classroom than in Alexis Brezinski's. Kramer spoke eloquently about collaboration being "a given part of the day." He wanted his students to learn respect and tolerance for people; he focused on social awareness and discussed social issues. Yet discussion of social issues also figured prominently in his classroom. In both classrooms, children worked on projects together and wrote to pen pals. They explicitly connected with their community, took field trips out into the community, and worked in the community.

Northeastern Teachers: Coherence, Integration, and Nuance

Compared to traditional teachers, and to teachers in the other schools in our study, Kramer and Brezinksi were strikingly similar to each other in their teaching practice, and to their Northeastern colleagues. These teachers' constructivist views of learning framed their practices. They saw learners as sense makers and were continually striving to understand their students' developing understandings. The teachers worked to acquire a deep knowledge of their students, and they used this knowledge in their conversations with students and in their teaching. Both Kramer and Brezinski followed students' interests in the choice of topics; during their interaction with students, they helped them elaborate their ideas, focusing more on content than on form, rather than substituting their own ideas for the students'. One difference between the two teachers was Kramer's additional use of peer response groups, in which students responded to each other's writing.

In both classrooms the degree of coherence and integration across subjects was impressive. Both teachers strove to make learning a seamless experience for students by making connections among reading aloud, conversing, writing, reading silently, and making meaning. They used their theme units to further these relationships. Reading and writing were major aspects of the study of ancient Greece in Brezinski's class, but other subjects also became important as the students worked on self-chosen projects. For example, building a scale model of the Parthenon involved mathematics, architecture, design, art, and other subjects.

In addition, both teachers endeavored to create curriculum that related to their students' experiences. Kramer constructed a theme unit that involved the study of the inner-city community in which Northeastern was located. One aspect of the curriculum then evolved from Kramer's students' writing letters to students in Vermont; after they visited Vermont, the Vermont students wanted to visit Northeastern's community. In contrast, most of the interest and knowledge of ancient Greece came from Alexis. Ancient Greece was an area that she knew a lot about, thought was important, and was interested in. Yet she strove to relate to students' experiences by having them choose projects in *their* areas of interest.

Negotiating the Constructivist Dilemma

Brezinski said she often "faced a dilemma" in her teaching.[1] It is an issue faced by many constructivist teachers who desire to build on students' experiences and understandings but realize that they, as teachers and adults, have developed some important understandings that might be useful for their children to know. These teachers wrestle with how and when to bring their own knowledge and understanding into the experiences of their students without displacing the students' own knowledge and experience. The dilemma arises particularly in the case of students like Jason, the "reluctant learners."

During the theme unit on ancient Greece, Brezinski said she faced the dilemma of whether or not to require all her students to read a version of the *Iliad* because of the importance of experiencing a text like this and getting to understand mythology through a primary source. While she felt uncomfortable insisting that her students read what she chose, rather than what they chose for themselves, she thought that most of the time what students chose for themselves was "not that terrific." As Brezinski put it:

> I just think that myths, like fairy tales, are stories that have immense meaning and different meanings to different individuals. Reading them and knowing them is a way of putting that meaning inside your head so that you can draw on it when you need to. The notion that this person Odysseus, who was very clever and quite manipulative and thoughtful of people, could control his life and control other people's lives and make things happen for himself and the world—I think that's a notion worth knowing. [Another notion is] that there are forces in nature that are not known and are just sort of there. Some are threatening, and some are encouraging. But they're there, and people deal with them. Myths and fairy tales and legends give kids images and ideas inside their heads that they can use, whatever way they decide to use them.

Kramer also faced this dilemma. Like Brezinski, he tended to start with children's knowledge, but he too realized that there were certain ideas children needed to know that they might not come upon themselves. For Kramer, managing this dilemma often involved more negotiation between teacher and student than it did for Brezinski. Yet even for him, there were some areas of knowledge that were nonnegotiable. For example, he had his students do a unit in which they planned "dream vacations." The "dream vacation" had to take place outside the United States because part of his goal was for the children to learn geography. While his students were completely free to choose their own countries, they could not create new worlds; they had to visit real parts of the world because he wanted his students to learn certain content.

In the end, the differences between Kramer's and Brezinski's classrooms seemed to be differences of degree rather than kind. Like the Eskimos who have a hundred different words for snow and are thus able to talk about the nuances among different types of snow, so too Northeastern teachers had developed multiple nuances of constructivist teaching, allowing them to converse about their practices.

Chapter Twelve

Learning Science

Dede Patterson and Dan Rollins

> Thoughts are our way of connecting things up for ourselves. If others tell us about the connections they have made, we can only understand them to the extent that we do the work of making these connections ourselves. Making connections must be a personal elaboration, and sometimes a person is simply not capable of making the connections that someone is trying to point out (Duckworth, 1987, p. 26).

In her analysis of Piaget's work, Duckworth suggests that students must come to understand ideas for themselves. The teacher's role is to create opportunities for students, who have differing levels of knowledge, to come to new understandings more or less on their own. Often citing Piaget as inspirational to their work with children, Northeastern teachers saw themselves as continually constructing roles to facilitate student understanding. Complex and fluid, these roles were central to restructuring practices at Northeastern. Two teachers, Dede Patterson and Dan Rollins, exemplify different approaches to this problem.

Dede Patterson: Discovery Learning or Confusion of Purposes?

Like many of the classrooms at Northeastern, Dede Patterson's third-and-fourth-grade classroom was filled with hands-on materials. Milk crates contained materials for students to build structures; paint, pipe cleaners, and fabric were readily available for student projects. Containers with separate places for funnels, weights, bottle caps, magnifying glasses, seashells, sand, magnets, pulleys, compasses, and protractors filled the room. Student dioramas, soap sculptures, hanging mobiles, a student-constructed playground, and other student projects were on display throughout the room. Photographs, posters, and student-generated questions related to the topic being studied—Eskimos, environments, or water, for example—added to the visual impact of Patterson's classroom. Tables were placed throughout the room for different purposes, and a small rug marked off one part of the room for discussions. Filled with student work and available resources, the room seemed to reflect student interests and gave an air of students being in charge.

In fact, it was somewhat difficult to find the teacher amidst the bustling activity around students' projects. Small and soft-spoken, she was assisting students in their work. Having experience in open-classroom settings, she felt comfortable with the high level of student activity.

Dede Patterson's Perspective on Learning

Patterson believed in providing students with many curricular choices. She found that she was beginning to limit the number of topics students would independently study because she could not keep up with all of them. She decided to have students choose topics within a broad theme. Because she wanted students to have a great deal of responsibility for their own learning she encouraged student responsibility by having them teach others. She explained, for instance, that Jesse had fallen behind in mathematics and Ruben was helping him. She was pleased with the result because Ruben took on the role that she herself did when teaching: asking questions but not giving students answers. She reported in an interview how she responded to Ruben's teaching:

> I said, "Oh, you're a wonderful teacher. You're not giving any information; you're just asking questions. It's wonderful to do that." Or if the kid's stuck on something, I'll say, "Oh, fraction work. Go get the egg cartons; show him how." Then I say, "Don't forget, now. Set him a few problems, and let him do it. And you watch him." So I sort of try to teach them my method of asking the questions and letting the person do the work. Otherwise, I don't want them to do

the work for somebody, because then that person hasn't learned anything. So they know that when I say help somebody, their job is to try to think of the questions to ask the other person. And they do it pretty well.

Patterson also believed that students would learn by having opportunities to experiment with concrete materials. The teacher's role, she argued, was to set up experiences for students and pose questions.

Patterson's Beliefs and Practices During the Water Unit

When setting up experiences for a water unit, Patterson had two major goals for her students: (1) to have some beginning experiences and understandings of concepts of physics, and (2) to use the scientific method. She wanted students to see that the same laws of physics that applied to soap bubbles also applied to raindrops or other liquids.

> I'm really looking for them to have some beginning experiences in what is basically I think physics, without naming it as that. Without necessarily having the advanced concepts, but seeing those things about the work that they're doing that do apply to other aspects of liquids so that there is some tying together of stuff. For instance, the soap bubbles—I was rereading last night some material I had read—a book on patterns of nature, which was a wonderful book, which was hard for me to read. I read it over and over trying to get it. Beautiful. Like to work with soap bubbles; they'd look at the shapes of soap bubbles, for instance. The same laws of physics and space that make for a circle shape in soap bubbles apply to raindrops, apply to drops of oil, apply to all kinds of other liquids, so that at some later point when they get further into the physics, hopefully they'll say—"Oh, yes, I know that, because I had this experience with the soap bubbles. I remember when. . . ."

Such concepts as the effects of pressure, displacement, surface tension, and density were the ideas she hoped students would understand through participation in various experiences. Her goal also included the development of "scientific thinking": making observations, making comparisons, testing out hypotheses, and coming to new conclusions.

To begin the unit, students brainstormed ideas related to water: pollution, water cycles, glaciers, oceans, pond water. Then Patterson constructed a flow chart by grouping students' ideas. They worked in small groups on a self-selected project for at least three days to answer research questions that interested them about their topic, before writing reports to inform others about the topic. Students ended up involved in projects with clay boats, a terrarium, soap bubbles, erosion, saline solutions, submarines, and sewer water.

As students participated in the water unit, however, it began to become clear to Patterson that things were not going as planned. For instance, students were keeping scientific logs of their observations, intending to share them with others, but they did not have an opportunity to do so. She realized she had not trained students "to chair a group" and could not reach all of the groups to record their ideas. As a result of the difficulty in monitoring so many projects, she expressed concerns about what students were learning from the experience: "So I've been in a state of panic almost from the beginning of this. I wasn't really sure how deep the knowledge was going; I don't know whether they're doing a speck here, a speck there, a speck there, not really being aware of what they're learning."

On a day-to-day basis, certain factors created a feeling of confusion for her. For instance, while the scientific experiments were occurring, some students were doing writing or talking to the teacher about "author's day," a big event at Northeastern occurring simultaneously. She was trying to coordinate several science projects and discuss authors at the same time. Meanwhile, students were expected to do both "a project in the room for exploration with water and to have signed up for a research project, which may or may not be what they're working on here." The teacher and students were juggling many topics and events simultaneously.

One example of this juggling involved Jesse, who had been studying the submarine as part of the unit. Patterson attempted to extend Jesse's research into other types of boats by asking him what other kinds of boats he was interested in studying. When he mentioned battleships, she brought up the idea of making a papier-mâché map of the harbor area in which they lived, identifying different kinds of boats and including a submarine. Before this conversation was finished, one student had asked to go to the library and another discussed an upcoming visit from a parent. Patterson returned to the discussion about making different kinds of boats but then told another student she wanted to read with him. At this point, Juan asked her for help with his work on dilutions. Patterson then approached Melba, who read aloud the story she was writing. Before she could respond to Melba's story, another student indicated it was time to go to an author's day event. Patterson then tried to find out which students were at music and which were meeting with authors. Besieged by different students pursuing a variety of topics and goals, Patterson had difficulty focusing the students. Discussions of the theme units were interspersed with conversations about reading and writing as well as with logistics concerning author's day and parent-teacher conferences. Although she described the day from which these observations came as being more chaotic than most, the level of activity was only slightly higher than that of other days we observed in her classroom.

Besides the complex balancing act that she was trying to maintain with students and theme units, Patterson believed that some students contributed to the problems by not staying on task. She was occasionally frustrated by students' misbehavior, saying, "this group of boys—unless there's an adult standing there—cannot keep themselves from mixing, trying, spoiling the colors, not cleaning their straws in between. And they make me furious." These comments were connected to a particular project that a group of students were working on. She referred to this project as "the dilutions group."

Discovering Density Through Colored Mixtures

The group of students were experimenting with various colored mixtures that contained differing amounts of salt and thus differed in their density. Students were to mix colored solutions, observe what they saw, and record their observations. Patterson seemed to want the students to gain an understanding of why particular colors rose to the top; presumably the least dense solutions would rise to the top while the densest would remain at the bottom. She was not explicit in discussing her goals with them but tried to elicit information from them, as is evident in the following dialogue:

Lennie: Blue tried to get to the top. But to get the top, the green would meet with blue, so it mixed.

Patterson: All right. Now, there's another reason why it mixed, you think? The blue's trying to get to the top, right? Which one are we talking about, this one?

Meredith: It tried to get up there, and it mixed with whatever color was in there.

Patterson: What other colors were you—which one are you doing, this one here? So we had red, blue trying to get to the top, and had to go through the green, right, and this way with blue. So it makes—okay. Now, I think I see what you see. There are really two reasons—we've got them sort of stuck in together. Blue tried to get to the top, and green is made with blue, so it mixed. Did it mix up with the red also?

Lennie: Yeah, I think so.

Patterson: Yeah, I think it did too, because it was also trying to get through the red, right?

In this conversation, neither Patterson nor the students were making a direct connection between the colors of the solutions and their densities. It was almost as if the colors themselves were the important concepts rather than what the colors represented in salinity or density. The conversation continued:

Damon: [*Inaudible*] . . . all three of them.

Patterson: I think so. Yeah? So could you add that?

Lennie: It mixed with red and blue too.

Patterson: Because?

Lennie: Because they're also made with blue.

Patterson: Are they? Is red made with blue?

Lennie: No.

Patterson: No. So what's the other reason? See, you only have two reasons. Help him think it out. This is the order of what he did. Look. He put in red first, clear next, green next, and blue. And they mixed. And his thinking—the blue was trying to get to the top. Remember we said blue always seems to be on the top? So on its way up, it got mixed in with the other colors?

Damon: I think so.

It is unclear whether Patterson had two or three reasons in her mind for why the "blue" should rise to the top. It seemed that the students were also confused about why the blue was rising. She attempted to clarify it by restating what the colored solutions did when they were mixed together:

Patterson: A group problem? Well, [*to Josh as he enters*] How are you? You weren't here this morning, so listen to these guys. Here's what he did. He put in red first; clear; green; and blue. And then he wrote [that] blue tried to get to the top, but green is made with blue, so it mixed. And Damon was pointing out—and Meredith—that blue was trying to get through the red also, and mixed up with the red. And then he said yes, because red is made with blue, which it isn't, right? So—green has blue in it, which tended to mix up the color. What's the other reason that the blue mixed with the red and the green?

Josh: You mean the red and the clear.

Patterson: The red and the clear, right.

Lennie: The blue goes through the red and the green—

Patterson: Yeah, and it mixed with those.

Josh: —and the clear.

Patterson: They put the blue in last, right?

Lennie: Because clear—it mixed with everything?

Josh: No.

Patterson: No, because they put it in last.

Patterson observed that the colors mixed but then focused on what color was added last, though it wasn't clear why she was doing so. The students continued to offer observations, and she asked several questions:

Patterson: The green was maybe the strongest color, but it did mix. But now why would blue be mixing with all these other colors—

Damon: I don't understand. If it turns all green, then why should it go on top?

Patterson: —because in fact that's not what happened. What happened was, as he wrote, mixed, it all got mixed. He put in the red first, then he put in the clear, then he put in green. The last color he put in at the bottom was blue, and it ended being a big old fat mix. Now why would blue be mixing up with green and with clear and with red?

Lennie: Because . . . I guess since red is a primary color . . . I don't know.

Patterson: You do know, from the dilution that you did before. All right, so maybe it mixed with green because blue is part of green, but what about red? Why did clear and red and blue mix together? It's not that hard. Think about it. Get your yesterday's work. Remember yesterday's work, you guys? Damon, help a little. That we discovered when we were doing pairs of colors that blue always went where?

Although the students seem to be struggling with what concepts Patterson wanted them to understand, she did not directly answer their questions. She referred back to what the students should already have known from some previous experience, but again not explicitly. In the next part of the discussion she continued to make observations and ask questions, yet it is not clear what answers she hoped they would provide:

Lennie: To the top.

Patterson: All right. So here he goes, he puts blue in last. So what is blue trying to do?

Damon: Go to the top.

Patterson: Trying to go the top. And if you put it in last, it has to go through—

Students: Green, red, clear—

Patterson: Yeah. So, it's moving through all the other colors, and it's mixing as it goes. Yeah? So, it turned all green because maybe green has blue in it, and it's stronger, but it also turned—

Josh: I know why the clear mixed with blue too, because when I did it yesterday, the blue turned the white into a light blue. So since the blue turned green, it turned the clear into green.

Patterson: Okay. So one color rising through another tends to mix, right? And so if you put in last the color that needs to rise because it's the least salty, it's going to probably mix up. So you really have two reasons—one is [what] you've talked about. The green has some blue in it, so it would turn to hide the color, and the other reason is that the blue is the least—

Lennie: So it has to come up.

Patterson: The least what? The least . . . salty, yeah? So it has to come up. So it's traveling through the other colors. Could you add that so it's a little clearer? There really are two reasons, yeah? At least we think there are two reasons. Thank you. All right, okay. Good. [*Turns to address student teacher*] Susan, I think we are supposed to take them to look at books.

Finally, Patterson made the connection between the solutions and salinity. However, neither she nor the students elaborated on the connection or the reasoning that led to it. Before it could be ascertained whether the students were clear about the concepts, she closed the discussion by saying "thank you" and organizing them to move on to their next activity.

What happened in this exchange among teacher and students? What learning seemed to occur? First, Patterson did not connect the colored solutions to their salinity or density for the students. It is not clear from the students' responses whether they understood the relationship on their own. They did not use the term *salinity;* only the teacher used it, at the end of the exchange. The focus was on the colors themselves, and there seemed to be confusion between the properties of colors and the properties of salinity and density. This confusion seemed to be aggravated by the use of green, a compound of yellow and blue; had she used all primary colors, the process might have been less confusing. Although she tried to get the students to build on their prior knowledge, as when she told Josh he knew what was happening from doing it before, it may have been Patterson herself who was drawing on some prior knowledge to make the connection.

The next day she alluded to her own lack of clarity about the concepts: "I haven't internalized what should happen. So there I am, not knowing myself what would happen and [I] say 'well, let's mix up,' and getting kind of like this because I'm not sure what is going on. But what amazed me was that the group I got together yesterday . . . they know more about it than I do. They had, in spite of all the messing around, messing up the colors, actually figured out which was the least saline and the most saline and the ones in between."

One way of making sense of her response is to suggest that she herself may not have had the scientific knowledge to know what the students were discovering. Another way to consider her response, however, is to see an unusual openness to students' ideas and her pride in her students' discoveries. Throughout the conversation, students were engaged in the process; they were trying to figure out the solution to a somewhat ill-defined problem. The conversation had a kind of fluidity, suggesting that she probably thought the students were understanding the larger ideas. Perhaps because she was committed to the discovery method—that by having experiences with science materials and ideas students would absorb the ideas when they were ready—she believed students had learned the concepts despite the lack of clarity of the lesson.

Tensions Between Patterson's Goals and the Students' Ideas

Patterson seemed to experience tension between following what students wanted to do and her own original goals. The result was somewhat chaotic. For instance, although the unit was supposed to focus on water, some students proposed an electricity table and "we added that, because some kids said, 'Can I please study electricity' and I said, 'Sure, why not?'" She also tried to take advantage of serendipity. For instance, students had been inventing their own boats out of various materials such as clay and aluminum foil, and then oil from another experiment intruded on their boat making. "And then the oil spill happened, so I thought, 'the bird flew in the window, you know?'" This offered the opportunity for discussion, yet only a few students were involved and it was not sustained.

These aspects of the curriculum that emerged from serendipitous events or students' ideas provided the opportunity for hypothesizing and discussing; yet it was not clear how Patterson related them back to the large ideas of the water unit. Juggling multiple curricular areas during theme-and-project time while she was trying to monitor many different projects about water contributed to a general sense of confusion in the classroom. It was not clear how the electricity table linked up to the water unit, nor how various activities such as the oil spill, boat making, and the dilutions unit were connected. Did she have whole-group discussions about the basic ideas related to physics? There was no indication that she did. Instead, students had opportunities to pursue a huge range of activities loosely related to the theme of water.

Patterson's enactment of the water unit raises two questions. Might her commitment to a Piagetian discovery method have detracted from students' understanding of the concepts? And what role did her own lack of scientific background or knowledge play in the confusion?

First, research has suggested that simply providing students with materials and encouraging them to discover scientific concepts has not been successful in developing substantive learning. Gelman, Massey, and McManus (1991) reported on their extensive efforts to create a museum environment to foster informal learning in science and mathematics. They found that provision of manipulatives and materials was not enough to increase students' understanding. They concluded that "it is unlikely that children's constructivist tendencies alone will suffice for learning math and science" (p. 255) and that social and cultural inputs are needed. For example, "mathematics and science have languages of their own, and to interpret objects correctly for use in mathematics and science, one has to use these languages" (p. 254). Patterson did not use the language of science in her salinity discussions with students; to a large extent, they were left on their own to interpret the findings for their discoveries.

Perhaps if she had provided more explanation of the relationship between the colored solutions and salinity, or introduced students to the language used to understand density, they might have come away with a clearer idea of the concepts of density. However, in answer to the second question, she would not have been able to provide such explanation easily if she were unclear about the ideas herself. It is unrealistic to expect elementary teachers to have a deep understanding of all the important concepts for each of the subject areas; however, Patterson's own self-professed lack of clarity about the ideas may have led to her students' not understanding the important concepts within the theme units. Encouraging students to pursue simultaneously many areas of study compounds the task of being knowledgeable about the subject areas at hand.

The issues of commitment to discovery and teachers' knowledge come into sharper focus as we examine the case of Dan Rollins. Like Dede Patterson, Rollins valued science, providing many opportunities throughout the year for students to engage in scientific thinking and construction of projects. Both teachers encouraged students to experiment with scientific ideas and to articulate their ideas. However, Rollins's case contrasts with Patterson's in relation to his emphasis on more explicit instruction in science.

Dan Rollins: Balancing Discovery with More Explicit Instruction

Dan Rollins had extensive experience working with young children. He had worked in day care or nursery schools for about eight years before coming to Northeastern; the beginning of our study marked his eighth year at this school. His strongest interest was science: "In another life I would have been in some form a biologist. . . . I went to school as a natural scientist." Before completing his degree in science, he went into the social sciences and later got a teaching credential.

One of Rollins's greatest concerns about public education was student assessment. He lamented his own daughter's experience of receiving sixteen S's for satisfactory in a regular public school where the teacher did not indicate a single aspect where his daughter excelled. In contrast, because of Northeastern's focus on individual student progress, its alternative evaluation system, and the collegial discussions about children, Rollins felt at home there and believed it was a school that placed students at the center of learning.

Rollins's third-and-fourth-grade classroom consisted of twenty-five students, one-third African American, one-third Hispanic, one-third European American. He noted that about one-fifth of the students were biracial.

Rollins put a class schedule on the board each day to remind students of the subjects they would work on that day. He began and ended the day with large-group discussions around the rug that often centered on interesting and unusual topics, such as what color Christ was. Student preparation of a snack, Rollins reading aloud from a novel, journal writing, quiet reading, math, and theme units occurred daily. Additionally, because Rollins played the guitar, students often sang a repertoire of songs, including some from their black history unit.

Used for meetings at the beginning and end of the day and for whole-group discussions, a large rug occupied the central part of the room. Around the periphery of the room were several long tables that were used for reading, writing, or constructing projects. During the life cycle unit, large posters of insects decorated the room, and many books about topics related to animals, life cycles, and eggs were both on display and accessible to students. An aquarium containing tadpoles, eggs, and an incubator; scales for weighing the eggs; magnifying glasses; and materials for assembling papier-mâché "mini-beasts" were set throughout the room.

Rollins's Reflection on the Life Cycles Theme

Rollins's reflection on his day of teaching about life cycles captures to a large extent his own excitement about the topic as well as his perspective on student learning. He focused on one particular boy, Raymond, in making his point that many students were excited by the discoveries related to eggs and egg cases.

> When the room's brimming over with life and energy and excitement and—everything that I think a classroom should be . . . I'm thrilled. Look at Raymond—he's the boy who broke the egg. I mean, all day long, he was just deeply engrossed in one pursuit or another, of questions and how this worked, and first it was his beetle, his mealworm beetle, and then it was the eggs, then the weighing, and how his triple beam balance worked. . . . At each point, he was just deeply engrossed, and that was true of a lot of the kids. You know? I mean, the discoveries about the egg—I mean, this is an object they see every day of their life, and yet, there was this awe of discovery of what's really there. I think giving children the opportunity to do that and explore and think about it, I think that's what it's all about. And there has to be some discipline in what's the next

step and where do you go from there, and they are disciplined. What do we then do in terms of following up on the eggs, and what's happening inside? But the initial enthusiasm, I think, will carry us a long way.

Rollins was committed to providing many experiences for his students related to the life cycle theme. He believed that enthusing students initially about a topic would help them learn about it.

Rollins developed this enthusiasm by providing several related experiences in the life cycle unit, throughout the day. During project time students observed the praying mantis egg cases or designed models of different insects out of papier-mâché. During quiet reading time, many students read books about insects, while during journal time many students wrote poems about insects. The formal egg study occurred before lunch, when Rollins led the students in an observation and discussion about eggs. Even the snack of deviled eggs tied into the egg topic.

Project Time

Project Time began first thing after the morning meeting. Students worked individually or with partners on one of the projects listed on the board under the heading "Mini-Beast Study":

Drawing, painting, clay figures of beasts

Crossword puzzles

Concentration game

Computer

Model making, papier-mâché

Model of habitats

Poetry and stories

Magazines—nature study

Animal studies experiments

Surveys

Reports and research

Weigh chicken eggs

Parts of an egg drawing

During this time about ten students were in the class while the rest were working with the art teacher or visiting the authors-and-illustrators program. Students were engaged in many of the projects listed on the board. Two boys were writing a report together about stick bugs, while two girls wrote a poem about the praying mantis. Using vocabulary such as *pupa* and *larva,* one boy with magnifying glass in hand explained to the researcher about how the mealworms were going to turn into beetles. Several students were feeling a raw egg, describing it as "slimy" but also identifying the different parts of it, such as *blastoderm.* Their discussion continued until one of the students broke the egg after weighing it. All the while, a couple of students were preparing the deviled egg snack, mixing eggs and mayonnaise. One boy worked by himself on his booklet about insects.

Rollins went around the room offering advice to individual students as they worked on their projects. Much of his time was spent with the students who were constructing large papier-mâché models of insects. His assistance took the form of doing logistical tasks such as collecting materials or pointing out where students could find things. Students were very involved and carried out tasks independently. Project time continued into reading time; later on, he did a more formal lesson with the students in discussing egg cases.

Praying Mantis Egg Cases

To conduct the observation and discussions of the praying mantis egg cases, Rollins called the class to meet together on the rug. He sat on the rug with the aquarium that held the egg cases and began the discussion by asking why people other than scientists might be interested in the praying mantis. One student responded that the praying mantis would eat the insects that ate the crops. The teacher then continued to lead the discussion by asking what was inside an egg, differences between eggs and egg cases, and why egg cases were like bags. After students gave responses to those questions, Rollins asked them to guess how many eggs might be in an egg case he held up, about one and one-half inches in diameter. They gave responses ranging from five to a thousand eggs in each egg case. He then gave them some hints. The interchange continued as follows, until a student, Johnny, asked an interesting question:

Rollins: How big are the adults? The adults grow to about four or five inches. How big are the eggs? I'm not sure. If we knew how many eggs were in there, we could make a reasonable guess. How big are the babies? The babies come out about a centimeter. Well, the answer to the first question is about 200. Somewhere—there are about 200 eggs in here. Somewhere between 150 to 200 to 300. Johnny?

Johnny: Forget it.

Rollins: No, we'd like to hear.

Miguel: No, I'll tell them, because I heard the question. He said, if they're a centimeter when they're hatched, how could there be 200 or 300?

Rollins: Because it doesn't seem like there's room for 200 centimeters inside of there, does it?

Johnny: Uh-huh.

Rollins: When you see a woman who's pregnant, it often doesn't seem to me that there's room for a baby that comes out 18, 19, 20 inches. Doesn't seem that there's room. What position is the baby in? [*Rollins positions himself into a ball*]

Miguel: He's balled up.

Rollins: I wonder what position the praying mantises are in when they're in there. Do you think they all get their own spaced out room, with their legs all stretched out? Remember whose praying we're talking about?

Rollins then held up a needle, simulating a tree branch from which the praying mantis hangs in nature. He asked for suggestions about where he could hang the needle with the egg cases in the classroom. One student offered that they could put it up in a cage. Before solving that problem, the teacher and students went on to discuss when the eggs would hatch. After students gave dates that corresponded to about two weeks from then, Rollins got them to focus on how the animals would know when it was time to hatch.

Rollins: One of the things I'd like to do—when they got these, how do the egg cases—how do the animals inside know that it's time to hatch?

Martha: They don't.

Rollins: They just hatch anytime?

Jim: They get so big that—

Rollins: Just wait a minute.

Jim: —they just break out.

Rollins: When was this egg case laid?

Jason: Do they come from China?

Rollins: No, they originally—the first praying mantis came from China, but these are all over this part of the country. Can anybody make a guess—was it laid yesterday?

Lisa: No.

Rollins: A week ago?

Chantelle: Yes.

Johnny: We don't really know when this is going to hatch.

Rollins: Well, it's not—I'll give you a hint. A lot of animals, in the fall, lay their eggs for the spring. These egg cases were actually laid last fall. And they've been outside all winter, they've been on different branches of bushes—

Lisa: Then they should be hatched already.

Rollins: Well, if they hatched in the winter, what would happen?

James: They would die.

Rollins: Why?

James: No food.

Maria: Too cold.

Rollins: How is it controlled how they hatched?

Lisa: The weather—when it's hot, whatever.

Maria: Maybe they can feel how warm it is.

Miguel: Solar energy.

Rollins: Precisely. What if we wanted these two to hatch, what if we wanted these egg cases to open, and then we wanted these egg cases to open a little bit later?

James: Put those in a cold area, and those in a warm area.

Rollins: All right, do we have a cold area around here?

Manuel: No.

Lisa: Yeah.

James: The refrigerator.

Rollins: Would you put this in [another teacher's] refrigerator, please? Make it think it's still winter for another week. And then next week, we'll put it in [a warmer place].

Although this was a teacher-directed discussion, students had opportunities to ask questions as well as answer Rollins's. Students provided different answers without his evaluating each response. While he encouraged them to provide suggestions, he also focused students by asking specific questions such as what would happen if the eggs hatched in winter. By placing the eggs in the refrigerator, he implied that they would be doing an experiment to find out what happened in different temperatures. One girl brought over a book that indicated the refrigerator should be at 55 degrees. Before ending the discussion and observation session, Rollins asked students to figure out what kind of top they could put on the egg cases to prevent them from being all over the room after they hatched. Students provided many different answers, from plastic to tin foil, and others noted the need for air holes. The discussion ended when a girl volunteered to make a top out of some material that Rollins indicated he had.

Observing Chicken Eggs

More observations and discussion of eggs occurred in the afternoon, when Rollins showed the poster-size diagram of an egg that he had drawn. As he pointed out different parts of the egg, he asked students what they thought the functions of different parts were, such as the shell and the albumen. At times, he clarified and expanded students' guesses by bringing in his own knowledge. For instance, when discussing the red spot, the following exchange occurred:

Rollins: Now, there's two more very important parts to go. Ali? Anybody have an idea what the blastoderm is? Blastoderm? The little spot on top of the yolk. No, it's not the sperm. Juaniki?

Ali: It's the baby—

Rollins: *Embryo* is the word you're looking for.

Juaniki: It's the thing forming.

Rollins: It's the chicken forming. That's a good way to put it. Another way—the chicken forming. Another way—the scientific word would be embryo, which means an animal life that is forming, that is not yet formed. It's the beginning form of what will become, if it is a fertilized egg, will become the chicken.

Here Rollins poses questions and supplies the scientific words for the students' responses. He both values Juaniki's answer and explains further what the embryo is.

Students became particularly engaged when Rollins got a dozen eggs, had students find partners, and then gave each pair an egg. After cracking open the eggs, students made observations to each other about what they saw. Some walked around the room talking about their observations or merely saying, "Ick!" Many students identified the parts of the egg and wanted to share their observations with the teacher. A sense of excitement was apparent as the students called Rollins over to show him what they had found or to ask him questions:

Johnny: Dan, can you help us so we can see the air cell?
Lisa: What's the white part, Dan?
Juaniki: Look, Dan—the rounded part of the egg—
Rollins: That's the membrane—
James: Dan, can we have this?
Ali: We found it!
James: We found it first!
Miguel: Dan, quick, come here!
Rollins: That's right, it actually breathes through there. The baby chick actually gets its air passing through there from outside.
Martha: Dan, you know the chalaza? We can see it, you can see it. Want to see it?
Rollins: That's right. That's the blastoderm, exactly.
Jason: What is this, Dan? This white thing?
Rollins: That's the chalaza.

Making Sense of Dan Rollins's Teaching

One of the things that is striking about Rollins's classroom is the sense of balance between the teacher's and students' knowledge. He provided opportunities for students to choose projects, but within a particular frame related to life cycles. During this time, students had opportunities to try out different projects, to work individually or in small groups, to write, create, observe, or experiment. Yet he also provided a more structured, whole-class period in which he used more explicit means of instruction. Students gathered together to talk about the praying mantis egg cases. The teacher interwove facts with speculation, explanation with questioning, and demonstration with observation. He balanced his own goals with students' responses. He was able to involve many different students in the discussion and both ask and answer questions. When discussing the parts of an egg, he provided focused discussion by pointing to the chart and asking students for guesses about the functions of different parts of the eggs. He also balanced this whole-group talk with pairings of students, where they had the opportunity to crack open and examine the inside of eggs. The activity was focused, with all students doing the same thing; yet students could share their individual observations with each other.

Rollins's practice seemed to be consistent with the goals he had for students. His selection of life cycles as the theme unit was based on his own knowledge and enthusiasm about the topic, his belief in immersing students in science, and his use of topics that were immediately available in the students' environment. He posed broad goals for student understanding of life cycles, such as "[understanding] that many animals go through changes in their life," but he was more concerned about getting students excited about the world than about knowing particular facts:

I'm just not interested in knowing 101 science facts extraneously. I'm really interested in their being curious and driven and excited and involved in the study, and if they—most of them—end up knowing *pupa* and *larva* and *metamorphosis* and all those words, and what it's all about, and they can answer it right on the dumb science test in fourth grade. But the point is, most of them, I mean I get very, very positive things from parents, saying, "You know, my kid was like driven, he'd turn over a log, and he'd say, 'Look at that millipede! And it's got four legs per segment, you can see the way it moves. The legs are underneath the body, but in a centipede the legs are splayed out. And you can see that it has the short antennas, whereas on a centipede, it has the long antennas!'" And I don't care even if they say it wrong. I don't care if they say, "The centipede has the legs underneath, and the millipede has the legs splayed out." Which is not true. It doesn't matter. I mean, do you care if a centipede has its legs splayed out? The point is, they have that drive of excitement about the natural world and to find out. And they pore over my field guides. I have Patterson field guides, and Audubon field guides, and they just—a couple of kids are just driven to know what they are, and how they work, and to research and figure it out and use books as a resource. That's what it's all about.

Rollins's goals are not focused on having students know particular kinds of information, but rather on learning to observe and challenge their own observations:

I'm interested in them knowing that what appears in front of you isn't necessarily what it is. So in other words, I don't think that whether it's egg or egg case, the point is to rethink what you're looking at. And I think that's what they get out of a lesson like that, is to say, "My God, what's in that? What's going on in there?" And Johnny's question was wonderful. When I said it comes out a centimeter, he said, "How could it come out a centimeter? There's not room for 200 centimeter-long insects in that thing." So again, it's sort of stimulation to think, "What's going on? What is in there that I don't see? How could it be?" And then the whole thing of the fetus, and comparing it to a human fetus, and which is say, we'll talk a lot about the egg, and what's going on with the chicken in there. How does that chicken fit there? So again, it's not a particularly useful piece of knowledge in the world to know the praying mantis comes out of egg cases and mealworms come out of eggs. I think it's useful to challenge your visual—information you get visually, and to think, "What is that? What's going on?"

Although Rollins tended to value the process of students' discovery and questioning, he was also knowledgeable enough to lead students to important understandings of scientific concepts, such as the effects of temperature on egg hatching. He balanced individual student discovery with more explicit whole-group instruction. He did not lecture about concepts but directed students' thinking by his questions.

Differences in Ways of Constructing Roles

Although Patterson and Rollins believed in the process of scientific discovery over memorization of facts and attempted to give students opportunities to discover scientific principles, they differed from each other in significant ways. Rollins's classroom reflected clarity of goals and purposes. Open to students' observations about chicken eggs or praying mantises, he had specific goals he wanted to accomplish. Patterson's goals, on the other hand, were less clear. She seemed to be so open to students' observations, and so vague about the underlying problem in the investigation, that the purpose of the experimentation with colored solutions was lost. While students had almost unlimited options in Patterson's class, including using the electricity table during the water unit, Rollins offered more limited choices; students could work on different projects during the specified time, but those projects were to be related to the egg unit. Additionally, in his class, students gathered together for a whole-group discussion of egg cases and chicken eggs. This discussion led to a sense of coherence and organization in Rollins's class that was not apparent in Patterson's.

Patterson and Rollins differed in two other significant ways: (1) their knowledge of their subject matter and (2) their relative commitment to the discovery method. Rollins had a clear interest in science coupled with a background in biology. Although he did not major in biology in college, he had extensive knowledge of particular topics gained through pursuing biology as a hobby and through some formal coursework. Patterson's knowledge of solutions and the principles of physics she wanted students to grasp was less evident. She seemed both unclear about the concepts themselves, as she confessed in her interview, and hesitant to impose her ideas upon students. This hesitancy seemed to be related to her commitment to allowing students to discover scientific principles for themselves. Not interfering with students' observations, Patterson's role was to allow students to focus on their observations and attempt to clarify what they were seeing in the colored solutions. However, this role appeared unsuccessful in ensuring that students understood the reasons for what was occurring and having a grasp of the underlying relationship between the solutions and salinity. By contrast, Rollins took a more directive role: asking students key questions, providing information when appropriate, and clarifying the observations about the eggs. Without lecturing to students, Rollins made students' understanding as well as his own more explicit in his interactions than did Patterson in a similar circumstance. Coupled with his knowledge of science, his balance of allowing students to discover ideas while providing more explicit instruction seemed successful in providing an exciting, hands-on curriculum where students had opportunities to understand key ideas. In Patterson's case, it is less clear what the students gained from the experience. While she attempted to juggle multiple goals, topic areas, and subject matters at once, some students may have gained from the experience while others may simply have been more confused than before.

The cases of Dede Patterson and Dan Rollins highlight the challenge of negotiating teacher roles. While committed to valuing students' ideas and offering opportunities for students to observe, discover, and discuss science, these teachers confronted the difficulty of meeting students' needs and interests at the same time they were establishing a coherent set of experiences for students. As with Alexis Brezinski and Brian Kramer, this tension resulted in a constructivist dilemma: a tension between the role of the teacher and the student in the joint construction of knowledge. Each had a different way of constructing his or her role in relation to this dilemma.

Chapter Thirteen

Fitting Structure to Practice

From the Northeastern case, what can we infer about the relationship between school structure and classroom practice?

Northeastern is distinctive on a number of counts. First, the beliefs and values of teachers are manifested in teaching practice to a degree that is not characteristic of the other schools in this book. Teachers are articulate in describing what their aspirations are for how students should learn, and they are quite successful at translating those aspirations into tangible actions in the classroom.

Second, there is a remarkable degree of consistency among teachers in both beliefs and practice. To an outside observer, Northeastern classrooms look and feel alike, but they are very different from the usual elementary school. Space is organized so that students interact with each other as much as with the teacher. The classrooms are organized to accommodate multiple activities simultaneously rather than single, teacher-centered activities. Teachers and students do similar things, and time is used comparably from one classroom to another. Students take significant responsibility for initiating and doing their own work within a structure broadly set by the teachers, rather than having teachers initiating and students doing.

While an outside observer is likely to see these similarities among classrooms, Northeastern teachers see many differences among themselves in the way they teach. From the teachers' perspective, differences in practice are complementary, rather than dissonant; they see their colleagues as having skills that complement their own more than having different views of teaching and learning. Teachers agree at a fundamental level on what good teaching practice is, while accepting important variations in the way it is actualized. They do not subscribe to the view that each teacher can have a distinctive "style" if it diverges from established good teaching practices, nor that teachers can disagree fundamentally on what good teaching is. It is precisely their common belief in certain basic principles that allows them to observe and capitalize on their differences. Differences in practice, then, are complementary rather than dissonant. Hence, differences lead to increased interdependence, rather than to inconsistencies in practice across classrooms.

Third, Northeastern is distinctive because teachers assert a high degree of control over their own affairs, and they use it to enhance the school's focus on its distinctive view of teaching and learning. Northeastern's tactics of control are subtle and not highly visible to the outside world, but they are nonetheless strong and purposeful. The school operates within a district policy framework that permits parents and students to choose which schools they will attend. While there is controversy over how "representative" Northeastern students are of the surrounding community, by virtue of their choice students and parents are required to make a commitment to the central values of Northeastern in order to attend the school. Additionally, its teachers exercise the determining influence over who will be hired to teach at the school, and they use that influence to find teachers who espouse the basic beliefs and values of the school, whether about teaching and learning or about the role of parents and the school's relationship to the community. Most decisions that directly affect teaching practice are strongly determined by people working in the school, including how to use staff development time; how the discretionary time of resource-room, art, and music teachers is used to create free time for regular teachers; and most importantly what will be taught and how. In other words, the people at Northeastern have assumed responsibility for the core organizational functions that allow it to nurture a particular view of teaching and learning.

Fourth, Northeastern tried a radical form of organizational structure and participatory governance before eventually settling on a simpler, somewhat more conventional organization that is consistent with its beliefs about teaching and learning. At the school's founding, Diane Mandel and the original group of Northeastern teachers tried a broadly participatory organization designed to eliminate distinctions between administrators and teachers. They tried putting all decisions into a schoolwide forum. Over three or four years and a modest crisis, the school evolved toward a more outwardly conventional structure: a full-time administrator, self-contained classrooms, and a more formal structure for making decisions. However, Northeastern's norms and modes of operating are anything but traditional. As noted above, teaching practice and classroom organization are very different from the teacher-centered model. In addition, the staff collaborate more informally and flexibly around key decisions in the school: teachers share significant responsibility for decisions about all students, teachers work on common organizational problems, and they open their classrooms to other staff. While on the surface Northeastern may appear to be conventionally structured, underneath it is anything but conventional.

Fifth and finally, Northeastern and its staff are awash in connections to the outside world. They participate continuously in research projects; they help to form other schools with similar points of view; and, perhaps most importantly, teachers have strong intellectual lives that draw them into outside study and work with other institutions. All of the schools we studied have outside connections, but at Northeastern these outside connections strongly reinforce and amplify its central beliefs and values. The school cooperates with outside institutions that share its view of teaching and learning, and from which it can learn something about itself. Individual teachers engage in their own continuous learning and development in large part because they believe that the basic idea of continuous development and learning is at the heart of what they are trying to teach their students.

Overall, then, we observe a strong connection between organization and teaching practice at Northeastern. Teachers know with some consistency what they are trying to accomplish in the classroom, and the organization of the school almost invariably supports and complements what teachers know or believe they should be doing. We think the strength of this connection between organization and teaching practice comes not from having chosen an organizational form that "results" in a particular kind of teaching practice, but from exactly the opposite: believing strongly in a particular approach to teaching and finding a structure that allows that practice to develop. What is significant about the structure of Northeastern is not how radical or unconventional it might be but rather how seamlessly it fits with the beliefs and values around which teaching practice occurs in the school. It took Northeastern a number of years to evolve this structure. The process was driven by a search not so much for the "right" structure as for one that would not get in the way of what teachers were trying to do in the classroom. Furthermore, the structure continues to change in small ways as teachers observe that it does not always support what they are trying to do.

Lurking underneath these issues of structure and teaching practice is a fundamental problem that we have called the "constructivist dilemma." Northeastern has been reasonably successful at creating a consistent view of good teaching practice that translates into remarkably consistent patterns of actual practice in the classroom. The school has also been successful at creating an organizational structure that complements and amplifies that practice. But these beliefs, values, and structures do not by themselves solve the fundamental problem of teaching children how to take control of their own learning. They simply provide a setting that is conducive to a continuous engagement with the constructivist dilemma. That dilemma emerges from our studies of teachers at Northeastern in the following way: on the one hand, it is the teacher's responsibility to provide structure and guidance for students to learn in ways that ultimately lead to their taking responsibility for their own learning; but on the other hand, the structures and guidance that teachers provide often prevent students from taking responsibility for their own learning. On the one hand, teachers are supposed to understand in a deep way the content and pedagogical knowledge necessary to teach students; but on the other hand, teachers' knowledge can overwhelm students' struggles to understand for themselves.

Teachers experience a constant tension between their desire to be open and accepting of children's views and at the same time to draw upon their own expertise as knowledgeable adults. Some teachers, like Dede Patterson, choose to allow students a great degree of latitude in discovering ideas for themselves, while others, like Brian Kramer and Dan Rollins, work to strike a more explicit balance between student discovery and teacher guidance. Alexis Brezinski literally expresses a dilemma between allowing students to choose their own areas of interest, while drawing upon her own considerable knowledge of ancient Greece. To a degree uncommon in most schools, all of the Northeastern teachers seem to struggle with the tension between providing opportunities for student initiative and using their own knowledge and expertise to structure those opportunities.

From the standpoint of teaching practice, Northeastern teachers are interesting not just because they have relatively advanced knowledge and skill in getting students to take responsibility, individually and collectively, for their own learning, but also because they have the capacity to reflect on the underlying dilemma at the heart of this conception of teaching. Northeastern teachers play an active role in shaping the learning of their students: by setting the structure within which students work, by bringing their own knowledge and passions to bear on what students learn, and by asking probing questions of students who are struggling with learning. Students in turn play an active role in shaping their own learning: by deciding what to write about, by consulting with their peers about what constitutes better and worse work, and by responding to constructive criticism from other students and their teachers. Some teachers and students do these things more fluently and successfully than others; no doubt some are more fluent in certain domains of knowledge than they are in others. As Dede Patterson's struggle with the complex idea of density suggests, it is hard to construct a situation in which students take responsibility for developing their own understanding when the teacher herself is struggling to understand the basic ideas and how to teach them. Patterson differs from many other teachers, however, in her capacity to reflect on what she has done. She understands, in ways that other teachers in our study do not, that her practice does not meet her own expectations.

This capacity to reflect on what it means to take responsibility for one's own learning as well as the learning of others permeates much of daily life of Northeastern. Teachers write detailed narratives of students and their work, drawing on their knowledge of the student and the student's work to draw conclusions about how they should teach the child. Teachers deliberate collectively on the progress and problems of students in staff reviews, sharing responsibility for the development of students. Teachers design project units in such a way that they set the general direction students will take, but students assume a large share of responsibility for specific parts of the project. Students work with each other to develop stories that capture what is important in their lives. Northeastern is a place where questions and deliberation are important.

Northeastern teachers are able to come to terms with the constructivist dilemma because they have the opportunity to reflect and deliberate about their own practice with sympathetic colleagues who share a common view of teaching. When Patterson's unit on density did not go as planned, she wondered aloud about her own understanding of the ideas. When Rollins sensed the eagerness of a particular student in the life cycle unit, he pondered the reasons why. When Kramer discussed his goals for students' capacities to understand their own community, he wondered about how well his teaching would promote that understanding. And when Brezinski wrote in her daily journal about the experiences of particular students, she was wondering about her own capacity, and the capacity of her colleagues in the school, to reach certain students.

Northeastern is a school with strong, shared views of what good teaching and learning consist of and a set of norms and structures that allow those views to develop and grow through the interaction of teachers and students. Northeastern did not get to this point by choosing a structure and hoping that certain beliefs, values, and practices—what Northeastern teachers call "habits of mind"—would follow. Rather, Northeastern focused on its central beliefs, values, and practices and then deliberately constructed an organization that made it possible for those to develop.

Chapter Fourteen

Conclusion
Restructuring Teaching

The Puzzle of Organization and Practice

We began this book with a seemingly straightforward problem: how do changes in organization affect teaching practice? School restructuring presumes that in order to change the way teachers teach schools must change the way teachers' and students' work is organized. We found in the introductory chapter that there is little support, either in the school-restructuring literature or in the broader research literature on school structure and student outcomes, for the view that changes in school organization lead directly to changes in teaching practice. But we also found a certain face validity to the claim by school reformers that the standard ways of organizing schools may limit teaching practice and undermine good teaching, which we define as teaching that has as its goal the development of a deep understanding on the part of all students.

Indeed, for most dedicated reformers the connection between school organization and teaching practice is so obvious as to be hardly worth examining. Many of the changes in teaching practice that reformers want to achieve—more flexible and responsive treatment of differences among students, more explicit connections between students' ways of knowing and teachers' ways of teaching, greater use of diverse teacher competencies, and more ambitious learning goals for all students—would seem to imply significant structural change in schools. Just what these structural changes might be is not immediately clear from looking at exemplary teaching practices. But it does seem plausible that significant changes in the organization of teachers' work might be related to changes in how teachers teach. If it is true, then, that changes in teaching practice seem to require changes in organization, why do we have so little evidence that changes in organization lead directly to changes in teaching and practice, and ultimately to changes in student learning?

In this chapter, we analyze this puzzle of school organization and teaching practice by drawing on the experience of the three schools in our study. Our analysis falls under four main headings. First, we discuss the similarities and differences among the three schools in our study and how these similarities and differences relate to conventional explanations of how schools change. Second, we discuss the three schools' experiences with structural reform. Third, we discuss how teachers, as individual practitioners, came to grips with the expectation that they would change their teaching practice. And fourth, we draw some conclusions as to how to think about structural reform and teaching practice in the future, both in the design of research and in the practical task of changing schools.

Similarities and Differences Among the Three Schools

It is a truism of qualitative research that every school is unique and special. At some level this is true of the schools in our study. Yet in the welter of details that make each school special, it is easy to overlook their similarities.

Organizational Structure

Each of the schools we studied made significant changes in its organizational structure. Lakeview changed the structure of the school day, breaking the day into two parts, with different grouping strategies and different content in each part. Lakeview also created multi-age student groups and teams of teachers for instruction in reading and math. Webster created teams of teachers to work with common groups of students across the curriculum, encouraging teachers to develop a particular competence in a single subject. Webster also used multi-age grouping of students, combining teams across grades. Northeastern, in many ways the most conventional school of the three in terms of its formal structure, was organized around self-contained classrooms with cross-age student groups. But underlying this rather traditional structure was a strong set of norms for interaction among teachers and a flexible approach to grouping students, based on teachers' judgments about the appropriate class, grade, and teacher. So each school had made self-conscious departures from the traditional organizational forms of schooling, and each was far enough into the implementation of these changes to provide us with an opportunity to observe the relationship between changes in organization and changes in teaching practice.

Vision

Likewise, each of the schools had undergone a group experience of committing itself to a common vision, based on a more ambitious conception of student learning. Lakeview teachers and their principal, Laurel Daniels, devised their new structure during a summer workshop. Thereafter, they met regularly, during the school year and summers, to renew and refine their ideas about how Lakeview should be organized. Their vision was based on the precept that all children could learn at high levels and that students should not be labeled as underachievers by the way they were grouped or by the way school was organized. Webster teachers and their principal, Cheryl Billings, likewise met at a summer retreat and devised a vision statement for the school, "Expect the Best, Achieve Success," and committed themselves to an agenda of structural and curriculum changes. This commitment was sustained by regular staff development and steady expansion of the team structures each year. The teachers at Northeastern and their principal, Diane Mandel, were drawn together around the vision of creating a child-centered alternative school shaped by the views of a network of early-childhood educators. This model was progressively refined as the staff composition of the school changed and the teachers came to increasing agreement on what they meant by good teaching and learning. Each school, in other words, went through some formative experience of committing itself to a common purpose, and some continuing process of renewing and reinforcing that purpose. Each subscribed to the belief that all children could learn at high levels of understanding, that schools should change the way they are organized in order to achieve that purpose, and that teachers should change the way they teach to accommodate this aspiration.

Leadership

Each school had a strong and dynamic leader as its principal, although the principals differed considerably in their leadership style. Lakeview's Laurel Daniels was a skilled practitioner of creative noncompliance, using her educational instincts and her growing knowledge of her environment to carve out an organizational and political niche for the school and to pry resources out of federal, state, and private donors. Webster's Cheryl Billings was more a product of her environment. She took advantage of the district's considerable resources, support, and encouragement to develop her own capacities and to exploit opportunities for Webster teachers to learn and develop their own talents. Diane Mandel was recruited to start Northeastern because of her prior experience in alternative schools; she developed her leadership capacities as the school developed. Luisa Montoya followed in Mandel's footsteps, emerging from the ranks of teachers at Northeastern with the strong support of her peers. While the leadership styles of the principals differed, each was a strong figure in her setting and each created an environment within the school that set a positive value on challenging conventional ways of organizing schools.

The principals of the schools were similar in another way: they each assumed considerable authority over recruitment and personnel issues in their schools. Daniels became adept at working the district's personnel system, using it to recruit teachers with an interest in Lakeview's agenda. She also exercised considerable influence over teachers' work assignments within the school, for example moving a teacher who had been ill from a regular classroom assignment into teaching art. Similarly, Billings worked to encourage teachers who were interested in the school's reform agenda and to politely discourage resistant teachers from staying there. Over time, she began to exert increasing influence over who taught at Webster and over the opportunities that Webster teachers had for access to learning outside the school. Mandel had more or less complete control over who taught at Northeastern from the beginning as a consequence of being asked by the district superintendent to form a new school. She exercised such influence, for example, by recruiting an art teacher and then arranging for that teacher to do a year's internship with an art teacher at an exclusive private school before she was introduced to Northeastern. As Northeastern developed its cohesive culture, the teachers in the school assumed increasing informal influence over recruitment and selection of new teachers, as in selecting a new teacher from student teachers working in the school.

Length of Process

Alongside these similarities, there were some major differences among the schools. One of the most significant was how long the schools had been engaged in the process of change. Lakeview and Webster were relatively new to the business of restructuring. Lakeview had been at work on its agenda for about three years when Daniels decided to leave. Webster had been working on its agenda for about the same period when our research was conducted, and its principal, Cheryl Billings, seemed determined to stay. Northeastern had been more or less continuously engaged in the same agenda for about fourteen years, under Mandel and then Montoya, at the time of our observations. For about nine or ten of those years the school had been in a reasonably steady state, pursuing the same basic operating norms, structures, and classroom processes. Thus the differences in the degree of success in developing new forms of teaching practice might have been largely a function of the amount of time they had been engaged in the process of change.

But time alone probably does not entirely account for the differences we observed in success in changing teaching practice. Northeastern had been working with stable leadership over the whole period of its restructuring. Lakeview and Webster were at earlier stages of development, one with unstable leadership, the other with stable leadership. Along the same lines, Northeastern was consistent in pursuing its agenda, had deep agreement among teachers about the nature of what they regarded as good practice, and enjoyed the cumulative learning that occurred among teachers over that period. While consistency and cumulative learning require time, neither is necessarily the sole, inevitable consequence of time. Schools can, and frequently do, wander aimlessly from one innovation to another over long periods of time, gaining little in the way of cumulative understanding and little common learning among teachers. Likewise, teachers may subscribe in principle to the idea of changing their practice but make only small changes that do not accumulate over time. So while the schools in our study differ in the length of time they have been in the process of restructuring, it is more important to know what schools do over time to reinforce new forms of practice than it is to know or impart too much significance to how long they have been engaged in change.

The District

Another important source of differences among the schools in our study was the district environment in which they operated. Lakeview and Laurel Daniels faced a district administration that was at best indifferent and at worst hostile to their reform agenda. Daniels was perceived to be a renegade in the district. She was admired by parents, state and federal policy makers, and community members for her passion and dedication to changing traditional forms of schooling. She had formidable entrepreneurial skills, generating money and political support for her reform ideas. But in many ways her visibility in the community and outside the district undermined her position within the district. District administrators gave only symbolic support to Lakeview's agenda, reacting cautiously to Daniels's constituency but unenthusiastically to her substantive goals for Lakeview. When Daniels became frustrated and left, the district responded by moving a person they regarded as more reliable, and less visible, into the principalship of Lakeview. Daniels's successor also perceived the district to be less than supportive of Lakeview's agenda.

Webster, on the other hand, operated in a district environment explicitly designed to provide support and reinforcement for what it was doing. The school's agenda was, in basic terms, the same as the district's agenda. The school was regarded as a flagship of the district's broader restructuring and professional development programs. Cheryl Billings skillfully exploited the complementarity of school and district aims, bringing a formidable array of resources to the school.

The Fairchild School District had made a highly visible commitment to school restructuring. They created the Masters Center, an ambitious professional development initiative, with a substantial infusion of private money and charged it with the task of providing support to schools undergoing restructuring. They employed resource teachers to work in schools, helping to develop new approaches to teaching. They offered professional development for teachers and principals, and they supported travel by teachers and principals whether to outside professional development activities or to other schools and districts to learn new practices. Webster was the beneficiary of all these resources. District administrators and staff of the professional development center were careful in public to show consistent support for Webster's effort, including providing the school staff an opportunity to present their innovative report card to the school board. In broad terms, then, Webster operated in a generous and supportive district environment, and this environment delivered many direct benefits to the school and its staff.

In more specific terms, however, Webster demonstrated both the strengths and weaknesses of the district's reform strategy. The district's strategy of providing resource teachers to work in classrooms with Webster teachers did have a direct and tangible impact on the practice of at least one teacher at Webster. On the other hand, most teachers at Webster did not have access to this highly focused attention and seemed to be floundering with very basic issues of content and pedagogy. The professional development center staff had an aversion, for both bureaucratic and substantive reasons, to working with district curriculum specialists in the district's school restructuring efforts. They saw the district curriculum staff as representing an outmoded, subject-matter-based view of teaching and learning, although the curriculum staff's connections to networks of knowledgeable people could have been helpful to Webster teachers.

Process Versus Content

This split between district restructuring and curriculum staff in Fairchild represents a deeper problem in the conception of school reform. The district restructuring staff's concept was primarily process-centered; they saw themselves as supporting a process of change in schools. They sponsored certain specific innovations— notably, site-based decision making, multi-age teaming, and hands-on curriculum—but their main focus was getting schools engaged in the *process* of changing themselves. Even the resource teachers, who brought some valuable advice to teachers, were given no specific charge to focus on certain areas of *content or practice,* but rather were told to engage teachers in something they, the teachers, would find useful in their classrooms. The district curriculum staff, on the other hand, were mainly concerned with what teachers were actually teaching, rather than with the process by which schools and teachers learned to do things differently. These two concerns—one for the process of change, and the other for content of teaching and learning—are in principle complementary, and they should operate in tandem. In Fairchild, at the time of our study, they did not. Because the restructuring team was more influential in district decisions, the focus of assistance to Webster and other schools tended to be more on process than on content and pedagogy. The consequences at the school level were visible: teachers were actively engaged in the process of changing Webster, but they were relatively unsupported in their attempts to learn new ways to teach content.

Northeastern also operated in a supportive district environment, but one considerably different from Webster's. Northeastern too was a flagship school of the district's reform strategy. But this district strategy was based on the development of distinctive alternative schools representing different approaches to teaching and learning. Rather than attempting to establish a districtwide agenda that would be represented in each school, Antonio Amada, the district superintendent, promoted the idea that teachers should form groups and design their own schools. In Amada's view, the district's role was to make it possible for these schools to operate, and make it possible for parents to choose the school they thought was appropriate for their children. Hence Northeastern's district was generally supportive of the school, but it did not pursue a specific agenda about what the school should be doing instructionally. Nor did the district provide professional development opportunities directed at making specific changes in Northeastern.

Within this district environment, Northeastern formed its own philosophy and pedagogical approach and gradually became more autonomous in all essential features of its organization and management, including assuming major responsibility for recruitment and hiring of staff. Northeastern teachers solved the problem of how to get access to new knowledge essentially by taking control of their own staff development. They planned schoolwide activities and designed their responsibilities within the school to mesh with those activities. They also developed strong norms that teachers should be actively engaged in intellectual pursuits outside the school as part of their professional life, and that these pursuits should be integrated into their classroom experience. They developed strong ties with other schools sharing their philosophy and used those ties to augment their own knowledge of teaching and learning. In the absence of direct support for teacher development, Northeastern developed its own strategy, one consistent with the district's objective of allowing a high degree of school autonomy.

The three schools show how diverse the effects of district administrative systems can be on schools pursuing reform agendas. Lakeview struggled against a sometimes indifferent, sometimes actively hostile district that did little to support the school's agenda. Webster operated in a district environment that was actively supportive, although the district's strategy introduced a division between process and content that did not seem to work well for Webster. Northeastern operated in a more laissez-faire environment, in which the district was highly supportive of the school's autonomy but not very directive in terms of an overall district strategy for teaching and learning.

All three schools were committed to structural reforms, which they thought would lead to different ways of teaching students, and they manifested this commitment in common activities designed to galvanize a common vision of schooling. All three had strong, committed leaders willing to take control of key functions of the organization, notably recruitment and hiring of teachers. They differed markedly in their experience with restructuring, although all had enough experience to discover the main difficulties in changing well-established structures and practices—difficulties well illustrated by district environments ranging from hostile to fully supportive.

Structural Reform in the Three Schools

At the level of organizational structure and process, all three schools in our study looked like models of enlightened practice according to the current literature on school restructuring. They all provided supportive collegial environments for teachers. Teachers were actively involved in deciding how the schools would be organized and what their responsibilities would be in the new structures. They all endorsed ambitious learning goals for children. Each school subscribed to a shared set of beliefs about the importance of all children learning at high levels. Furthermore, these beliefs were widely shared and well represented in the structures that the schools developed. They were all willing to make significant changes in the conventional structure of schools to reflect their beliefs about teaching and learning. Each school altered in some significant way how students were grouped, how teachers related to each other in their daily work, how academic subjects were allocated time, and how they made decisions about organizational matters. In other words, each school was actively involved in changing the conventional structures and processes of schooling. They were, in this sense, actively restructuring themselves.

Below the level of organizational process and structure, however, we found a rather different picture. Teaching practice in two of our three schools, Lakeview and Webster, was highly variable to say the least. Some teachers in these schools enthusiastically pursued new ways of teaching but demonstrated a lack of understanding of how to make the new practices work successfully with students. Some teachers thought they were teaching in bold new ways, when in fact they seemed to be using slight modifications of what they said they had previously done. Other teachers demonstrated a shaky command of the content they were teaching, which undermined their attempts to pursue new practices.

In the third school, Northeastern, we found a rather different picture. We saw teachers and students engaged in ambitious teaching and learning with far greater consistency than we observed in the other two schools. There was variability at Northeastern too, but largely restricted to teachers grappling in different ways, at a relatively high level of expertise, with some of the fundamental dilemmas of constructivist teaching. For the most part, what we observed at Northeastern was a group of teachers with a strong set of commonly held norms about what constitutes good teaching, and a high level of success at translating those norms into classroom practice. As we moved from classroom to classroom, we were struck by the similarities in how classrooms were organized, how teachers organized students' work in classrooms, how content was portrayed in classroom activities, the role students played in their own learning, and the strategies teachers used to elicit students' ideas. Yet when we interviewed Northeastern teachers they expressed the view that practice varied considerably among teachers within Northeastern. They focused on the unique strengths of individual teachers, expressed in terms of a teacher's command of a particular academic subject or of special expertise in dealing with a particular kind of problem student. Where we saw uniformity, they saw variability.

The Northeastern case is complicated in that, as noted earlier, it was the most conventional, perhaps least "restructured" school of the three. It was organized around self-contained classrooms, with a single teacher having virtually full-time responsibility for a single group of students. Both Lakeview and Webster chose to break this convention because of their beliefs about student learning and the importance of teacher collegiality. Northeastern chose not to. In addition, while the instructional practice of teachers at Northeastern was quite distinctive and consistent from classroom to classroom, there were minimal formal structures within the school to promote teacher collegiality. Teachers were not organized into teams, for example, nor did the school invest substantial amounts of time in group work among teachers organized around specific curriculum objectives. Similarly, Northeastern chose not to make a major break with the conventional age-grade structure for grouping students. Classrooms did include multi-age groups, and teachers worked to make sure that students were assigned to classrooms in which the teacher and the content were appropriate for the student's needs; but the formal structure of Northeastern looked much like that of any elementary school.

The Collaborative Environment at Northeastern School

In order to discover what was special about Northeastern, we had to probe below the formal and into the informal structure of collegial relations within the school. At that level, Northeastern was quite distinctive. Teachers talked regularly to each other about students and about the problems they were facing in getting students to engage in learning. They met regularly, at least weekly, in loosely structured meetings focused alternately on administrative business or on teaching and learning issues—in the latter case, often focused on specific students and their work. Teachers and other outsiders moved freely in and out of classrooms. Teachers exercised considerable influence, albeit largely informal, over key decisions such as who would be allowed to teach in the school. They each had serious intellectual outside interests that they brought into the school, and for which they were acknowledged as experts by their colleagues. These informal structures supported a common view of teaching and learning. In fact, they seemed to be the main device by which teachers at Northeastern expressed their common values and interests.

In large part, Northeastern's solution to the problem of the relationship between structure and teaching practice had to do with its unique history. The school was formed as a community of like-minded educators. It went through a long period of experimenting with what it meant to be a community, including a traumatic early crisis over who would determine the future of the school. Through this experimental period, Northeastern became a strong, focused, cohesive community; it assumed major responsibility for key decisions about what would be taught, what constituted good teaching, and who would teach in the school. It should not be surprising, then, that one consequence of this steady development of a community of interest was a high level of agreement on what good teaching and learning would look like, at both the level of principle and enacted practice. Neither should it be surprising that such agreement was absent from Lakeview and Webster, with their histories so different from Northeastern's.

One might argue that Lakeview and Webster are more like "real schools," in the sense that they operate within constraints more typical of public schools, while Northeastern is an atypical school because of its special history. Northeastern could evolve into a more coherent school, one might argue, precisely because it was exempted from many of the pressures that operate on typical schools. Teachers formed the school out of a common interest, parents chose to send their children there, and the school assumed de facto control over most of the administrative functions affecting its capacity to do what it wanted with teaching and learning. These factors would not be present in a typical school in the "real world," the argument might continue, where principals have to work with teachers who are not necessarily of their own choosing and deal with many external constraints on their capacity to shape a school's destiny.

We take a somewhat different view. None of the three schools in our study was "typical"; all were pushing against the constraints imposed by their own preconceptions of teaching and learning as well as external influences on their organization and practice. From this perspective, Northeastern might be seen as a *more highly evolved version* of what Lakeview and Webster were trying to become. Northeastern was formed under conditions that allowed it to exercise considerable influence over teaching and learning, and it evolved an informal structure for expressing that influence; Lakeview and Webster also showed signs of taking increasing responsibility for conditions that would support a cohesive view of teaching and learning (for instance, as Daniels and Billings clarified their views of good practice and asserted greater influence over recruitment of new teachers). Northeastern brought in people who shared its view and progressively refined it over time through extensive informal relationships among teachers. Struggling to create their own cohesive visions, Lakeview and Webster were moving fitfully in that direction through staff development and the creation of structures that encouraged teachers to interact with each other around issues of practice.

When we designed this study, we set out to find exemplars of current thinking about school restructuring. It appears we did, in that all three schools exemplified what the literature on school restructuring might call enlightened practice: collegial decision making on a broad range of issues, visible changes in the structures by which students were assigned to teachers and by which teachers related to each other, frequent staff development focused on broadening the skills of teachers, and active collaboration among principals and teachers on issues of teaching and learning. Amid this welter of restructuring, however, we found a high degree of variability in teaching practice in two schools—and the one school in which we found consistency and the most ambitious version of teaching for understanding was, in a formal sense, the least "restructured" school in the study.

Teachers and Teaching Practice

All the schools in our study, and all of the teachers within those schools whose practice we have described and analyzed, were enthusiastic advocates of a certain kind of teaching, which they understood to be different from the teaching that usually occurs generally in elementary schools. They subscribed to more student-centered views of pedagogy, in which students' ideas and understandings were the central focus of teachers' concerns in the classroom. Rather than taking their cues exclusively from what the textbooks and materials said students should know, they were committed to understanding how students understood the things they were teaching. The teachers were also committed to engaging students in more active learning and a more hands-on classroom experience for students. They were committed to exposing students to concrete learning activities, whether by using manipulatives in mathematics; constructing models of buildings to learn history, design, and mathematics; or exploring scientific ideas by conducting experiments and investigations. And teachers were committed to providing equal opportunities for students to engage in these ambitious forms of learning. They wanted students of diverse aptitudes and backgrounds to work together in the same classrooms; they wanted to design classroom activities that would equally acknowledge and assist student learning; and they wanted diverse students to work together in groups and learn from each other. They were, in other words, advocates of an ambitious pedagogy, what in the introductory chapter we called *teaching for under-standing,* or "constructivist" teaching.

Each of the schools added its own particular spin to these ideas.

Lakeview teachers subscribed to the view that teachers and students were characterized by very different individual "learning styles," and that these differences would determine how teachers would teach and students would learn. The result of this view was a high degree of variability in teaching practice and much discussion of the nature of individual differences and their impact on teaching and learning.

Webster teachers, on the other hand, seemed to be groping—and persistently pushed by Cheryl Billings—toward a common view of practice, in which teachers would specialize in certain content areas within their teams for the purpose of bringing new ideas into the school, but they would share a common view of teaching and learning. Webster teachers took their subject-matter responsibilities seriously, although with highly variable results in the classroom.

Northeastern teachers as a group were more sophisticated and concrete in their ability to articulate ideas about good practice, and more consistent in applying these ideas in the classroom. While they focused a great deal on individual student differences in the classroom, they would not have subscribed to the "learning styles" beliefs of Lakeview teachers. Nor would they have given nearly as much weight as Webster teachers to subject-matter specialization. Northeastern teachers saw themselves as specialists in the intellectual growth and development of children, which they expressed through the teaching of academic content. To be sure, they saw each teacher as having a unique body of knowledge and special interests, but these interests translate not into subject-matter specialization but into different emphases in a given teacher's choice of what to teach at any given moment.

Thus each of the schools in our study took the core ideas of ambitious teaching (child-centered pedagogy, active learning, and equal access) and expressed them in different ways.

All of the teachers in our study were struggling—some more actively than others—with how to make their classroom practice approximate more closely their own ideas, and the ideas of others, about what a more student-centered, active, and equal approach to learning would look like. Lakeview's Lisa Turner struggled, very actively but not altogether successfully, with how to put structure in her students' rambunctious forays into the school playground to find and count ants. Trudy Garrett approached a similar task by spending most of the class time meticulously organizing students into groups in which each student had a clearly identified role, and having them chant back her instructions. Students took away from these two exercises remarkably different views of what inquiry was about, though neither teacher left sufficient time in the exercise to listen to and discuss what students had actually learned. Contrast their approaches with that of Dan Rollins at Northeastern, carefully cajoling his students through a discussion of praying mantis egg cases. First he set out the larger framework of life cycles; then he let students explore eggs in various forms; and finally he listened to students talk and ask questions about what they were observing in their being focused on the praying mantis egg cases. While his practice looked both spontaneous and seamless, it had a strong undercurrent of careful planning, forethought, and inquisitiveness about students' modes of thought.

Similar differences can be seen in how teachers helped students learn to deal with text through reading and writing. Lakeview's Peg Ernst was so preoccupied with how her students felt about what they were doing, so determined that each student should get some positive reinforcement from the learning experience she had created, that she neglected to pay attention to exactly what students were supposed to learn. Her colleague Lynn Horn, on the other hand, jumped into the poems her students were creating, inserting her own words and editing suggestions, seemingly without regard for whether students understood what she was doing or why she was doing it. Contrast their approaches to that of Julie Brandt at Webster, carefully cajoling students into selecting a topic from a list she had created and then using questions to draw them into expressing their thoughts about the topic. Similarly, Northeastern's Brian Kramer and Alexis Brezinski found ways not only to draw students into writing but also to create an environment in which students were able to help each other solve the routine problems that occur in the process of written expression. Much of the conversation in Kramer's classrooms was between students, working together on text and narrative, sharing a common language for how to construct text in ways that made sense to both writer and reader. Kramer created the setting in which these discussions occurred, but students took a large share of the responsibility for making the discussions work.

Teacher Knowledge

These examples illustrate that ambitious teaching practice is difficult and demanding work. Good teaching is not simply a matter of individual taste or style; it is a matter of deep, complex, and hardwon understandings of how to construct teaching that is consistent with one's views of how children ought to learn. What distinguishes Rollins, Brandt, Kramer, and Brezinski from Turner, Garrett, Ernst, and Horn is not their espoused views of pedagogy; they all talked very similarly about the kind of teaching they would like to do. Nor are these teachers greatly distinguished from one another by the effort they invested in their teaching; all of them were trying very hard to do a good job. The main distinction among these teachers was in their levels of sophistication in understanding what students are actually doing when they are actively understanding something, and their capacity to create settings in which that understanding occurred consistently for most students. Deep, systematic knowledge of practice—in both abstract and concrete terms—is what distinguishes teachers who do ambitious teaching from those who are struggling to do it.

The more successful teachers also had a command of the subject they were teaching and confidence in their ability to connect content with the experience of children. Webster's Joanna Griffin and Melissa Benton were clearly working hard to teach mathematics in a "new" way, but they were just as clearly constrained by their lack of fundamental knowledge of the mathematical concepts they were teaching. Griffin insisted that place value in a base-ten number system could be taught effectively through Roman numerals, a numerical system in which there is effectively no place value, despite an abundance of advice to the contrary—some of it in the textbook from which she was teaching. Both Griffin and Benton were more comfortable with a modified form of drilling students in basic facts and algorithms than they were in trying to understand how students made sense of the mathematical ideas they were teaching. To have the sort of confidence and fluency in teaching mathematics that their colleague Julie Brandt had in teaching writing, Griffin and Benton would have to have a similar familiarity and comfort with mathematical ideas. Neither Benton nor Griffin had studied mathematics after high school, and despite the Fairchild district's ample staff development program neither had an opportunity to study mathematics in a serious way as part of their experience with the new math curriculum. Dan Rollins at Northeastern was a self-confessed amateur in science, but he had clearly cultivated the knowledge of the subject matter necessary to engage his students in a serious discussion of biological life cycles. Knowing something about the content and structure of the knowledge you are trying to teach, and how students come to understand it, is clearly a component of the knowledge necessary to teach ambitiously.

For most teachers, getting access to fundamental content knowledge is a difficult problem. Elementary school teachers have a particularly difficult version of this problem. They are expected to know enough about the diverse subjects they teach, and about the way children approach those subjects, to be "expert" in these domains. Little in their educational background equips them for this role, and even in settings where they have access to professional development, they often do not get access to knowledge in a form that is useful in changing their classroom practice. The schools in our study are exceptional in the degree to which they involved teachers in professional development, and even in these schools teachers had a difficult time translating the "big ideas" of ambitious teaching into practices they were comfortable with in the classroom. The approaches that seemed to have the most promise were Jay Ross's careful work with Julie Brandt—a relationship in which Ross acted as both consultant and mentor with an active role in Brandt's classroom—and Northeastern's strategy of selecting teachers who were already committed to and relatively well-schooled in a new kind of teaching and putting them in an environment where discussion and observation of teaching was a matter-of-fact part of every day's work. In the first instance, Brandt was able to observe someone teaching in a setting that she understood: her own classroom. In the second instance, teachers thought of themselves as practitioners of a common approach to teaching and used each other's experience as a guide to their own learning and discovery.

The approaches to augmenting teachers' knowledge that seemed least effective were those that relied on exposure to one-shot staff development programs or lessons in the use of prepackaged materials. Lakeview School was virtually overrun with staff development; the list of discrete staff-development activities for Lakeview teachers in a given year ran to a dozen or more. Teachers were both grateful for and exhausted by Laurel Daniels's persistent attempts to bring outside knowledge into the school. But the form in which the knowledge came did not encourage teachers to work seriously on transforming their practice. Teachers would agree collectively on a list of topics they needed to work on, and Daniels would bring in experts in those topics to talk with the teachers. Teachers would also acquire curriculum units from outside experts; the ants and snails units from Turner's and Garrett's classrooms were provided by a consultant from a neighboring university. But no one worked through the complex process of bringing these ideas to fruition in the classroom with Lakeview teachers. *The assumption was that if the teachers had access to good ideas they would know how to put them into practice.*

Consider that the Fairchild district was pursuing one of the country's most sophisticated districtwide staff-development strategies. Still, Julie Brandt was the only teacher at the time of our visits who had experienced the benefit of deliberate, careful attention to practice and thereby gained insight into how her teaching might be different. Griffin's and Benton's experience with staff development was more typical of what other teachers at Webster received: access to district-sponsored workshops and to meetings outside the district at which experts spoke, without any direct scrutiny or observation of their resultant practice. In other words, even schools and districts that invested heavily in professional development for teachers often did so in ways that had little direct connection to teachers' practice.

Northeastern's solution to the problem of teacher knowledge is worth exploring in greater detail, because it is both unconventional and seemingly quite effective in influencing teachers' practice. Northeastern had little access to district-sponsored staff development, largely by choice. The district provided certain types of workshops for teachers, and Northeastern teachers took advantage of these workshops; but in our interviews, teachers did not cite these workshops as being particularly important to them or influential in their teaching. Sometimes teachers referred to these workshops as a sort of mild nuisance, something they were obliged to participate in but did not expect to gain much from. Nor did the school provide much in the way of formal staff development for itself, although individuals and groups of teachers were crafty at getting access to outsiders to come and help them solve specific problems within the school.

Northeastern solved the teacher-knowledge problem in three main ways: by setting very high expectations for entering teachers, by creating and reinforcing a norm that every teacher should have a consuming intellectual interest that he or she should bring into the school, and by forming internal and external networks of like-minded practitioners who were available to consult on problems of practice.

Northeastern teachers were expected to be practitioners of a certain kind of teaching when they entered the school. Some teachers were selected from the population of student teachers who regularly circulated through the school; some came to the school through professional networks; and in at least one case a teacher was "apprenticed" to another school for a year to learn how to teach art before being hired at Northeastern.

All the teachers at Northeastern expressed a consuming interest in some domain of knowledge that was their personal passion. And they all found a way to bring that personal interest into the experience of their students.

Northeastern teachers were all connected to other teachers outside the school who shared a common interest in what they were doing. The school had a partner relationship with a small alternative school in Vermont, to which teachers often went to recharge their intellectual batteries and think about their practice. For Northeastern, in other words, staff development was not an administrative function but a seamless part of the culture of the organization. It was not distinct and apart from their teaching practice or from who they were as practitioners; it was part of what they expected to do, and part of what they expected of each other. Teachers acquired knowledge at Northeastern by being part of the organization and by accepting its norms and values.

Whether one chooses to solve the problem of teachers' knowledge by creating a specialized staff-development function or by knitting teacher learning into the fabric of the organization, our studies suggest that it is probably unreasonable to expect teachers to transform their practices in response to big ideas without careful observation and sustained work with outsiders in their own classrooms. It was not especially difficult to get the teachers in our study to subscribe to ambitious ideas about teaching. Nor was it particularly difficult to get them to try out new curricula and practices in the classroom. All of the teachers in our study did these things, often with great enthusiasm. But if the schools in our study are any indication, it is extraordinarily difficult to get teachers to engage in sustained reflection and criticism of their own work that leads to fundamentally different ways of teaching. Access to external staff development and new materials may be helpful and is probably a necessary component of changing teaching practice. But that access is far from sufficient. Teachers need direct experience with the kind of practice they are expected to engage in, either by working with an expert or by being in an organization in which the practice is part of the air they breathe.

The Constructivist Paradox

All of the teachers in our study were grappling with a fundamental problem embedded in the new, more ambitious kind of teaching they were expected to practice. In the Northeastern case study, we called this problem the "constructivist dilemma." In question form, the dilemma might be expressed as, What is the role of the teacher in a student-centered model of learning? Alternatively, if the object of teaching is to get students to develop their own understanding of the subject matter, how much should the teacher actively intervene to set the conditions of the student's learning?

The most skilled practitioners of this form of teaching in our study worried about the dilemma frequently, vocally, and persistently. Alexis Brezinski struggled with whether to require her fourth and fifth graders to read selections from the *Iliad* as part of the unit she was doing on ancient Greece. Her passion was ancient Greece, her knowledge of the subject was deep, and her convictions about what students needed to know in order to understand that culture were well formed. But these influences were in tension with her views about how children learn. By requiring them to read the *Iliad*, she felt she was setting up a situation in which students would do the reading because they were expected to do it, not because they were drawn to it by a need or desire to know something that would be helpful in increasing their own understanding. In a way, she had already answered her own question by setting the parameters of the project on ancient Greece; by using her own passion for the subject as the major source of student motivation she was getting them to study something they probably would not otherwise have studied. In the end the students did read the *Iliad*—probably believing somehow that they were doing it because they had discovered for themselves that it was important.

A somewhat less successful illustration of a teacher grappling with the constructivist paradox was Dede Patterson at Northeastern. She embodied active learning and discovery in her attempt to teach the concept of density by using colored liquids. In her words, she was "asking questions and letting them [the students] do the work." But she had extreme difficulty carrying the idea off. She herself sounded confused at various points in the lesson about whether it was the color or the density of the liquid that was important, and students picked up this confusion. When she finally got to the issue of density, she did not have enough time to get students engaged in a thorough discussion of what it meant. In the end, however, what distinguished her from other less successful practitioners of ambitious teaching was her capacity to reflect on what she did wrong. She volunteered that she had difficulty focusing students' attention and that "I haven't internalized what should happen in the demonstration." In other words, Patterson had not dealt with her own role in clarifying the knowledge underlying the learning experience she was bringing to students and in thinking through what good student learning would look like.

On the other hand, Patterson's colleague at Northeastern, Dan Rollins, led students through a detailed discussion of their observations of praying mantis egg sacks, deftly supplying scientific terms for many of the things the students were observing, but letting students' observations drive the process of discovery. He set the theme of life cycles to hold students' learning together, but he provided multiple options for them to do specific things they were interested in to learn about the larger topic. In the process, he realized his goal to impart "drive and excitement about the natural world" by teaching students how to ask productive questions.

What marked many of the other teachers in our study was their lack of inquisitiveness, awareness, or even interest in the problems posed by the constructivist dilemma. Turner at Lakeview was a whirlwind of activity in her lesson on ants, but she was apparently not particularly bothered that students had experienced something whose significance they did not seem able to explain. Her colleague Trudy Garrett employed vestiges of Distar (a direct-instruction pedagogy) to lead students through the exercise, chanting responses along the way, with no evidence that she appreciated the irony of the tension between her pedagogy and the nature of the task she was asking students to perform. Likewise, Joanna Benton doggedly pursued the problem of place value by using Roman numerals without much concern for whether her own understanding of the content was a constraint on her capacity to create settings in which students would understand the content better.

In other words, some teachers were pursuing a pedagogy without really understanding the thicket of intellectual and practical questions they had gotten themselves into. They were not doing a particularly good job of implementing the kind of teaching they aspired to, nor did they adequately reflect on the degree to which they fell short of their goals. For all her limitations, Patterson knew when she had gotten herself into deeper water than she could manage, and she was in an organization that could toss her a lifeline if she called for help.

Teaching in the ambitious ways espoused by the teachers in our study involves grappling with the most fundamental problems of the teacher's role, the role of knowledge, and the role that students play in constructing that knowledge. There is no predetermined set of solutions to these problems. The fact that the teachers in our study were trying to do things differently with an eye to how students actually learn is testimonial to their commitment to their work. But most of the teachers in our study were not in settings— schools, networks of colleagues, professional communities—in which they were routinely exposed to such people as Alexis Brezinski and Dan Rollins, accomplished practitioners and articulate in their descriptions of the problems of their practice. In the absence of such connections, it is no wonder that enthusiastic and energetic teachers often cannot make the connection between their aspirations and their practice and cannot reflect on the complexities involved in making that connection. To be accomplished practitioners, people have to be committed, enthusiastic, knowledgeable, and skilled, which all the teachers in our study were to one degree or another; but they also have to have the capacity to reflect on their practice in a community of colleagues who know deeply what the problems are. Only a few of the teachers in our study were so fortunate.

The teachers in our study had essentially opened a new chapter in their professional lives and were struggling to understand the message embedded in that chapter. All the teachers subscribed to the notion of active student learning, but most did not yet understand that they were obliged to know deeply how students made sense of things independently of how they as teachers made sense of things. Many teachers clung to repetition and recitation, rather than developing techniques for listening to students express their own ideas. Teachers routinely supplied answers to questions they themselves had asked, often, they said, to spare students the embarrassment of not knowing the "right answer." But in the process they set up the expectation that the object of classroom discourse was to guess what the teacher was thinking. And teachers routinely put themselves in the position of being the source of students' learning—supplying facts and algorithms for students, sometimes supplying words for students' writing—rather than creating situations in which students were obliged to construct their own knowledge. These practices permeate American classrooms, and they permeate the professional knowledge and backgrounds of teachers in most American classrooms. If teachers want to change these practices, then our study suggests they have to be put in the presence of influences more powerful than the ones found in at least two of the three schools in our study.

Solving the Puzzle of Structure and Practice

The schools in our study were doing what enlightened researchers and practitioners generally recommend that all schools should do:

- They were changing the way students were grouped for purposes of instruction.

- They were creating opportunities for teachers to share knowledge by working in teams.
- They were taking greater responsibility for the fundamental decisions in their schools on budget and personnel matters.
- They were changing the conditions of their work to accommodate professional development as part of their regular responsibilities.

They were, in other words, trying to change teaching and learning by changing the structure of the organizations in which they worked.

Our study leads us to some tentative conclusions about this approach to changing teaching and learning.

The first conclusion we provisionally draw from these examples is that *the relationship between changes in formal structure and changes in teaching practice is necessarily weak, problematic, and indirect; attention to structural change often distracts from the more fundamental problem of changing teaching practice.* The idea that changing the structure of schools leads teachers to teach differently seems even more improbable to us after analyzing our cases than it did after analyzing the literature on the relationship between school structure and student learning.

Reformers focus on changing structures because these changes have a visible impact on schools. People inside schools can see changes in structure and feel the impact of these changes on their daily work lives: children come to teachers in different types of groups, teachers see each other in different settings for different purposes, and the daily routines of organizational life about who does what when are carried out differently.

From the perspective of outsiders—administrators, parents, policy makers—schools involved in structural change appear to be "doing something." That is, they are involved in visible activities that seem to be responsive to the demands of external constituencies. For these reasons, structural change is seductive and energizing, both for the people who participate in it and for those who observe it.

Relative to structural changes, changes in teaching practice are considerably more difficult both to achieve and to see as they are taking place. Changes in teaching practice are also, as we have commented, quite sensitive to the knowledge and skills of the people who are trying to bring them about.

It should come as no surprise, then, that people within and outside schools find changing structure more interesting and engaging, more motivating and energizing, than changing teaching practice. The one is highly visible and sexy; the other is more difficult and indeterminate.

The slippery relationship between structure and teaching practice grows out of this fundamental tendency to displace the core problems of teaching practice by focusing energy on structure. All three of the schools in our study did this. They invested enormous energy and commitment to changing their work routines, while professing a high commitment to changing teaching practice but spending less focused energy on that activity. Lakeview and Webster stayed in this mode throughout our observations. Northeastern began to move out of this mode after about four years and to focus less on structural change and more on fundamental problems of teaching and learning. In all cases, though, attention to structure did not work as a road into changing teaching practice; it seemed in some instances to serve as a detour from attention to practice.

As a corollary of this first conclusion, we assert that *there probably is no single set of structural changes that schools can make that will lead predictably to a particular kind of teaching practice.* Reform advocates often speak, intentionally or unintentionally, as if making some specific change in structure, such as changing student grouping practices or enhancing teacher collegiality, will lead inexorably to a different kind of teaching, which in turn will lead inexorably to students' learning in different ways, which in turn will lead to students' knowing different things. Our study should cause readers to be very skeptical of this kind of logic.

The problem with such reasoning is evident from our cases. How teachers teach at any given time is a composite of how they taught in the past, how they think they ought to be teaching in the present, and how they reconcile the latter with the former. Teachers are not ciphers for their organizations; they do not simply and immediately translate the prevailing ideas about teaching practice in their schools into some new form of teaching. Teachers are active decision makers who are constrained in their capacities to act on new ideas by their past practice, by their judgments about what is worth doing, and by deeply rooted habits that are often at odds with their own espoused views of what they ought to do. It is highly implausible that putting them in a new kind of structure—in which they confront different groups of students than they have confronted before, and in which they are expected to behave differently toward their colleagues—will somehow cause teachers not only to teach differently but to do so in predictable ways across classrooms. Teachers may be, indeed many *will* be enthusiastic partisans of the new structures, and of the new views of teaching and learning that are alleged to come with those structures. But the structures themselves do not lead to or cause the changes in teaching practice; they simply create the occasion and legitimate the opportunity to engage in changes in practice.

Structure offers little leverage on how teachers teach, and such leverage as it does offer is decidedly unclear and unpredictable in its effects. Structural change is simply a way of calling the attention of the school and its environment to the necessity to work on a set of problems. Whether those problems are addressed successfully by individual teachers depends more on the intensity, knowledge, and skill with which teachers engage the problems, and less on the structure in which they engage them.

Hence, our third conclusion is that *it is just as plausible for changes in practice to lead to changes in structure as vice versa.* One way to think about the distinction between Lakeview and Webster on the one hand and Northeastern on the other is that the former believed that changing structure would change teaching practice, while the latter moved away from such a belief to a much more pragmatic view that they would be comfortable with any structure that would not get in the way of implementing their fundamental beliefs about practice. In other words, Lakeview and Webster saw themselves as using structure to drive teaching practice. Northeastern, in its mature state, saw teaching practice—and the norms, knowledge, and competencies that support it—as more important than any particular structure. Northeastern faculty were in fact willing to be quite pragmatic about structure so long as it did not get in the way of practice. At Northeastern one might say practice drove structure.

Northeastern, of course, went through a phase early in its existence when Diane Mandel and her faculty believed that a school had to be radically structured in order to work well educationally. They evolved, however, toward a structure that was radical only in the sense that it fit their distinctive pedagogy like a glove, not in the sense that it looked radically different from other schools. In fact, as we have said several times, Northeastern is in many ways the most conventionally structured school in our study. What is therefore important about the Northeastern example is not the structure itself, but the fit between structure and pedagogy.

Our fourth and final conclusion is that *the transformation of teaching practice is fundamentally a problem of enhancing individual knowledge and skill, not a problem of organizational structure; getting the structure right depends on first understanding that problem of knowledge and skill.* One of the reasons teaching practice varied so markedly within the schools in our study was that despite changes in organization and despite high levels of staff development, teachers simply did not have access to the knowledge and skill necessary to transform their teaching.

Lakeview was virtually inundated with staff-development and external-curriculum assistance. Teachers found these experiences stimulating and energizing, but virtually none of the experiences that Lakeview teachers had confronted the basic problem of how to transform teaching practice. The experiences all assumed that teachers knew how to transform their own practice and that all they needed was access to new ideas about what to do.

Webster is a somewhat more complicated story. The Fairchild School District had a strategy which, if it had been implemented on a wider scale, might have addressed the problem of how to transform individual teaching practice more directly: the strategy of using collaborating teachers to work in schools with individual teachers in the way that Jay Ross worked with Julie Brandt. But few teachers got access to that kind of assistance, and the effect at Webster was that for most teachers the assistance was weak and ineffectual.

Northeastern solved the problem of knowledge and skill through careful recruitment and a rich set of organizational norms that encouraged teachers to consult regularly on problems of practice. In the absence of attention to this basic problem of where teachers are to get assistance in developing their knowledge and skill, organizational changes are likely not to have much effect.

In some instances, teachers simply did not know the subject matter they were teaching well enough to make the transition to a more ambitious kind of teaching. In some instances, they were behaving inconsistently with their professed beliefs about how teaching should occur. In some instances, they were using teaching strategies that were unsuccessful adaptations of how they had taught before. In all instances, their practice was unlikely to change without some exposure to *what teaching actually looks like when it is being done differently,* and exposure to someone who could help them understand the difference between what they were doing and what they aspired to do. This sort of problem has to be solved first at the individual level before it can be solved at the organizational level. Indeed, increasing collegiality by changing the structure of schools but without some attention to change at the individual level could simply result in teachers' reinforcing questionable practice through collegiality rather than confronting the difficulties of teaching differently.

To be sure, these individual-level transformations are bound to have organizational implications. In order for teachers to work closely with someone who has a grasp of the knowledge and skill required to teach differently, teachers have to open up their classrooms to outside observers and consultants. They might also have to make modifications in the timing and sequence of when certain things are taught. And ultimately the experience will probably be more powerful if it is shared by a number of teachers who have the opportunity to discuss it. All of these things have organizational consequences. But one does not get to the problem of teachers' knowledge and skill by first talking about organizational changes. Rather, it is done by first talking about the fundamental problem of knowledge and skill and then asking what organizational arrangements support solutions to that problem.

Recommendations

If we were to advise *educational practitioners,* based on our limited study of these matters, we would say that attention to the problem of providing access to new knowledge and skill for teachers should supersede attention to the problem of how to restructure schools.

Structural problems arise as teachers become aware of the demands that accompany new ways of teaching; structures undoubtedly have to be changed to address these demands. But the energy required to change structures first does not seem to pay off in terms of broad-scale changes in teaching practice. It is also important to acknowledge that teachers themselves do not necessarily possess the knowledge and skill required to transform their own teaching practice in response to structural change, any more than other professionals possess the ability to dramatically alter their modes of practice without considerable outside assistance. It is not an indictment of teachers to say that changing teaching practice necessarily means putting teachers in some kind of new relationship with people who have more knowledge and skill than they do.

The tremendous symbolic value of changes in structure no doubt means that ambitious administrators and policy makers will continue to advocate structural change as a solution to the problem of how to improve teaching and learning. Structural changes may in fact be an important way to focus the attention of certain important constituencies on how to transform teaching and learning. Ultimately, however, focusing on structural changes draws attention away from the more fundamental problem of whether teachers have access to the knowledge and skill they need to respond to higher expectations about teaching and learning. In the absence of a solution to that problem, continued focus on "restructuring" is likely to increase disillusionment and cynicism about school reform.

If we were to advise *researchers,* based on our study, we would urge much more attention to understanding the various ways in which people learn new approaches to established tasks, and the ways in which their work environment influences their acquisition of new knowledge and skill. A key premise of the school-restructuring movement is that teachers discover new ways to teach simply by being exposed to new ideas and by working in organizations where the structure promotes interaction. We are more than a little skeptical of this assumption, and we think that the problem of how teachers acquire new knowledge and skill is considerably more complex than either reformers or researchers have acknowledged.

What seems important in our case studies is that in some settings teachers actually began to acknowledge that teaching to enable students' understanding required not just a new way of teaching but a new way of thinking about their role as practitioners. Julie Brandt began to think of herself not just as teaching differently but as having a different relationship to knowledgeable people in her field, and of being willing to have her practice scrutinized by others and vice versa. In other words, she changed not just her view of how to teach but also her view of how knowledge about teaching is developed, understood, and communicated to others. Likewise, this view of teaching seemed to be "hardwired" into the organization at Northeastern, where teachers were connoisseurs of their particular brand of teaching for understanding as well as active participants in networks of other teachers who share their views. What these teachers knew, in other words, they knew as a consequence of an extensive set of social relationships around the practice of teaching, not simply their personal knowledge. It would seem important for researchers to focus on these various influences on teaching practice and on how to create stronger, more extensive, and more pervasive versions of these influences.

Critics and commentators may read this book as arguing that "structure doesn't matter" in the determination of teaching practice. This would not be an accurate portrayal of our conclusion. Rather, we argue that the way schools are structured *might* matter a great deal to teaching practice, *if* we understood what kind of teaching practice we wanted, and *if* we understood the conditions necessary to give teachers access to the skill and knowledge they need to engage in that practice. We would rather map backward from an understanding of teaching practice to an understanding of what a good school structure might be—recognizing that the solution to that problem will vary for different schools—than we would map forward from structural changes in schools to changes in teaching practice.

Once again, our study affirms what extraordinarily complex and demanding work teaching is and how little we know about how to create good teaching on a large scale. We think we have added to this understanding an appreciation first of how important it is to focus on good teaching practice, and the conditions that enable it, as the central issue of educational reform, and second of how important it is to put structural reform in a new, more productive relationship to teaching practice.

Notes

Preface

1. All names of cities, schools, and individuals in this book have been changed to protect the confidentiality of participants in the study.

Chapter Two

1. Information on communities, schools, and individuals is current as of our last interviews in the spring of 1991.
2. Later, the grouping arrangement was changed to K–1, 2–4, and 3–5. The overlap in the latter two groups allowed for still greater flexibility in assigning and moving students from one group to another.

Chapter Eleven

1. Brezinski herself used the term *dilemma* to describe the tensions she often felt in her teaching. She said that she preferred this term to *problems*. She may have gotten this term from other constructivist teachers who studied at the same school in Vermont with which Northeastern has been affiliated since its founding. Other constructivist teachers talk about "managing dilemmas" in teaching (see Lampert, 1985; Lampert, 1990; Ball, 1993; and Peterson and Knapp, 1993).

References

Ball, D. L. "With an Eye on the Mathematical Horizon: Dilemmas of Teaching Elementary School Mathematics." *Elementary School Journal,* 1993, *93*(4), 373–397.

Baroody, A. "How and When Should Place Value Concepts Be Taught?" *Journal for Research in Mathematics Education,* 1990, *21,* 281–286.

Bereiter, C., and Scardamalia, M. "An Attainable Version of High Literacy: Approaches to Teaching Higher-Order Skills in Reading and Writing." *Curriculum Inquiry,* 1987, *17*(1), 9–30.

Burk, D., Snider, A., and Symonds, P. *Box It or Bag It Math.* Salem, Oreg.: The Mathematics Learning Center, 1988.

Calkins, L. *The Art of Teaching Writing.* Portsmouth, N.H.: Heinemann, 1986.

Cohen, D. K. "A Revolution in One Classroom: The Case of Mrs. Oublier." *Educational Evaluation and Policy Analysis,* 1991, *12,* 311–330.

Cohen, D. K., McLaughlin, M. W., and Talbert, J. E. (eds.) *Teaching for Understanding: Challenges for Policy and Practice.* San Francisco: Jossey-Bass, 1993.

Cuban, L., and Tyack, D. *Tinkering Toward Utopia: A Century of Public School Reform.* Cambridge, Mass.: Harvard University Press, 1993.

DeLany, B. "Allocation, Choice, and Stratification Within High Schools: How the Sorting Machine Copes." *American Journal of Education,* 1991, *99*(2), 181–207.

Duckworth, E. *"The Having of Wonderful Ideas" and Other Essays on Teaching and Learning.* New York: Teachers College Press, 1987.

Ehlert, L. *Color Zoo.* New York: HarperCollins, 1989.

Elmore, R. F. "School Decentralization: Who Gains? Who Loses?" In J. Hannaway and M. Carnoy (eds.), *Decentralization and School Improvement: Can We Fulfill the Promise?* San Francisco: Jossey-Bass, 1993.

Elmore, R. F. "Teaching, Learning, and School Organization." *Educational Administration Quarterly,* 1995, *31*(3), 355–374.

Elmore, R. F., and Associates. *Restructuring Schools: The Next Generation of Educational Reform.* San Francisco: Jossey-Bass, 1990.

Fendel, D. M. *Understanding the Structure of Elementary School Mathematics.* Boston: Allyn & Bacon, 1987.

Finn, J., and Achilles, C. "Answers and Questions About Class Size: A Statewide Experiment." *American Educational Research Journal,* 1990, *27*(3), 557–577.

Fleischman, L. I. *Whipping Boy.* New York: Greenwillow Books, 1986.

Fullan, M., with Stiegelbaure, S. *New Meaning of Educational Change.* New York: Teachers College Press, 1991.

Fuson, K. C. "Conceptual Structures for Multiunit Numbers: Implications for Learning and Teaching Multidigit Addition, Subtraction, and Place Value." *Cognition and Instruction,* 1990a, *7,* 343–404.

Fuson, K. C. "Issues in Place-Value and Multidigit Addition and Subtraction Learning." *Journal for Research in Mathematics Education,* 1990b, *21,* 273–280.

Gamoran, A. "The Stratification of High School Learning Opportunities." *Sociology of Education,* 1987, *60*(3), 135–155.

Gamoran, A., and Berends, M. "The Effects of Stratification in Secondary Schools: Synthesis of Survey and Ethnographic Research." *Review of Educational Research,* 1987, *57*(4), 415–435.

Garet, M., and DeLany, B. "Students, Courses, and Stratification." *Sociology of Education,* 1988, *61*(2), 61–77.

Gelman, R., Massey, C., and McManus, M. "Characterizing Supportive Environments for Cognitive Development: Lessons from Children in a Museum." In L. B. Resnick, J. M. Levine, and S. D. Teasley (eds.), *Perspectives on Socially Shared Cognition.* Washington, D.C.: American Psychological Association, 1991.

Glass, G., and Smith, M. L. "Meta-Analysis of Research on the Relationship Between Class-Size and Achievement." *Educational Evaluation and Policy Analysis,* 1979, *1,* 2–16.

Graves, D. *Writing: Teachers and Children at Work.* Exeter, N.H.: Heinemann, 1983.

Heaton, R., and Lampert, M. "Learning to Hear Voices: Inventing a New Pedagogy of Teacher Education." In D. Cohen, M. W. McLaughlin, and J. E. Talbert (eds.), *Teaching for Understanding: Challenges for Policy and Practice.* San Francisco: Jossey-Bass, 1993.

Konigsburg, E. L. *From the Mixed-Up Files of Mrs. Basil E. Frankweiler.* New York: Dell, 1977.

Kouba, V. L., Carpenter, T., and Swafford, J. "Numbers and Operations." In M. M. Lindquist (ed.), *Results from the Fourth Mathematics Assessment.* Reston, Va.: National Council of Teachers of Mathematics (NCTM), 1989.

Lampert, M. "How Do Teachers Manage to Teach? Perspectives on Problems in Practice." *Harvard Educational Review,* 1985, *55*, 178–194.

Lampert, M. "Connecting Inventions and Conventions." In L. P. Steffe and T. Wood (eds.), *Transforming Children's Mathematics Education: International Perspectives.* Hillsdale, N.J.: Lawrence Erlbaum, 1990.

McCarthy, B. *The 4-Mat System: Teaching to Learning Style with Right/Left Mode Techniques.* Arlington Heights, Ill.: Excel, 1980.

McCarthey, S., and McMahan, S. "From Convention to Invention: Peer Interactions During Writing." In Rittertz-Lazarowitz and M. Miller (eds.), *Interaction in Cooperative Groups: The Theoretical Anatomy of Group Learning.* Cambridge, England: Cambridge University Press, 1992.

Malen, B., Ogawa, R., and Krantz, J. "What Do We Know About School-Based Management? A Case Study of the Literature—A Call for Research." In W. Clune and J. Witte (eds.), *Choice and Control in American Education, Vol. 2, The Practice of Choice, Decentralization, and School Restructuring.* New York: Falmer Press, 1990.

Murphy, J. *Restructuring Schools: Capturing the Phenomenon.* Beverly Hills, Calif.: Sage Publications, 1991.

Murphy, J. and Hallinger, P. "Equity as Access to Learning: Curricular and Instructional Treatment Differences." *Journal of Curriculum Studies,* 1989, *21*(2), 129–149.

National Council of Teachers of Mathematics. *Curriculum and Evaluation Standards for School Mathematics.* Reston, Va.: National Council of Teachers of Mathematics (NCTM), 1989.

Nelson, J. *I'll Build a Zoo.* Cleveland: Modern Curriculum Press, 1989.

Newmann, F. M., Marks, H. M., and Gamoran, A. *Authentic Pedagogy: Standards That Boost Student Performance.* Issues in Restructuring Schools, report no. 8. Madison: Spring Center on Organization and Restructuring Schools, University of Wisconsin, 1993.

Oakes, J. *Keeping Track: How Schools Structure Inequality.* New Haven, Conn.: Yale University Press, 1985.

Oakes, J. *Multiplying Inequalities: The Effects of Race, Social Class, and Tracking on Opportunities to Learn Mathematics and Science.* Santa Monica, Calif.: Rand Corporation, 1990.

Peterson, P. L., Fennema, E., and Carpenter, T. "Using Children's Mathematical Knowledge." In B. Means, C. Chelemer, and M. S. Knapp (eds.), *Models for Teaching Advanced Skills to Disadvantaged Students.* San Francisco: Jossey-Bass, 1991.

Peterson, P. L., and Knapp, N. F. "Inventing and Reinventing Ideas: Constructivist Teaching and Learning." In G. Cawelti (ed.), *The 1993*

Yearbook of the Association for Supervision and Curriculum Development. Washington, D.C.: ASCD, 1993.

Peterson, P. L., Carpenter, T. P., and Fennema, E. L. "Teachers' Knowledge, Students' Knowledge, and Cognitions in Mathematics Problem Solving: Correlational and Case Analyses." *Journal of Educational Psychology,* 1989, *81*(4).

Resnick, L. *Education and Learning to Think.* Washington, D.C.: National Academy Press, 1987.

Robinson, G. "Synthesis of Research on the Effects of Class Size." *Educational Leadership,* April 1990, *47,* 80–90.

Rockwell, T. *How to Eat Fried Worms.* New York: F. Watts, 1973.

Rucker, W. E., Dilley, C. A., and Lowry, D. *Heath Mathematics Teacher's Edition: Level 4.* Lexington, Mass.: D. C. Heath, 1983.

Rucker, W. E., Dilley, C. A., and Lowry, D. *Heath Mathematics Teacher's Edition: Level 5.* Lexington, Mass.: D. C. Heath, 1983.

Slavin, R. "Ability Grouping and Student Achievement in Elementary Schools: A Best-Evidence Synthesis." *Review of Educational Research,* 1987, *57*(3), 293–336.

Slavin, R. "Achievement Effects of Ability Grouping in Secondary Schools: A Best-Evidence Synthesis." *Review of Educational Research,* 1990, *60*(3), 471–499.

Smith, F. *Understanding Reading: A Psycholinguistic Analysis of Reading and Learning to Read.* New York: Holt, Rinehart & Winston, 1971.

Smith, F. *Essays into Literacy.* London: Heinemann, 1983.

Smith, F. *Joining the Literary Club.* Portsmouth, N.H.: Heinemann, 1988.

Sorenson, A. and Hallinan, M. "Effects of Ability Grouping on Growth in Academic Achievement." *American Educational Research Journal,* 1986, *23*(4), 519–542.

Talbert, J., and McLaughlin, M. "Understanding Teaching in Context." In D. Cohen, M. McLaughlin, and J. Talbert (eds.), *Teaching for Understanding: Challenges for Policy and Practice.* San Francisco: Jossey-Bass, 1993.

Wilder, L. I. *Little House in the Big Woods.* New York: HarperCollins, 1953.

Wood, T., Cobb, P., and Yackel, E. "Change in Teaching Mathematics: A Case Study." *American Educational Research Journal,* 1991, *28,* 587–616.

Index

A

Active learning, 81, 226; in mathematics, 92–111. *See also* Hands-on activities

Administrative support, 51–52, 56–57, 146–147

Alternative schools, 18–19, 141. *See also* Northeastern Elementary School

Amada, A., 139, 143–144, 145

Ancient Greece unit, 171–173, 180, 182–183, 233–234

"Animals in Our Immediate Environment," 36–45

Ants lesson, 37–41

Art, for self-expression, 54–56, 57–58

Art teacher, 150, 151

Assessment, student: alternative report cards for, 82; evaluative, 147, 195

Author's chair, 118–119, 124–125

B

Baroody, A., 107

Beliefs: teaching practice coherent with, 170–171, 179–181, 207, 210, 227–228, 235–236; teaching practice contrary to, 62–67, 70–73

Benton, M., 93, 99–105, 229–230, 235

Bereiter, C., 5

Billings, C., 78–84, 216–217

"Box It or Bag It Math," 103–104, 107

Brainstorming, in classroom, 37–38

Brandt, J., 112–120, 228, 230, 243

Brandt, T., 84–85

Brezinski, A., 171–181, 182–183, 228, 233–234

Budgeting, school-site, 82

Burk, D., 93, 108

Busing, 77

C

Calkins, L., 161, 165

Carpenter, T., 107, 109

Chicken eggs science unit, 201–202

Class size: effects of, on learning, 11; strategies for reducing, 19–20, 21

Classroom arrangements, 113, 121, 150, 184–185, 196

Classroom discussion: of fieldwork, 39–41, 45; of science projects, 198–202

Clerihew poetry, 58–62

Cobb, P., 109

Cohen, D. K., 105

Collaborative learning, 162, 163–165, 181. *See also* Cooperative learning; Teacher collaboration

Community interaction, pedagogical, 153, 154–155, 169

Community settings, of case study schools, 17–18, 77, 141–143

Constructivist approaches, 6, 108–109, 181, 226–227; dilemma in, 182–183, 206, 212, 233–236, 245; effects of, on substantive learning, 194

Cooperative learning, 23, 26, 180–181; effects of, on student learning, 48–49; effects of, on teaching practice, 69–70; in mathematics lessons, 97, 99–103, 185–186; role assignment for, 42–44; in science lessons, 36–45. *See also* Student response peer groups

Cross-subject approaches, 2, 3, 20, 25, 36–50. *See also* Curriculum; Themes approach

Curriculum: active problem-solving focus in, 81, 92–111; cross-subject focus in, 2, 3, 20, 25, 36–50; mathematics, 92–111; reading, 113–114; science, 36–45; writing, 54–62. *See also* Mathematics instruction; Reading instruction; Science instruction; Themes approach; Writing instruction

Curriculum experts: contact of, with larger expert community, 106–108, 136–137; in mathematics examples, 93–105; as school consultants, 87–88; teachers as, 81, 92–93, 134–135, 227

Curtis, C., 33–34, 65–66

D

Daniels, L., 15, 18–34, 51–52, 216

Decision making: collaborative, 148–149, 209; collective, 144–145, 148; participatory, 22–23, 24, 78–79, 128–129

Density science unit, 188–193, 195

Desegregation, 77

Discovery learning: balancing of, with explicit instruction, 195–206, 210–211; in examples, 184–193, 195–204; problems with, 193–195, 204–206

Distar, 20, 46, 235

Duckworth, E., 184

E

Egg-crate structure, 3

Elmore, R. F., 1, 7, 8

Engagement, in classroom, 5

Ernst, P., 53–56, 62–67, 228

F

Faculty meetings, 149

Family involvement, 153–154

Federal compensatory education policy, 28, 29

Fendel, D. M., 105–106

Fennema, E. L., 109

Fieldwork, in Lakeview School examples, 39, 44

From the Mixed-Up Files of Mrs. Basil E. Frankweiler, 122

Fullan, M., 8

Fuson, K. C., 107

G

Gamoran, A., 9

Garrett, T., 36–37, 42–45, 46, 48, 49–50, 228, 235

Gelman, R., 194

Government funding, obstacles to, 28–31

Graves, D., 118, 165

Griffin, J., 93, 94–99, 229–230

Grouping: ability, 3, 9–11; flexible, 21, 22, 69, 80, 226; homogenous, 9; in school restructuring, 2, 4; traditional, 3, 9. *See also* Multi-age groups; Multiple ability groups

H

Hallinan, M., 9

Hallinger, P., 9

Hancock, J., 120–126

Hands-on activities, 226; in mathematics, 94–99; in science, 36–45, 49–50. *See also* Active learning

Hands-on materials, 184–185

Heath Mathematics Level 8 (D. C. Heath), 94, 99, 105

Heaton, R., 109

Horn, L., 52, 56–62, 63–67, 228

How to Eat Fried Worms, 121, 122

I

Iliad, 174, 182–183, 233–234
Income levels, at case study schools, 18, 77, 142–143
Intentional learning, 4–7
Interaction, in classroom, 5

J

Journaling: for K-1 class, 54–56; teacher's, 180; writing, 175

K

Kouba, V. L., 107
Kramer, B., 160–171, 183, 228–229
Krantz, J., 8

L

Labeling of students: avoidance of, 22, 23; and government funding restrictions, 28
Lakeview School, 15–73; administrative support in, 51–52, 56–57; core values of, 22–24, 215; description of, 17–18; and government funding, 28–31; principals of, 18–20, 33–34, 216; relationship of, with school district, 27–31, 68–69, 218, 221; restructuring of, 20–24, 68–73, 214, 217; self-esteem/self-expression focus at, 53–67; staff development at, 21–22, 25, 33, 231, 240; student grouping at, 21, 22, 69; teaching practice at, 227, 228, 235; teaching practice at, changes in, 24–27, 35–36, 45–50, 62–67, 68–73, 222; teacher teams at, 36–50
Lampert, M., 109
Leadership, in case studies compared, 216–217. *See also* Lakeview School; Northeastern Elementary School; Webster Elementary School
Learning, for deep understanding, 4–7, 110. *See also* Literary understanding; Scientific understanding

Learning styles approach: as core value, 23–24; effects of, on teaching practice, 47–48, 49, 72, 227
Life cycles science unit, 196–204
Life-long learning, 155, 179
Literacy instruction. *See* Reading instruction; Writing instruction
Literary understanding, connection of, to self-expression activities, 71–72
Little House in the Big Woods, 121–122

M

McCarthy, B., 47
McCarthy, S., 118
McLaughlin, M. W., 6
McMahan, S., 118
McManus, M., 194
Malen, B., 8
Mandel, D., 143, 144, 145, 216, 217
Massey, C., 194
"Masters Center," 77–78, 84–90, 219
"Math Their Way," 104–105
Mathematics: active learning in, 92–111; constructivist approaches to, 108–109; "old" versus "new" theories of, 105–108; student-designed tests in, 151; teacher knowledge of, 229–230; textbook, 94, 99
Montoya, L., 146–147, 216
Multi-age groups, 2; at Lakeview School, 21; at Northeastern Elementary School, 149–150; at Webster Elementary School, 80, 133; for writing instruction, 114
Multiple ability groups, 23
Murphy, J., 8, 9, 12
Music instruction, 150, 151

N

National Assessment of Educational Progress (NAEP), 107
National Council of Teachers of Mathematics (NCTM), 107

National Council of Teachers of Social Studies, 180

National Curriculum Standards, 107

Newmann, F., 7, 12

Northeastern Elementary School, 139–212; admissions process of, 143, 148, 153–154; administrative role in, 144, 145–147; administrative support in, 146–147; collaborative environment at, 148–149, 209, 224–226; core beliefs/cohesiveness at, 144, 147–148, 215, 232; description of, 141–143; directors of, 144, 145, 216, 217; founding of, 143–145; norms and structures of, 148–156, 209, 215, 217–218; original organization of, 144–145; political conflicts and, 145, 148; reorganization of, 145–148, 158, 208–209; school district's relationship with, 220–221; staff development at, 147, 221, 230–232, 240–241; student grouping at, 149–150; teacher responsibility/control at, 144–145, 146, 156, 208, 224–225; teaching practice at, 158–159, 227, 228–229; teaching practice at, for reading/writing instruction, 159–183; teaching practice at, related to structure, 207–212, 223–224; teaching practice at, for science instruction, 184–206, 234–235

O

Oakes, J., 9

Ogawa, R., 8

Open education movement, 143, 144

Organizational change, dimensions of, 8. *See also* School restructuring

Organizational structure, in case studies compared, 214–215. *See also* School restructuring

P

Patterson, D., 184–195, 204–206, 234

Peterson, P. L., 109

Phonics skills instruction, 122–123, 124–125, 126

Piaget, J., 184

"Place value" mathematics lessons: activity-based, 94–105; "old" versus "new" theories of, 105–108

Poetry writing lesson, 56–62

Praying mantis egg cases unit, 198–201, 204

Principals: restructuring driven by, 18–34; roles of, 78–84, 216–217, 144, 145–147. *See also* Lakeview School; Northeastern Elementary School; Webster Elementary School

Principals' Center, Harvard Graduate School of Education, 79

Process-writing approach, 161, 165

Professional communities, teacher contact with, 106–108, 136–137, 155, 209, 233, 235

Project Time, 197–198

R

Racial composition, of case study schools, 18, 77, 142–143

Reading instruction: basal versus literature-based, 120–121, 126; for constructing meaning, 173–174, 182–183; examples of, 113–114, 121–122; interrelated with writing, 159–162, 172–173; thematic, 120–122

Reflection, teacher, 64–67, 211–212

Relationships: teacher-student, 23, 25, 147, 150, 193–195; among teachers, 224–225. *See also* Cooperative learning; Teacher collaboration; Teacher teams

Report cards, alternative, 82

Research instruction, 162

Research study design, 12–14

Resnick, L., 5

Resource teachers, 85–90, 130–131, 136–137, 220

Rollins, D., 195–206, 228, 230, 234–235

"Roman fold" activity, 95–97

Ross, J., 88–90, 130–131, 136–137

S

Scardamalia, M., 5

Schedule, school-day: in Lakeview School, 21; in Northeastern Elementary School, 150–151, 196; in school restructuring, 2; traditional, 3

School district: collaborative support of, for alternative school, 143–144, 156, 218, 220–221; collaborative support of, for school restructuring, 77–78, 84–90, 132–133, 218–219, 220; effects of, on school restructuring, 218–222; hinderance by, of school restructuring, 27–32, 34, 68–69, 218, 221; "Masters Center" established by, 77–78, 84–90, 219

School restructuring: to accommodate teachers' needs, 51–52, 56–57; defined, 1–3; effects of, on teaching practice, 1, 2–3, 6–14, 213–239; essentials of, 4; length of process of, 217–218; politically motivated, 8; precipitants to, 7–8; principal-driven, 18–34; process versus content orientation to, 220–222; relationship of, to teaching practice, 1, 2–3, 6–14, 68–73; research study on, 12–14; school district-driven, 77–78, 84–90, 132–133, 143–144, 156, 218–219; in study schools compared, 222–226; and teaching for understanding, 6–7. *See also* Lakeview School; Northeastern Elementary School; Webster Elementary School

School restructuring movement, 1, 242

School-site management, 82, 85–86, 132

School structure, traditional, 3–4

Science: discovery approaches to, 184–206; explicit instruction in, 196–206; facilitating students' understanding of, 184–206; hands-on approaches to, 36–45, 49–50

Scientific understanding: connection of, to hands-on learning activities, 49–50; and discovery learning, 194–195, 203–204; facilitating understanding of, 186–188, 203–204

Self-contained classrooms, 150–151

Self-directed learning, 5, 195–206, 210–211, 226, 228. *See also* Constructivist approaches

Self-esteem focus: and administrative support for teachers, 51–52, 56–57; in classroom practice, 53–62; at classroom and school levels, 52, 53–67; as core value, 23, 52; with self-expression activities, 54–62; and teaching practice, 62–67, 110

Self-expression focus: as core value, 52; through journaling, 54–56; through poetry writing, 56–62; for teachers, 57–58, 66; and teaching practice, 62–67, 70–72

Shared vision, 78–79, 132–133, 215–216

Slavin, R., 9

Slugs and snails lesson, 42–45

Smith, F., 159–160, 161

Snider, A., 93, 108

Social studies instruction, 171–173, 180, 182–183

Sorenson, A., 9

Special education policy (Public Law 94–142), 28, 29

Staff development: for content and pedagogical knowledge, 230–233, 240–241, 242; at Lakeview School, 21–22, 25, 33, 231, 240; at North-

eastern Elementary School, 147, 221, 230–232, 240–241; at Webster Elementary School, 78–79, 80, 231, 240
Staffing arrangements, flexible, 21–22. *See also* Teacher teams
Standardized test performance, at Lakeview School, 28
Student achievement: effects of class size on, 11; effects of homogeneous grouping on, 9–10; with restructuring, at Lakeview School, 28
Student peer response groups, for writing, 162, 163–165. *See also* Cooperative learning
Students, understanding of, 147, 150, 162, 180
Swafford, J., 107
Symonds, P., 93, 108

T

Talbert, J. E., 6
Teacher collaboration: in Lakeview School, 22–23, 24–27; in Northeastern Elementary School, 148–149, 209, 224–226. *See also* Teacher teams
Teacher teams: consultant for, 89–90; development of, 129–131; effects of, on teaching practice, 48, 70, 93, 128–131, 135–136; inducement for, 86–88; in Lakeview School, 21–22, 25, 36–50, 70; in Northeastern Elementary School, 144–145; teaching style differences within, 127–128, 129–130; in Webster Elementary School, 80–81, 112–131, 127–128
Teachers: administrative support for, 51–52, 56–57, 146–147; connection of, to outside professional communities, 106–108, 136–137, 155, 209, 233, 235; as curriculum/content experts, 81, 92–93, 134–135, 227, 229–231; hiring of,

156, 217; influence of, on teaching practice, 226–241; knowledge needed by, 179, 229–233. *See also* Staff development
Teaching practice: for building self-esteem, 53–62; and class size, 11; coherence of, with philosophy, 62–67, 70–73, 170–171, 179–181, 204–206, 207, 210, 222–227–228, 235–236; constructivist approaches to, 6, 108–109, 181, 182–183, 206, 212, 226–227, 233–236, 245; effects of cooperative learning on, 69–70; effects of learning styles approach on, 47–48, 49, 72, 227; effects of restructuring on, 1, 2–3, 6–14, 213–239; effects of restructuring on, length of process, 217–218; effects of team structure on, 48, 70, 93, 128–131, 135–136; effects of themes approach on, 49–50; and homogenous grouping, 10–11; influence of, on school structure, 239–244; research study on, 12–14; for self-esteem development, 53–62; and teacher qualities, 226–236; teacher reflection on, 64–67, 211–212; transformation of, 240–241; for understanding, 4–7, 227. *See also* Lakeview School; Northeastern Elementary School; Webster Elementary School
Teaching styles: adaptation of, based on student learning styles, 47–48, 49, 72; different, within a similar philosophy, 207–208; different, within teacher teams, 127–128, 129–130, 134–135; and structural/curricular change, 83–84; and teacher reflectiveness, 64–67
Team learning. *See* Cooperative learning; Student peer response groups
Team teaching. *See* Teacher teams

Tell, P., 98, 107

Themes approach, 35; effects of, on teaching practice, 49–50; problems with open-ended, 186–195; for science, 36–45, 186–195, 196–204; for social studies, 171–173, 180, 182–183; for writing/reading, 162, 168–182

Thompson, P., 84–85

"To Fifty and Back," 104

Tracking, 9–11. *See also* Grouping

Turner, L., 36–41, 45–46, 47–48, 50, 228, 235

V

Values, core, 22–24; effects of, on teaching practice, 51–67, 70–71. *See also* Beliefs; Shared vision

W

Water science unit, 186–188, 194

Webster Elementary School, 75–137; description of, 77–78; mathematics instruction at, 92–111; principal of, 78–84, 216–217; reading instruction at, 113–114, 120–122; resource teacher for, 88–90, 130–131; restructuring of, 80–91, 132–137, 214–215, 217; school district's relationship with, 77–78, 84–90, 132–133, 218–219, 220; shared vision of, 78–79, 132–133, 215; staff development at, 78–79, 80, 231, 240; student grouping at, 80, 114; teaching practice at, 227, 228; teaching practice at, changes in, 92–93, 97–99, 103–105, 108–111, 120–121, 125–126, 128–131, 222; team structure in, 80, 89–90, 112–131; team structure in, and teacher change, 128–131, 133–137; variability at, 133–136; writing instruction at, 114–128, 122–126

Whipping Boy, 122

Whole-language approach, 161

Wood, T., 109

Writing instruction: author's chair technique in, 118–119, 124–125; based on students' experiences, 168–170; collaborative, 114–120; integration of, with content, 162, 168–182, 182; interrelated with reading, 159–162, 172–173; in multi-age groups, 114; preparing students for, 122–123; process approach to, 161, 165; for self-expression, 54–62; teacher conferences for, 115–118, 123–124, 165–168; teacher problems with, 58–62, 71–72; and teaching practices, 228–229; topic selection for, 114–115, 122, 165–168; and types of writing, 162; whole-language approach to, 161

Y

Yackel, E., 109